Apache Jakarta Commons

BRUCE PERENS' OPEN SOURCE SERIES
http://www.phptr.com/perens

- *Java™ Application Development on Linux®*
  Carl Albing and Michael Schwarz
- *C++ GUI Programming with Qt 3*
  Jasmin Blanchette and Mark Summerfield
- *Managing Linux Systems with Webmin: System Administration and Module Development*
  Jamie Cameron
- *Understanding the Linux Virtual Memory Manager*
  Mel Gorman
- *PHP 5 Power Programming*
  Andi Gutmans, Stig Bakken, and Derick Rethans
- *Implementing CIFS: The Common Internet File System*
  Christopher Hertel
- *Open Source Security Tools: A Practical Guide to Security Applications*
  Tony Howlett
- *Embedded Software Development with eCos*
  Anthony Massa
- *Rapid Application Development with Mozilla*
  Nigel McFarlane
- *The Linux Development Platform: Configuring, Using, and Maintaining a Complete Programming Environment*
  Rafeeq Ur Rehman and Christopher Paul
- *Intrusion Detection with SNORT: Advanced IDS Techniques Using SNORT, Apache, MySQL, PHP, and ACID*
  Rafeeq Ur Rehman
- *The Official Samba-3 HOWTO and Reference Guide*
  John H. Terpstra and Jelmer R. Vernooij, Editors
- *Samba-3 by Example: Practical Exercises to Successful Deployment*
  John H. Terpstra

Apache Jakarta Commons
Reusable Java™ Components

Will Iverson

Upper Saddle River, NJ • Boston • Indianapolis • San Francisco
New York • Toronto • Montreal • London • Munich • Paris
Madrid • Capetown • Sydney • Tokyo • Singapore • Mexico City

Many of the designations used by manufacturers and sellers to distinguish their products are claimed as trademarks. Where those designations appear in this book, and the publisher was aware of a trademark claim, the designations have been printed with initial capital letters or in all capitals.

The author and publisher have taken care in the preparation of this book, but make no expressed or implied warranty of any kind and assume no responsibility for errors or omissions. No liability is assumed for incidental or consequential damages in connection with or arising out of the use of the information or programs contained herein.

The publisher offers excellent discounts on this book when ordered in quantity for bulk purchases or special sales, which may include electronic versions and/or custom covers and content particular to your business, training goals, marketing focus, and branding interests. For more information, please contact:

    U. S. Corporate and Government Sales
    (800) 382-3419
    corpsales@pearsontechgroup.com

For sales outside the U. S., please contact:

    International Sales
    international@pearsoned.com

Visit us on the Web: www.phptr.com

Library of Congress Catalog Number: 2004115288

Copyright © 2005 Pearson Education, Inc.

Pearson Education, Inc.
Rights and Contracts Department
One Lake Street
Upper Saddle River, NJ 07458

ISBN 0-13-147830-3

Text printed in the United States on recycled paper at R.R. Donnelley & Sons Company in Crawfordsville, Indiana.

First printing: February 2005

For Cynthia.

About Prentice Hall Professional Technical Reference

With origins reaching back to the industry's first computer science publishing program in the 1960s, and formally launched as its own imprint in 1986, Prentice Hall Professional Technical Reference (PH PTR) has developed into the leading provider of technical books in the world today. Our editors now publish over 200 books annually, authored by leaders in the fields of computing, engineering, and business.

Our roots are firmly planted in the soil that gave rise to the technical revolution. Our bookshelf contains many of the industry's computing and engineering classics: Kernighan and Ritchie's *C Programming Language*, Nemeth's *UNIX System Administration Handbook*, Horstmann's *Core Java*, and Johnson's *High-Speed Digital Design*.

PH PTR acknowledges its auspicious beginnings while it looks to the future for inspiration. We continue to evolve and break new ground in publishing by providing today's professionals with tomorrow's solutions.

Contents

Preface xiii

Acknowledgments xvi

About the Author xvii

1 Overview 1
   Proper Versus Sandbox 2
   License 4
   Obtaining and Installing 4
   Configuration Under Eclipse 5
   From Here 9

2 FileUpload 11
   Web and User Interfaces 11
   FileUpload Design 13
   Building an Application with FileUpload 16
      FileUpload Application User Interface 16
   Sample FileUpload Application Code 17
      Application Presentation 18
      Application Logic 20
   Limitations and Security Issues 26
   Summary 27

3 HttpClient 29
   A Simple Cookie-Based Web Site 31
   Understanding HttpClient 32
   Simple Swing Client 37
      Swing Client User Interface 37
      Swing Client Code 38
   Summary 43

4 Net 45
Net Overview 46
FTP Functionality 48
FTP Implementation 49
NNTP Functionality 54
NNTP Implementation 56
Summary 66

5 Pool 67
Interfaces and Implementation 69
Thread Pool Example 69
Object Factory Example 74
Worker Thread 75
Summary 77

6 DBCP (Database Connection Pool) 79
Standalone DataSources 81
    Client Connectivity 81
    Building the DataSource 83
Legacy JDBC Driver 86
Summary 89

7 BeanUtils 91
Understanding BeanUtils 93
Using BeanUtils to Generate Forms 94
    Sample JavaBeans 95
    Presenting the Form 95
    FormBean 97
    FormBeanUtils 101
Summary 103

8 JXPath 105
Setting Up the Example Object Graph 107
Exploring the Hierarchy 110
XPath and JXPath Syntax 113
    Basic XPath 113
    Complex XPath 114
    JXPath Extensions 115
Supported Data Types 116
Summary 117

9 Logging 119
Trace Levels 119
Using Logging 120
Logging Output 122
Summary 125

10 Lang 127
Base Lang Classes 127
- ArrayUtils 128
- BitField 128
- BooleanUtils 128
- CharRange, CharSet, and CharSetUtils 129
- ClassUtils 130
- ObjectUtils and ObjectUtils.Null 130
- RandomStringUtils 130
- SerializationUtils 131
- StringEscapeUtils 131
- StringUtils 132
- SystemUtils 134
- Validate 134
- WordUtils 134

Builder 135
Enum 136
Exception 136
Math 136
Time 137
Summary 137

11 Collections 139
Collections Concepts 140
- Bag 140
- Bean 142
- BidiMap 144
- Blocking 145
- Bounded 145
- Buffer 147
- Circular 147
- Closure 147
- Collating 150
- Comparator 150
- Composite 151
- Cursorable 151
- Factory 152
- Fast 152
- Fifo 152
- FixedSize 152
- Flat3 153
- Functor 153
- Hash 153
- Identity 153
- Lazy 154

>   Linked
>   List 154
>   LRU 156
>   Map 156
>   Multi 158
>   NodeCaching 158
>   ObjectGraph 158
>   Ordered 159
>   Predicate 160
>   Reference 160
>   Set 160
>   Singleton 160
>   StaticBucket 162
>   Synchronized 162
>   Transformed/Transformer 162
>   Typed 163
>   Unmodifiable 163
> Summary 164

12 Codec 165
Character Encodings 166
Base64 Encoding 170
URL Form Encoding 171
Hash Generation 173
Phonetic Analysis 175
Summary 176

13 CLI (Command-Line Interface) 179
ClassPathTool Overview 179
Building a Command-Line Interface 181
Running Command Line 184
Behind the Scenes with ClassPathTool 186
Summary 191

14 Other Projects 193
Additional Commons Proper Projects 193
>   Betwixt 193
>   Chain 193
>   Configuration 193
>   Daemon 193
>   DbUtils 194
>   Digester 194
>   Discovery 194
>   EL 194
>   IO 194
>   Jelly 195

Contents   xi

       Jexl 195
       Latka 195
       Launcher 195
       Math 195
       Modeler 195
       Primitives 195
       Validator 196
   Sandbox Projects 196
       Attributes 196
       Cache 196
       Clazz 196
       Compress 196
       Convert 196
       Email 197
       Events 197
       FeedParser 197
       Functor 197
       Id 197
       JJar 197
       Mapper 197
       Messenger 198
       Resources 198
       Scaffold 198
       SQL 198
       ThreadPool 198
       Transaction 198
       VFS 198
       Workflow 199
   Summary 199

A Lang Reference **201**

B Apache License, Version 2.0 .... **327**

   Index **331**

Preface

I originally noticed the Jakarta Commons libraries while working with Apache Jakarta Tomcat. At some point, Tomcat started to include a suite of small libraries with commons in the name. They started to show up everywhere, in all sorts of other open source projects. At first, it was slightly off-putting—what exactly is commons-lang.jar, and why is this tiny library showing up in all of my software?

Exploring the Jakarta Commons, I first found a broad suite of what I would characterize as "utility" code—things that often wound up in my software in packages named things like "util." Digging deeper, I found useful libraries to solve common problems, interesting algorithms, and more. In brief, by using the Jakarta Commons, I found I spent less time reinventing the wheel, and more time solving the problem at hand.

Virtually every Java developer can take advantage of various Jakarta Commons components—from the utilities provided by the Collections and Lang packages, through the networking components afforded by the HttpClient and Net packages. These components underlie Apache Tomcat, Struts, and countless other projects, helping move forward both the Java industry and the Java platform.

The first few chapters cover the more web-specific packages, including FileUpload, HttpClient, and the Net suite of protocol implementations. The Pool and DBCP packages are useful for a broader range of applications. BeanUtils and JXPath provide easier ways to work with objects. Logging, Lang, and Collections are a suite of tools applicable to almost every application. Codec provides a suite of specialized conversion routines, useful for data transfer, security, and (interestingly) phonetic analysis. Finally, the CLI package provides support for building command-line applications.

Chapter 1: Overview

This chapter shows you where to download the various Commons components, and also how to install both the libraries and the documentation into Eclipse.

Chapter 2: FileUpload

This chapter shows how to easily add file upload capabilities to your web application.

Chapter 3: HttpClient

This chapter shows how to programmatically access HTTP resources. HttpClient provides many features, including cookie management and support for a broad range of features.

Chapter 4: Net

This chapter shows how a wide variety of common Internet protocols can be accessed, including FTP, NNTP, and others.

Chapter 5: Pool

This chapter demonstrates the use of a suite of configurable object pools.

Chapter 6: DBCP (Database Connection Pool)

This chapter covers the DBCP package, useful for Swing applications and other situations in which a container is not managing database connectivity for you.

Chapter 7: BeanUtils

This chapter shows how the information provided by JavaBeans-style objects can easily be accessed at run-time.

Chapter 8: JXPath

As you build applications composed of complex graphs of objects, traversing those objects can become tedious. JXPath provides an easy mechanism for walking through these graphs.

CHAPTER 9: LOGGING

Virtually every application can benefit from configurable logging—and the logging package is a good place to get started.

CHAPTER 10: LANG

Lang is one of the most useful packages, but one of the hardest to get started with. This chapter provides an overview of the Lang package, helping you get oriented.

CHAPTER 11: COLLECTIONS

This chapter covers powerful tools for working with collections—richer object relationships.

CHAPTER 12: CODEC

This chapter shows how to use a suite of specialized conversion routines useful for data transfer, security, and phonetic analysis.

CHAPTER 13: CLI (COMMAND-LINE INTERFACE)

Learn how to present consistent, useful command-line configuration and help information—with a bonus class path search tool.

CHAPTER 14: OTHER PROJECTS

This chapter provides a roadmap for a broad suite of other Commons projects—both the proper and sandbox.

DOWNLOADING THE CODE

The code presented in this book is available for download from `http://www.cascadetg.com/commons/`.

Acknowledgments

Many, many thanks to Mark Taub for pulling this book together and being such a pleasure to work with.

Thanks to my agent, Laura Lewin of StudioB, without whom this book would not exist.

Thanks to the technical reviewers for taking the time to provide such excellent feedback, including Sylvain Gibassier, Mark Ferkingstad, and Lance Young. Any remaining mistakes are my own.

On a personal note, thanks to friends and family for their support. In particular, that includes adoor, alzo, dionysusdevotee, gaaneden, grandmoffdavid, hansandersen, jephly, jrpseudonym, merovingian, musae, p_fish, phoebek, preciousjade, rogerothornhill, sajin, and zunger. And finally, thanks to Cynthia, Diane, and Mom. You are, quite simply, the best.

About the Author

Will Iverson has been working in the computer and information technology field professionally since 1990. His diverse background includes developing statistical applications to analyze data from the NASA Space Shuttle, product management for Apple Computer, and developer relations for Symantec's VisualCafé. For nearly five years, Will ran an independent J2EE consulting company with a variety of clients including Sun, BEA, and Canal+ Technologies. He currently serves as the application development practice manager for SolutionsIQ. Will lives in Seattle, Washington.

CHAPTER 1

Overview

The Apache Jakarta Commons project (http://jakarta.apache.org/commons/) is a collection of reusable Java software components. Each Commons project represents a unit of functionality smaller than a full application—all of the various Commons projects are intended to help a Java developer build a useful application more quickly by leveraging existing components. Despite the range of functionality included in the various Commons projects, many developers have not taken the time to understand or make use of these libraries, despite their inclusion in many of the most popular open source projects such as Tomcat and Hibernate. On the other hand, considering that the Commons project (as of this writing) consists of twenty-nine released proper components and twenty sandbox components, it's easy to understand why some developers may find the project intimidating. Nonetheless, virtually every development project of any scope can benefit from the introduction of an appropriate Commons package. The Lang package alone contains a broad suite of simple utilities needed by almost every web application, such as a utility function for escaping a bit of HTML or SQL, or a quick class to make it easier to return a Date object formatted to a particular locale.

The difficult thing about the Commons package is not the complexity associated with any particular project, but rather simply remembering what functionality is present. Therefore, the goal of this book is to provide an overview of the most useful Commons package for the broadest array of Java developers. Certain packages solve hard problems—for example, it's easy to identify a need for the HttpClient package after hitting a wall with the built-in JDK HTTP connectivity suite. Implementing HTTP file upload capability from scratch is somewhat difficult, but the FileUpload package takes care of things nicely. Introspection is great, but BeanUtils is easier. And so on.

Even the small bits add up quickly—it may seem easy to write your own utility methods, but those thirty minute one-offs can start to add up, especially considering the time needed to track down and fix minor bugs. Even more critically, other developers familiar with various Commons packages will immediately know where to find and how to use the utility routines in your project.

PROPER VERSUS SANDBOX

The maintainers of the Commons project divide contributed code into two main areas, a "proper" suite and a "sandbox." The proper code is considered stable (and popular) enough to warrant a certain level of commitment—the interfaces are expected not to change without warning, and the code is considered to have been tested well enough for production use. The sandbox, on the other hand, is open to anyone already accepted as a committer on another Jakarta project.

The bulk of this book is devoted to the most popular and useful of the proper components—for more information on the sandbox components, see Chapter 14, "Other Projects."

The proper components from the Commons package identified in Table 1-1 are covered in this book.

Table 1-1 Covered Proper Components

BeanUtils	Chapter 7	Easy-to-use wrappers around the Java reflection and introspection APIs.
CLI (Command Line Interface)	Chapter 13	Provides a simple API for working with command line arguments, options, option groups, mandatory options, and default help output.
Codec	Chapter 12	Contains phonetic encoders, Hex, Base64, and a URL encoder.
Collections	Chapter 11	Extends and augments the Java Collections Framework.
DBCP	Chapter 6	Database connection pooling services. Based on the Pool component, described in Chapter 5, "Pool."
FileUpload	Chapter 2	Adds robust, high-performance, file upload capability to servlets and web applications.
HttpClient	Chapter 3	A framework for working with the client side of the HTTP protocol.
JXPath	Chapter 8	Utilities for manipulating Java classes that conform to the JavaBeans naming conventions using the XPath syntax. It also supports maps, DOM, and other object models.
Lang	Chapter 10	A very common set of utility classes, including routines for escaping text, enums, math, and time.
Logging	Chapter 9	A wrapper around a variety of logging API implementations (including log4j and JDK logging).
Net	Chapter 4	A collection of network utilities including Telnet, FTP, and NNTP clients.
Pool	Chapter 5	A generic object pooling interface, with classes for creating object pools and several general purpose pool implementations.

The proper projects listed in Table 1-2 are not covered by this book. Some of these projects merely provide implementations of certain standards (e.g., the JSP Expression Language), are handled by other frameworks (e.g., DbUtils), or are too narrowly focused for coverage in this text.

Table 1-2 Additional Proper Components

Betwixt	Services for mapping JavaBeans to XML documents, and vice versa.
Chain	Provides a "Chain of Responsibility" pattern implementation for organizing complex processing flows.
Configuration	Tools to assist in the reading of configuration/preferences files in various formats.
Daemon	An alternative invocation mechanism for Unix-daemon-like Java code.
DbUtils	JDBC helper library that factors out mundane resource cleanup code for common database tasks.
Digester	An XML-to-Java-object mapping utility commonly used for parsing XML configuration files.
Discovery	Provides tools for locating resources (including classes) by mapping service/reference names to resource names using a variety of schemes.
EL	An interpreter for the Expression Language defined by the JavaServer Pages (TM) specification, version 2.0.
IO	Collection of I/O utilities.
Jelly	XML-based scripting and processing engine.
Jexl	An expression language that extends the Expression Language of the JSTL.
Latka	An HTTP functional testing suite for automated QA, acceptance, and regression testing.
Launcher	Cross-platform Java application launcher. Eliminates the need for a batch or shell script to launch a Java application.
Math	Library of lightweight, self-contained mathematics and statistics components addressing the common practical problems not immediately available in the Java programming language.
Modeler	Provides mechanisms to create Model MBeans compatible with the Java Management Extensions (JMX) specification.
Primitives	Smaller, faster, and easier-to-work-with types supporting Java primitive types, with an emphasis on collections.
Validator	Simple, extendable framework to define validation methods and validation rules in an XML file. Supports internationalization of rules and error messages.

LICENSE

The Apache Software Foundation, which maintains the Jakarta Commons project, is dedicated to providing open source software. The standard Apache license, which governs the Jakarta Commons, is considered a "business friendly" license—anyone can build software using the open source Commons code without needing to disclose modifications.

For more information on the Apache Software Foundation license, including compatibility with other licenses (such as the GPL), see `http://www.apache.org/licenses/`.

OBTAINING AND INSTALLING

The Commons package (as well as the other Jakarta packages) is distributed in both binary and source forms. The binary releases can be found at:

`http://jakarta.apache.org/site/binindex.cgi`

The source code releases corresponding to the binary releases can be found at:

`http://jakarta.apache.org/site/sourceindex.cgi`

Finally, if you are interested in the latest (possibly unstable) release of Commons (or any other Jakarta software), instructions on CVS access are provided at:

`http://jakarta.apache.org/site/cvsindex.html`

Apache Jakarta

The Apache Jakarta project (`http://jakarta.apache.org`) simply refers to the Java-related projects conducted under the Apache Software Foundation's banner. Other popular Jakarta projects include the Tomcat web application server, the Cactus test framework, and the Velocity template engine. Certain projects, such as Struts and Ant, were originally part of the Jakarta project but have since "graduated" to exist as top-level Apache projects.

Generally speaking, you are advised to download the binary release at a minimum. The binary releases of the Commons projects covered in this book typically include a single JAR file, a README.txt, a LICENSE.txt file, and a docs directory. The JAR file should be added to your class path. For example, you would copy the JAR file to your WEB-INF/lib directory for a web application. You may also want to download the source distribution if you want to contribute to, debug, or examine the Commons package.

> **Directory Conventions**
>
> On my Windows development system, I install downloaded libraries into a single directory, `C:\devenv\`. This represents my personal repository of downloaded libraries (and associated documentation, samples, etc.). My development source trees are stored in another directory, `C:\devrep\`, which is controlled by a version control system (CVS, soon to be converted to Subversion). As libraries are required by projects, I copy the `.jar` files from the `C:\devenv\` directory into the appropriate location in `C:\devrep\`. Therefore, project-specific dependencies are resolved by relative paths, but upon occasion, interim development is done with references to the `C:\devenv\` directory. I don't use the `C:\Documents and Settings\<username>` directory because too many packages are confused by spaces in paths.
>
> On UNIX systems, I generally use `~\devrep\` and `~\devenv\`.
>
> There's nothing particularly magical about this strategy, but it does keep my tools and documentation nicely separated from my development tree.

CONFIGURATION UNDER ECLIPSE

Generally speaking, configuration of the various packages is development environment-specific. One of the more popular development environments is the free, open source Eclipse project (http://www.eclipse.org/). After downloading and installing the environment, you can add various Jakarta Commons components to your project(s). Assuming you are starting with an existing Java project, right-click on the project name and select Properties, as shown in Figure 1-1.

In the project properties, select the Java Build Path panel and then the Libraries tab, as shown in Figure 1-2.

If you have copied the JAR file to your project (for example, in the WEB-INF/lib directory), you can click the Add JARs . . . button to add the JAR file to the build path. Alternatively, if you wish to store the JAR file external to the project, click Add External JARs. . . . Either way, you will be presented with a dialog to select the JAR file. Select the file and click OK to exit the project properties. The JAR is now configured on the Eclipse class path, ready for development.

You may want to take advantage of Eclipse's additional features. To complete installation, right-click on the entry for the JAR file and bring up the properties, as shown in Figure 1-3.

Enter the path to the Javadoc for the distribution found in the docs/api directory of the binary release, as shown in Figure 1-4.

Next, if you have downloaded the source for the package, you can click on Java Source Attachment in the JAR properties dialog and set the source location,

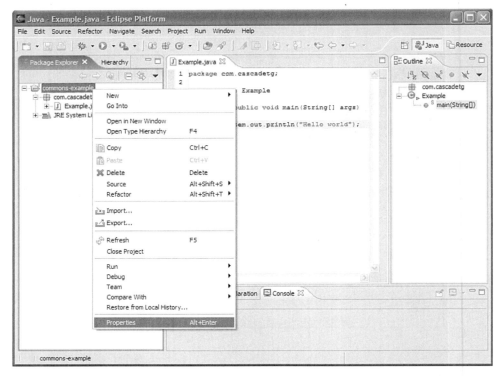

Figure 1-1 Opening project properties.

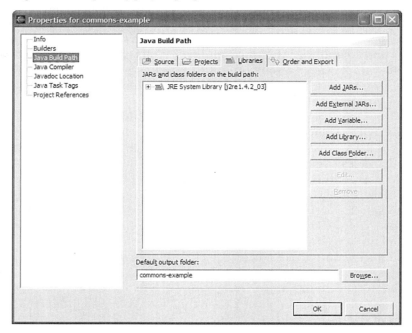

Figure 1-2 Java Build Path.

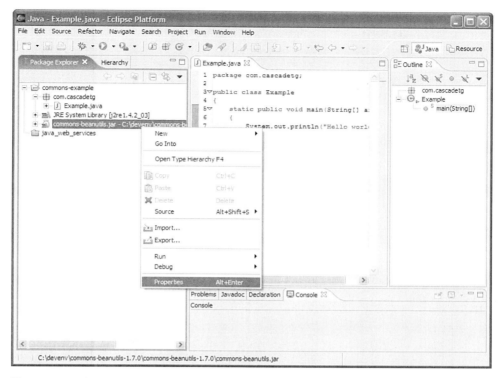

Figure 1-3 Opening JAR entry properties.

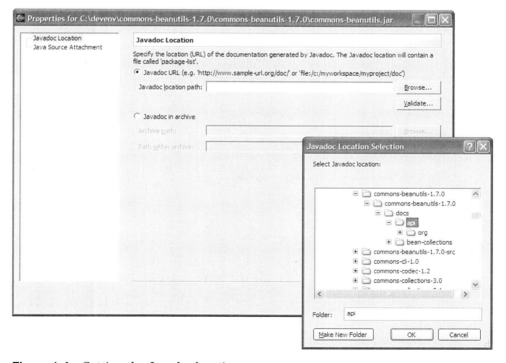

Figure 1-4 Setting the Javadoc location.

as shown in Figure 1-5. Note that the source is contained in the src/java directory.

By setting the Javadoc location, Eclipse will display the Javadoc contents in addition to the type-ahead information, as shown in Figure 1-6. Setting the source location will allow you to seamlessly bring up the source for the package when debugging.

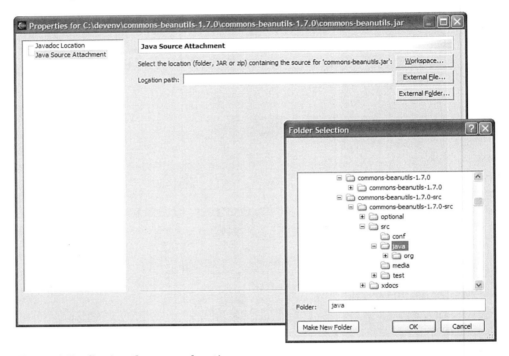

Figure 1-5 Setting the source location.

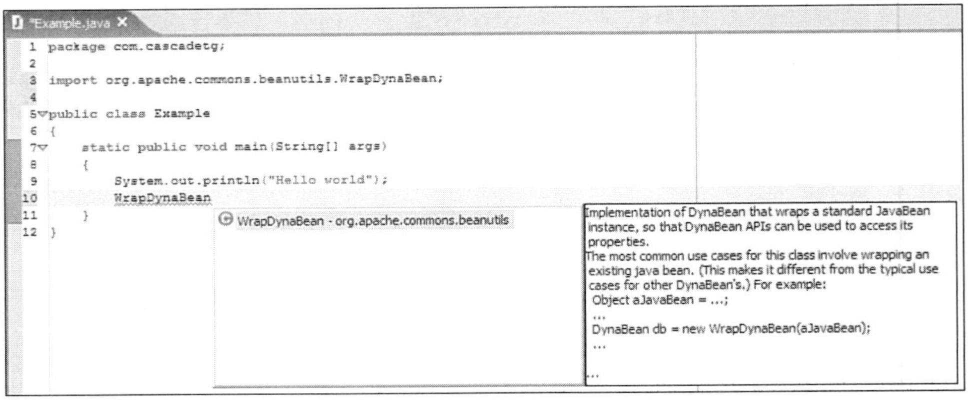

Figure 1-6 Quick Javadoc information access.

All of the Commons packages follow the same distribution structure and are downloaded from the same pages—the next step is to learn the actual packages.

FROM HERE

Each chapter except for the last provides an overview (and where appropriate, examples) for a major Commons proper package. The final chapter provides a bit more detail on the remaining packages, both proper and sandbox, including (where appropriate) a comment on the package status.

CHAPTER 2

FileUpload

The first Jakarta Commons component we will examine is FileUpload, an aptly named library that makes it easy to add file upload capability to your web application. By using this library, a user can send a file to a web server by simply selecting a file in a web form and clicking "upload." Anyone who has used a popular web-based email client to send a file attachment has seen file upload functionality in action (for example, Yahoo! or Hotmail).

In this chapter, we'll look at how this library works and show how to use the key classes.

WEB AND USER INTERFACES

When working with a JSP or servlet, you may be accustomed to retrieving data from a `javax.servlet.ServletRequest` using the `getParameter()` and `getParameterNames()` methods. This works great for simple HTML-based forms, such as the one shown in Listing 2-1. The standard servlet method, `request.getParameter("textfield")`, is used to retrieve data submitted when the user clicks the Submit button.

Listing 2-1 Simple Request JSP

```
<head>
  <title>Request Example</title>
  <meta http-equiv="Content-Type"
    content="text/html; charset=iso-8859-1" />
</head>

<body>
<%= request.getParameter("textfield") %><br />
<form name="form1" id="form1" method="post"
action="request_example.jsp">
  <input type="text" name="textfield" />
  <input type="submit" name="Submit" value="Submit" />
</form>
</body>
</html>
```

The JSP page as rendered in a browser is shown in Figure 2-1.

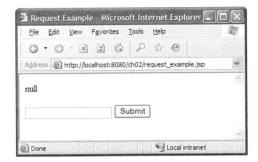

Figure 2-1 Simple request starting page.

As you can see in Figure 2-1, the initial page display shows "null" for the `request.getParameter("textfield")` call. Entering the words "Hello World!" into the text field and clicking the Submit button sends a page request back to the server (as specified by the `action` attribute). The server parses the request, and the form data is made available to the JSP. This can be seen in Figure 2-2.

Figure 2-2 Simple request parsed response.

This standard JSP/servlet mechanism works fine for normal HTML controls (check boxes, radio buttons, text fields, text areas, buttons, etc.). Unfortunately, it fails to handle file uploads using the `<input type="file" name="file_upload">` HTML tag.

Listing 2-2 Sample File Upload Form

```
<form action="request_example.jsp" method="post"
enctype="multipart/form-data" name="form1" id="form1">
    <input type="file" name="file" />
    <input type="submit" name="Submit" value="Submit" />
</form>
```

The code shown in Listing 2-2 is an example of an HTML file upload form. Notice the addition of the `enctype="multipart/form-data"` attribute to the form, as well as the `<input type="file" name="file" />` tag. The `enctype` attribute governs how the browser should package and send the data back to the server (for more information on this, read RFC 1867 at `http://www.ietf.org/rfc/rfc1867.txt`).

Figure 2-3 shows the `<input type="file" name="file_upload">` HTML tag as rendered by Internet Explorer.

Figure 2-3   FileUpload user interface.

The Jakarta Commons FileUpload component provides support for the file upload capability of a typical web browser, letting you go beyond the limitations of the parameter parsing of the standard servlet system. FileUpload will parse the data returned by the `multipart/form-data` form and file input type as sent by your browser.

FileUpload Design

FileUpload has two main points of interest to a user: the class `org.apache.commons.fileupload.DiskFileUpload`, which parses the incoming data, and the interface `org.apache.commons.fileupload.FileItem`, returned when the file upload data has successfully been parsed.

The class hierarchy for `DiskFileUpload` is shown in Figure 2-4.

To use `DiskFileUpload`, the application needs to set a temporary path on disk to spool file data and the size threshold. It's easy to envision applications that might require several megabytes to be uploaded at a time, and by using the `DiskFileUpload` class with appropriate thresholds, the application will try not to overload the server.

Be Aware of Performance Impacts

The Java servlet model uses a single thread per request. If your application server is set to provide a maximum of fifty threads for handling incoming requests, fifty file uploads can starve the server for additional requests. You may want to consider isolating the file upload capability of your application from the thread pool for the rest of the application. For example, in Tomcat, you may want to define a second HTTP connector on a different port with another thread pool for handling file upload requests. This is application server-specific functionality, but be aware that file uploads are typically much longer-lived, resource-intensive operations than simply handling an ordinary page request.

More seriously, a series of file uploads could easily be used to launch a denial-of-service attack. In a production environment, make sure that only authenticated users are allowed to initiate a file upload.

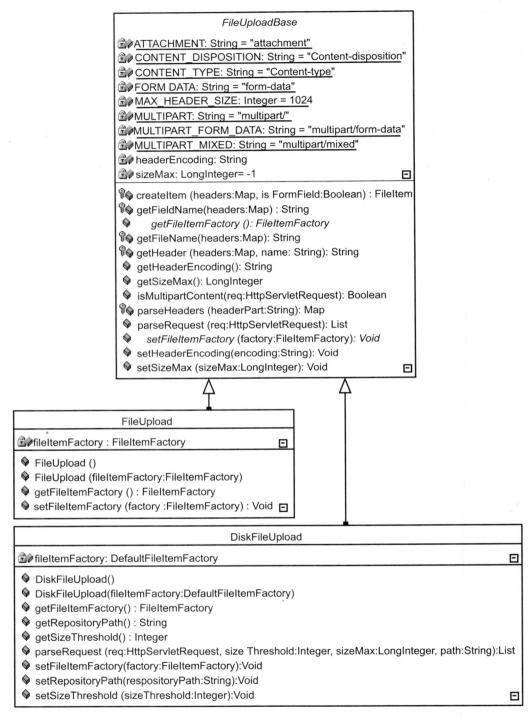

Figure 2-4 DiskFileUpload class.

FileUpload Design

The main `DiskFileUpload` method of interest is `parseRequest()`. It returns a `List` of `FileItem` objects, shown in more detail in Figure 2-5.

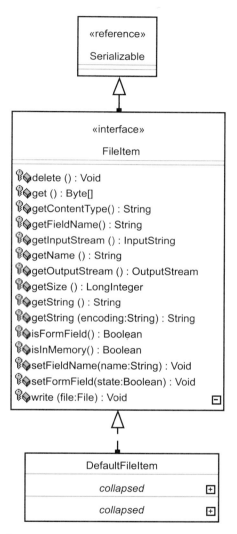

Figure 2-5 `FileItem` class.

The bulk of the methods of the `FileItem` interface are fairly self-explanatory. The most significant thing to be aware of is that using `get()` will load the entire file into memory at once, whereas `getInputStream()` allows for buffering and other stream operations.

BUILDING AN APPLICATION WITH FILEUPLOAD

Now that we understand the basic design of the FileUpload component, let's look at a simple application that makes use of FileUpload. As shown in Figure 2-6, the JSP pages provide a user interface, and a set of Java helper classes are used to configure and invoke the FileUpload component.

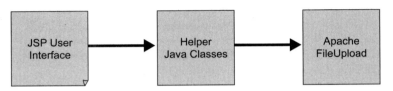

Figure 2-6 FileUpload application overview.

By centralizing the access to the FileUpload component in the helper classes, the configuration of the FileUpload component can be changed without updating the JSP pages. For example, you may want to configure the maximum permissible file size, the kind of files that may be updated, or the buffering of uploaded data to memory or disk.

FileUpload Application User Interface

A user visiting the file upload web application is first prompted to add a file, as shown in Figure 2-7.

Figure 2-7 Add File request.

Clicking the link takes the user to a file upload form, as shown in Figure 2-8. Clicking the Browse... button (a standard browser user interface widget) prompts the user to select a file on disk. Here, we've selected a file on the c:\ drive. Clicking Upload sends the selected file to the server.

The file is uploaded, and then the user is returned to the file list, as shown in Figure 2-9. You'll notice that the user can click on the file name to download the file again via HTTP, the file size is reported in bytes, and the MIME type (as reported by the browser) is listed. Additionally, the Location

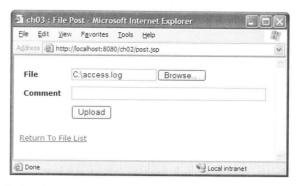

Figure 2-8 File Upload form.

Figure 2-9 Uploaded File list.

link points to the file location on the server's file system. Finally, clicking Delete will remove the file from disk.

The user interface is quite straightforward, and in the next section we'll look at the code required to build it.

SAMPLE FILEUPLOAD APPLICATION CODE

The code for the application consists of the following files:

- `index.jsp`—The main interface, as shown in Figure 2-7 and 2-8. Lists the files that have been posted.
- `post.jsp`—The file upload form, as shown in Figure 2-9.

These two JSP pages in turn make use of two Java classes.

- `Files.java`—Acts as the manager of uploaded files. Keeps track of information about the files that have been uploaded, such as the location on disk.
- `FileUploadHelper.java`—This application class wraps the Commons `FileUpload` class, making it easier to use in JSP pages. This provides a central location to keep track of the FileUpload configuration.

Application Presentation

The `index.jsp` page is shown in Listing 2-3. You'll notice a small bit of logic at the top to handle a file deletion. Otherwise, the bulk of the file deals with looping over the file list and other formatting.

Note that when your JSP page issues a `sendRedirect()`, as shown in the JSP scriptlet header, a `return` is used to avoid additional processing of logic on the page. This simple technique is used to avoid a variety of potential problems.

Listing 2-3 File Listing JSP

```jsp
<%@ page language="java" import="com.cascadetg.ch02.*" %>
<%
java.util.Hashtable myFilesHashtable = Files.getFiles();

java.util.Enumeration
    myFilesEnumeration = myFilesHashtable.elements();

if(request.getParameter("delete") != null)
{
    Files.deleteFile(application, request.getParameter("file"));
    response.sendRedirect("index.jsp");
    return;
}
%>
<head><title>File Upload Example</title></head>
<body>
<% if (myFilesHashtable.size() == 0)
    { %>
    No files posted.
<% } else { %>
<table width="100%" border="0" cellspacing="3" cellpadding="3">
  <tr>
    <td><strong>File</strong></td>
    <td><strong>Size</strong></td>
    <td><strong>Type</strong></td>
    <td><strong>Location</strong></td>
    <td> </td>
  </tr>
<%    while(myFilesEnumeration.hasMoreElements())
    {
        org.apache.commons.fileupload.FileItem
            myFile =
                (org.apache.commons.fileupload.FileItem)
                    myFilesEnumeration.nextElement();
%>
  <tr>
    <td><a href="<%=
        Files.getDownloadPath(request) +
            FileUploadHelper.getFileName(myFile.getName())
        %>"><%=
        FileUploadHelper.getFileName(myFile.getName())
        %></a></td>
    <td><%=myFile.getSize()%></td>
    <td><%= myFile.getContentType()%></td>
    <td><a target="_blank" href="file:///<%=
        Files.getUploadPath(application) +
```

(continues)

Listing 2-3 (continued)

```
            FileUploadHelper.getFileName(myFile.getName())
               %>">Local File</a></td>
    <td><a href="<%= "index.jsp?file=" +
        response.encodeURL(FileUploadHelper.getFileName(myFile.getName()))
            + "&delete=true" %>">Delete</a></td>
  </tr>
<%    } /* End of file display iteration */ %>
</table>
<% } /* End of file list display */ %>
<p><a href="post.jsp">Add File</a> </p>
</body>
</html>
```

The form used to upload a file to the server is shown in Listing 2-4. You'll notice that there is only a small bit of code—the heavy lifting is handled by the `FileUploadHelper` class.

Listing 2-4 File Post JSP

```
<%@ page language="java" import="java.sql.*" %><%

com.cascadetg.ch02.FileUploadHelper
    myFileHelper = new com.cascadetg.ch02.FileUploadHelper();

if(myFileHelper.doFilePost(request, application))
{
    response.sendRedirect("index.jsp");
    return;
}
%>
<html>
<head>
<title>ch02 : File Post</title>
<meta http-equiv="Content-Type" content="text/html; charset=iso-8859-1" />
<link href="default.css" rel="stylesheet" type="text/css">
</head>
<body>
<form action="post.jsp" method="post"
    enctype="multipart/form-data" name="form1" id="form1">
    <table width="100%"  border="0" cellspacing="3" cellpadding="3">
      <tr>
        <td width="25%"><strong>File</strong></td>
        <td><input type="file" name="file" /></td>
      </tr>
      <tr>
        <td width="25%"><strong>Comment</strong></td>
        <td><input name="Comment" type="text" size="50"
maxlength="250"></td>
      </tr>
      <tr>
        <td width="25%"> </td>
        <td><input type="submit" name="Submit" value="Upload" /></td>
      </tr>
    </table>
</form>
<p><a href="index.jsp">Return To File List </a></p>
</body>
</html>
```

Application Logic

The `FileUploadHelper` (diagrammed in Figure 2-10) handles the request, storing the uploaded files in one `Hashtable` and the form parameters in another.

This application doesn't actually make use of the form parameters, but it would be easy to add access methods to get to the data if it were needed. For example, you might want to allow a user to set a comment for a file on the same page as a form upload.

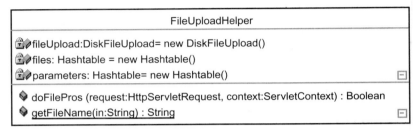

Figure 2-10 `FileUploadHelper` class diagram.

Listing 2-5 shows the declaration and three main bits of information tracked when a file is uploaded. First, it's possible that more than one file may be uploaded in a single POST (hence the `files` hash table). Second, the `parameters` hash table is used to track any additional non-file form data sent by the browser. In this example, we don't actually make use of the form parameters, but it would be easy to add access methods to get to the data if it were needed. For example, you might want to allow a user to send a comment for a file on the same page as a form upload. Finally, the third instance variable, `fileUpload`, contains a reference to the `DiskFileUpload` class. This object is used to actually perform the parsing.

Listing 2-5 `FileUploadHelper` (part 1)

```
package com.cascadetg.ch02;

import java.io.File;
import java.util.*;
import org.apache.commons.fileupload.*;
import javax.servlet.http.*;

/** This class is used to handle an uploaded file. */

public class FileUploadHelper
{
    /**   Used to store the uploaded files just uploaded. Note that
     * these are tracked by the Files class.   */
    Hashtable files = new Hashtable();

    /**   Used to track the additional parameters sent along with the
     * file. For example, you might send a textarea form element
```

(continues)

Listing 2-5 (continued)

```
    * along with a comment describing the file.  */
   Hashtable parameters = new Hashtable();

   /**   The org.apache.commons.fileupload.DiskFileUpload class used
    * to actually handle the upload processing.  */
   DiskFileUpload fileUpload = new DiskFileUpload();
```

Listing 2-6 shows that the `doFilePost()` method handles the file upload as sent by the JSP. First, some basic tests are performed to ensure that a form upload has actually been posted. Next, the `fileUpload` object is configured—the maximum file size, the maximum size to store in memory before spooling to disk, and the temporary location to spool the file are set. The value shown for the repository path is based on the current web application context—depending on the operating system and application server you are using, you may wish to set this to some other value.

The remainder of the class simply parses the incoming request and then loops through the returned response for additional information. Obviously, for a large file, the `fileUpload.parseRequest(request)` call may block for some time while the file is uploaded. You should consider this carefully when designing your web application.

You may notice that a simple utility method (`getFileName`) is provided for stripping the path information from the incoming form. As of this writing, Microsoft Internet Explorer 6 returns the full path of the uploaded file sent by the user (for example, `C:\myfolder\myfile.txt`), whereas Mozilla-based browsers (such as Firefox) only return the actual name of the file (`myfile.txt`). Similarly, some operating systems return the path with \ characters for the path separator, and others use the / character. For these and a multitude of other reasons, you'll want to test your web application thoroughly to ensure that it is compatible with a wide range of browsers.

Listing 2-6 `FileUploadHelper` (part 2)

```
   /**   Returns true if it's a file post, false if not. If it's
    * false, we know that we should use the standard servlet
    * methods for getting the parameters.
    */
   public boolean doFilePost(HttpServletRequest request,
         javax.servlet.ServletContext context)
   {
       if (request.getContentType() == null)
           return false;

       if (!request.getContentType().startsWith("multipart/form-data"))
       {
           // Not a multi-part/form-data post, which means we
           // should use standard servlet methods for getting
           // parameters
           return false;
       }
```

(continues)

Listing 2-6 (*continued*)

```
            // Maximum files size in bytes before a FileUploadException
            // will be thrown
            fileUpload.setSizeMax(10 * Files.MB);

            // maximum size that will be stored in memory before we
            // start spooling to disk
            fileUpload.setSizeThreshold(4 * Files.KB);

            // Set the location to spool temporary files
            fileUpload.setRepositoryPath(Files.getTempPath(context));

            try
            {
                // Use the fileUpload object (DiskFileUpload) to parse
                // the request.
                List fileItems = fileUpload.parseRequest(request);

                // Loop through the uploaded files and parameters
                Iterator i = fileItems.iterator();
                while (i.hasNext())
                {
                    FileItem file = (FileItem)i.next();

                    // MS IE reports the full path as the name, but
                    // we're only interested in the actual file name.
                    String fileName = file.getName();
                    fileName = getFileName(fileName);

                    if (file.isFormField())
                    {
                        // If it's a form field, we'll want to make it
                        // available as a parameter.
                        parameters.put(
                            file.getFieldName(),
                            file.getString());
                    } else
                    {
                        // If it's not a form field, we'll assume it's
                        // a file and add it both to this upload,to the
                        // list of posted files, and write the file to
                        // disk.
                        files.put(fileName, file);
                        Files.getFiles().put(fileName, file);
                        File upload =
                            new File(
                                Files.getUploadPath(context)
                                    + fileName);
                        file.write(upload);
                    }
                }
            } catch (Exception e)
            {
                e.printStackTrace();
            }
            return true;
        }
```

(*continues*)

Sample FileUpload Application Code

Listing 2-6 (*continued*)

```
    // A utility method to strip the path information away from the
    // submitted file. We assume that the / and the \ characters
    // are the only ones returned.
    public static String getFileName(String in)
    {
        String result = in;
        if (result != null)
        {
            if (result.indexOf("\\") > 0)
                result =
                    result.substring(
                        result.lastIndexOf("\\") + 1,
                        result.length());
            if (result.indexOf("/") > 0)
                result =
                    result.substring(
                        result.lastIndexOf("/") + 1,
                        result.length());
        }
        return result;
    }
}
```

The final code, as modeled in Figure 2-11, acts as an in-memory record of the uploaded files. You'll notice that a few attempts are made at security—for example, the application blocks certain extensions from being uploaded to the server in an attempt to avoid spreading viruses.

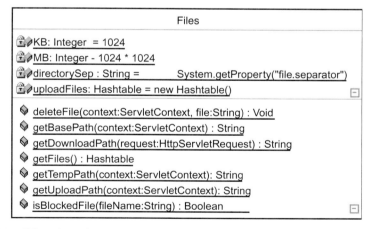

Figure 2-11   Files class diagram.

The source for the application's in-memory record, shown in Listing 2-7, deals with a number of platform-specific functions in addition to tracking the files themselves. For example, depending on your operating system, you may want to deny certain file names. A list of inappropriate file extensions for Microsoft Windows is shown—you may want to add more if you are using another operating system. Similarly, instead of the relatively permissive model shown, you may want to default to denying all files and only allow certain file types to be posted (for example, your application may only allow .zip archives, both to avoid potential security issues associated with other file types and to save space on the server).

You may notice that the temporary spool location (getBasePath) is inside the WEB-INF folder. This location is only used for random, unique temporary spool files—a user cannot overwrite a file in the WEB-INF directory in this fashion, but you may want to set this to an appropriate platform-specific temporary file location for increased security.

Uploaded files are placed in an upload directory. After a file has been uploaded, anyone can download the file by merely pointing his or her web browser to the proper location. If you want to protect the files, you may want to place them instead in a WEB-INF\upload directory, in a completely different directory outside of the web application, or even in a database. From there, a user who wanted to download one of these files would have to go through the authentication scheme you've chosen, and then your application would stream the data via a servlet as needed. Keep in mind that in that case, your web application is taking on a role (streaming static file content) that is otherwise handled by a different system (for example, Apache httpd or Tomcat's dedicated static resource handler). You will want to carefully consider the implications in terms of performance before putting this into production.

Listing 2-7 File Management

```
package com.cascadetg.ch02;

import java.io.File;
import java.util.*;
import org.apache.commons.fileupload.*;
import javax.servlet.http.HttpServletRequest;

/** This static class is used to manage the files posted to the
 * server. */

public class Files
{
    public static Hashtable getFiles()
    {
        return uploadedFiles;
    }
    private static Hashtable uploadedFiles = new Hashtable();

    /**     * List of blocked file extensions taken from the MS security
      * note posted at...
      * http://support.microsoft.com/default.aspx?scid=KB;EN-US;Q235309
      */
    static public final String[] blockedFileExtensions = {
        ".ade", ".adp", ".bas", ".bat", ".chm", ".cmd", ".com",
        ".cpl", ".crt", ".exe", ".hlp", ".hta", ".inf", ".ins",
```

(continues)

Listing 2-7 (continued)

```java
        ".isp", ".js", ".jse", ".lnk", ".mda", ".mdb", ".mde",
        ".mdz", ".msc", ".msi", ".msp", ".mst", ".pcd", ".pif",
        ".reg", ".scr", ".sct", ".shs", ".url", ".vb", ".vbe",
        ".vbs", ".wsc", ".wsf", ".wsh",
        // Also, don't allow people to upload code!
        "jsp", "php", "asp", "class", "java" };

    /** Useful constants */
    public static int KB = 1024;
    public static int MB = 1024 * 1024;

    /** Needed when working with files on disks */
    public static String directorySep =
        System.getProperty("file.separator");

    /**     * Used to determine if a file should not be uploaded based on
      * file extension. */
    public boolean isBlockedFile(String fileName)
    {
        String lowerCaseName = fileName.toLowerCase();
        for (int i = 0; i < blockedFileExtensions.length; i++)
        {
            if (lowerCaseName.endsWith(blockedFileExtensions[i]))
                return true;
        }
        return false;
    }

    /**     * The base path corresponds to the base directory of the
      * application context's WEB-INF directory. This means that
      * this directory is NOT visible to the end user.
      */
    public static String getBasePath(
        javax.servlet.ServletContext context)
    { return context.getRealPath("/") + "WEB-INF" + directorySep; }

    /**     * The temporary directory used to store files while they are
      * being uploaded.  */
    public static String getTempPath(
        javax.servlet.ServletContext context)
    { return getBasePath(context) + "tmp" + directorySep; }

    /**     * Gets the upload directory - used to indicate the local file
      * system storage area.
      */
    public static String getUploadPath(
        javax.servlet.ServletContext context)
    { return getBasePath(context) + ".." + directorySep + "ch02"
            + directorySep + "upload" + directorySep;
    }

    /**     * The path to the upload directory - used to retrieve a file
      * from the server.
      */
    public static String getDownloadPath(HttpServletRequest request)
    {
        return request.getScheme() + "://" + request.getServerName()
            + ":" + request.getServerPort() + "/" + "ch02/upload/";
    }
```

(*continues*)

Listing 2-7 (*continued*)

```
    /** Deletes the uploaded file. */
    public static void deleteFile(
        javax.servlet.ServletContext context,
        String file)
    {
        FileItem myFile = (FileItem)uploadedFiles.get(file);
        if (myFile == null)
            return;

        // Marks temporary file for deletion.
        myFile.delete();

        // Deletes the uploaded file
        File diskFile =
            new File(getUploadPath(context) + myFile.getName());

        if (diskFile.exists())
            diskFile.delete();

        // Removes from the in-memory hash.
        uploadedFiles.remove(file);
    }
}
```

LIMITATIONS AND SECURITY ISSUES

Before continuing, it's worth taking a moment to consider some of the limitations of the sample code as shown. Most of these limitations are easily solvable, but it's worth considering both the inherent limitations and the security implications of uploading file data to the server.

- ☞ The sample code shown previously stores the list of uploaded files in memory only (using a `Hashtable`)—if you're doing this "for real," you'll want to store data about the uploaded files with some sort of persistent mechanism (for example, using a relational database).
- ☞ The sample code shown previously stores files using the file name as the "unique identifier." This is a pretty simplistic mechanism, and it is prone to conflict if two files are uploaded with the same name. Again, the use of a database and a synthetic primary key may be your best bet.
- ☞ This is not an inherently transactionally safe operation—it's easy to think of situations that might "confuse" the application, such as uploading a new file with the same name as a file that is currently being downloaded.
- ☞ In general, error handling is limited to dumping an exception to the console. For a production application, you will want to handle all possible error scenarios as gracefully as possible.
- ☞ Some attempt is made to prohibit uploading potentially "dangerous" file types to the server. It may be more appropriate to store files in a fashion that doesn't preserve the original filenames on a file system—either by hashing the filenames or perhaps by storing the files in a database.

Similarly, you may only want to allow users to upload a certain set of file types and prohibit all others.
- ☞ It's terribly easy to choke your entire web application with a denial-of-service attack by simply initiating a large number of file uploads. Therefore, you will likely only want to allow users to initiate a file upload after they have authenticated. You may want to adopt a further strategy, such as a flag to only allow an authenticated user to upload a single file at a time, or you might want to use a pool to manage file uploads.
- ☞ No provision is made to protect file downloads. If a file is uploaded to a directory, anyone who has the URL can download it. If you want to protect the uploaded file in some fashion (for example, requiring a login), you'll need to add a mechanism to "hide" the file and only send it to approved users.

It's a truism that when considering the security of an application, you can't "trust" anything that comes from the client browser. This is doubly true when considering file uploads. When adding file upload capability, make sure you've fully considered the security implications.

SUMMARY

In this chapter, an application was shown demonstrating the use of the FileUpload component to add file uploads to a web application. In the next chapter, this will be flipped around to look at a library intended to help a client application download data from a web server.

Project Ideas

Use FileUpload in conjunction with the FTP component of the Net package (described in Chapter 4, "Net") to allow users to post files to an FTP server via a browser.

Create a web version of a file system browser. Add security and mechanisms for implementing common file system commands such as move, copy, rename, and delete. Use FileUpload to add file upload capability.

Use the Codec package (described in Chapter 12, "Codec") to encode files stored on disk uploaded via FileUpload.

Write a program to examine the different file upload characteristics as provided by as many different browsers as possible (e.g., Mozilla Netscape, Mozilla Firefox, different versions of Internet Explorer for Mac OS and Windows, Lynx, Mac OS X Safari, Opera . . .). Add performance metrics to compare different browsers. Does the servlet container (e.g., Apache Jakarta Tomcat) affect the performance?

CHAPTER **3**

HttpClient

It goes without saying that there is a staggering amount of data available on the Internet—specifically, available via the World Wide Web (HTTP). One of the wonderful things about the JDK is the built-in ability to access resources via HTTP—specifically, the `java.net.HttpURLConnection` class shows that simple HTTP resources can easily be downloaded by Java applications.

Unfortunately, the built-in HTTP connectivity in the JDK suffers from some significant limitations (for a partial feature set comparison, see `http://www.nogoop.com/product_16.html#compare`). Fortunately, these limitations are overcome when using the Commons HttpClient. A full list of features supported by HttpClient (including links to the relevant RFCs) can be found at `http://jakarta.apache.org/commons/httpclient/features.html`, but some of the most interesting features include:

- **Automatic Cookie Management**—Allowing access to web resources that require web form authentication and session tracking via cookies.
- **Multipart form POST for file upload**—See Chapter 2, "FileUpload," for more information on multipart form posts and file upload.
- **True request/response streams**—The 1.4.2 implementation of Java copies data into a byte array before sending and receiving data, whereas HttpClient passes the streams directly to the application.
- Built-in support for transparently handling redirects.

Glancing at Figure 3-1, which shows the non-Exception classes just in the `org.apache.commons.httpclient` package, you might think that the HttpClient package is complex and difficult to use. While exercising the full range of capability may be complex, we'll look at how we can use the HttpClient classes to easily deal with cookies and posting forms.

The biggest difference between HttpClient and the default JDK HTTP connectivity is the use of classes to implement each of the various HTTP requests. These classes are then passed to a persistent HTTP client object to execute. Listing 3-1 shows a simple GET request. The response to a particular method invocation is bound to the method object, not the client.

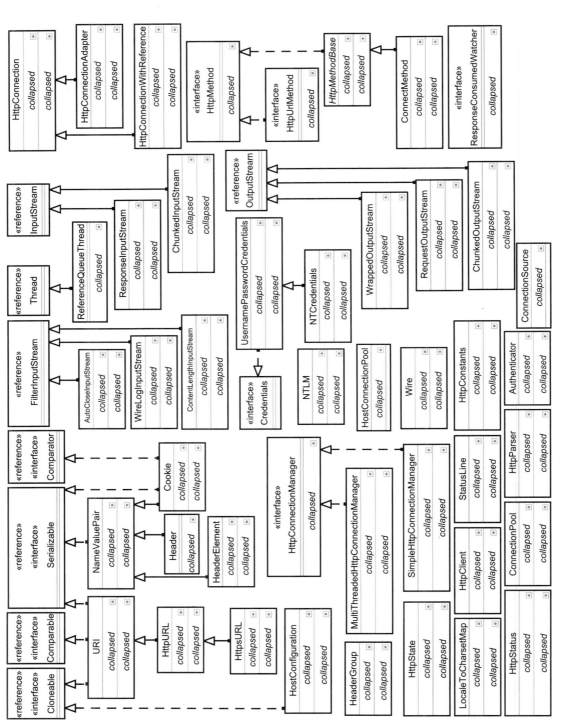

Figure 3-1 Main HttpClient classes.

Listing 3-1 Simple GET Request

```
HttpClient client = new HttpClient();
HttpMethod method = new GetMethod("http://www.cascadetg.com/");
client.executeMethod(method);
System.out.println(method.getStatusCode());
System.out.println(method.getResponseBodyAsString());
method.releaseConnection();
```

> **Redirects**
>
> One of the nuisances of dealing with the default JDK HTTP connectivity is the lack of support for server redirects. The server uses a redirect to indicate to a client that the requested page is no longer available and that the client should load an alternative page. Unlike the JDK implementation, this redirect is transparently followed by HttpClient (i.e., your application receives the content from the redirected URL). You can optionally configure the handling of redirects on a per-request basis with the `HttpMethod.setFollowRedirects()` method. You also can use the `HttpMethod.getPath()` method after the `execute()` to obtain the path that was actually finally read.
>
> If you only want to follow a certain number of redirects before failing, you should turn `setFollowRedirects()` to false and detect redirect status responses manually.

A SIMPLE COOKIE-BASED WEB SITE

Let's look at a very simple web page, as shown in Figure 3-2.

Figure 3-2 Simple web page.

You'll notice a counter is displayed—the server uses a cookie to track the number of times the page has been viewed. Each time the page is refreshed, the counter is increased. For this functionality to work, we need to support cookies on the client—otherwise, the counter won't update.

The other thing you'll notice is the form, which enables a client that does support cookies to reset the counter. Let's look at the JSP code for this simple web page in Listing 3-2.

Listing 3-2 Simple Cookie JSP

```jsp
<%@ page contentType="text/html; charset=utf-8" language="java" %>
<%
    Cookie myCookie;
    String counter = "0";
    if(request.getParameter("Submit") != null)
    {
        myCookie = new Cookie("counter", null);
        response.addCookie(myCookie);
    } else {
        Cookie[] cookies = request.getCookies();
        if(cookies != null)
            for(int i = 0; i < cookies.length; i++)
            {
                if(cookies[i].getName().compareTo("counter") == 0)
                    counter = cookies[i].getValue();
            }
        if(counter == null)
            counter = "0";
        if(counter.compareTo("null") == 0)
            counter = "0";
        counter = (Integer.parseInt(counter) + 1) + "";
        session.setAttribute("counter", counter);
        myCookie = new Cookie("counter", counter);
        response.addCookie(myCookie);
    }
%>
<html><head><title>Cookie Test Page</title></head>
<body>
<p>Counter: <%= counter %></p>
<form name="clear_form" id="clear_form"
method="post" action="index.jsp">
    <input type="submit" name="Submit" value="Clear Cookies!"/>
</form>
<p><a href="index.jsp">Reload Page</a></p>
</body>
</html>
```

You'll notice the use of cookie management facilities built into the standard JSP/servlet functionality. It's a shame that similar functionality isn't built into the standard Java SDK for accessing resources via HTTP—instead, we must turn to the Jakarta Commons HttpClient component for assistance.

UNDERSTANDING HTTPCLIENT

The basic object when working with HttpClient is, of course, HttpClient, as shown in Figure 3-3. This object represents a complete HTTP client, keeping track of state (e.g., cookies and authentication management), and it includes support for things like connection pooling and persistent connections.

Understanding HttpClient

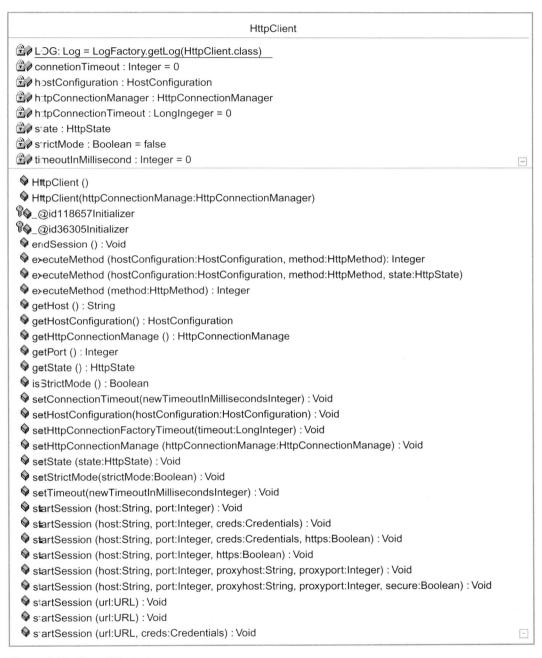

Figure 3-3 HttpClient class.

To actually make a connection, create a "method" object, corresponding to the type of request desired (for example, GET, POST, PUT, OPTIONS, HEAD, etc.). The most common methods are GET (a simple URI retrieval, e.g., "http://www.cascadetg.com/") and POST (sending form data back to a URI). For more information on the other methods, you may want to consult the RFC for HTTP 1.1 at http://www.ietf.org/rfc/rfc2616.txt. The hierarchy of methods can be found in Figure 3-4.

The main methods of interest for HttpMethod and HttpUrlMethod are shown in Figure 3-5.

You may want to inquire about the current status of the client, for example to determine the current state of the cookies that have been set. To do this, you use the HttpClient.getState() method. This returns an HttpState object, as shown in Figure 3-6.

So, to recap, you'll use an HttpClient object as a single representation of a client, you'll create an HttpMethod to make a connection, and you'll inspect the HttpState object to get data about the current client state.

Content Type

Given a particular URI, you may be curious about the type of content being downloaded. The content type is typically expressed in a notation known as MIME (see http://www.iana.org/assignments/media-types/). For example, text/plain indicates an ordinary text file, image/png indicates a PNG file, and application/msword indicates a Microsoft Word document. Depending on the type of content downloaded, you may want to take different action for dealing with the data.

Generally speaking, you have three options for determining the MIME type of a bit of content: the information supplied by the server, the file name, and guessing based on the actual bytes of the file content.

Ideally, the server should be configured to return the MIME of the data sent as a header, in which case you would use the HttpMethod.getRequestHeader("Content-Type") method to obtain the content MIME type. Unfortunately, the server may be set to send the incorrect type. In this case, you can use the static method java.net.URLConnection.guessContentTypeFromName(String fname) to attempt to guess the file type based on the file name and extension. Finally, if that doesn't work, you may want to try java.net.URLConnection.guessContentTypeFromStream(InputStream is). None of these methods is guaranteed to be correct—depending on your application, you may want to default to a particular method and document this behavior in your user documentation.

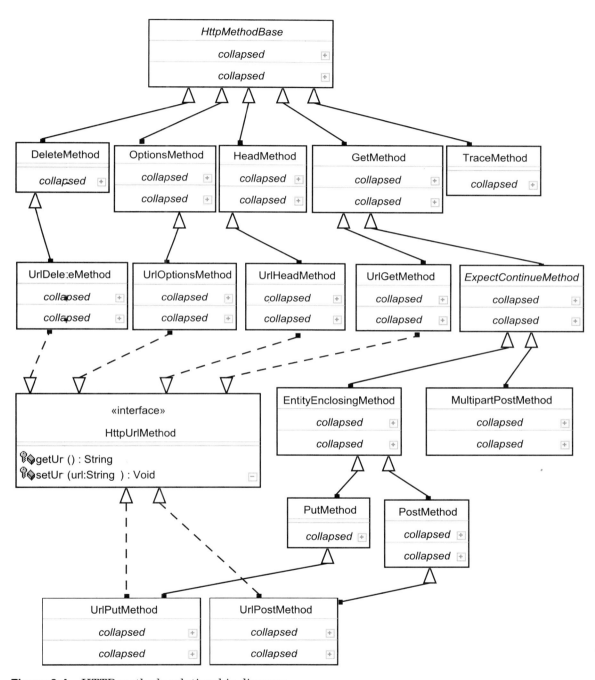

Figure 3-4 HTTP methods relationship diagram.

Figure 3-5 HttpMethod interface.

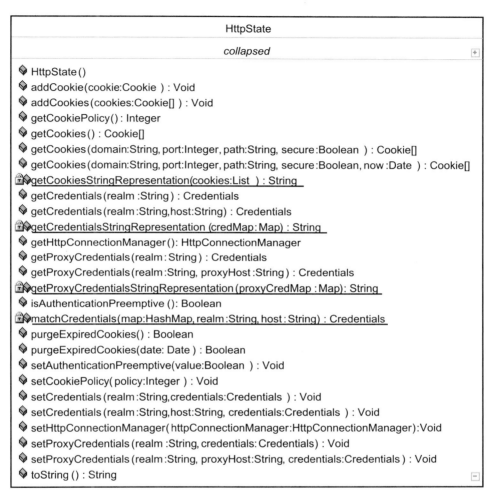

Figure 3-6   HttpState.

SIMPLE SWING CLIENT

Now that you understand how HttpClient is put together, let's consider a simple Swing client designed to talk specifically to the JSP shown in Listing 3-2. Before diving into the code, let's look at how our Swing client works.

Swing Client User Interface

Figure 3-7 shows the initial user interface. Notice the text field at the top, allowing the user to specify a URL, and the two buttons.

Figure 3-7 Initial Swing client view.

Figure 3-8 Viewing cookies.

Clicking the Load button sends a GET request to the specified URL. Figure 3-8 shows the client after clicking the Load button three times—you'll notice that the counter cookie, displayed at the top of the page (along with the session cookie), is now set to three. The main text area shows the content of the retrieved page, and the bottom bar displays the response code as sent by the server.

Clicking the Clear button sends a form POST back to the server, as shown in Figure 3-9. The JSP being posted to (see Listing 3-2) is set up to clear the cookies when that form data is received.

Swing Client Code

Now let's look at the actual code behind this Swing application, starting with Listing 3-3. The main method of interest is the testCookies() method. Depending on the URL retrieved, you may also get cookie data.

Simple Swing Client

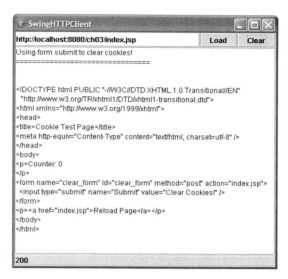

Figure 3-9 Clearing cookies.

Listing 3-3 Swing Client GET

```
package com.cascadetg.ch03;

import org.apache.commons.httpclient.*;
import org.apache.commons.httpclient.methods.*;
import java.awt.*;

public class SwingClient extends javax.swing.JFrame
{

    HttpClient client = new HttpClient();

    public SwingClient() { initComponents(); }

    /** Gets a page via http and displays the cookies and the page */
    public void testCookies()
    {
        // Sometimes the Internet is slow.
        this.setCursor(Cursor.WAIT_CURSOR);

        // We set up a GET request using the URL entered in the URL
        // textfield.
        HttpMethod method =
            new GetMethod(this.urlTextField.getText());
        try
        { client.executeMethod(method);
        } catch (Exception e) { e.printStackTrace(); }

        // Set the response label to the returned value.
        this.responseCodeLabel.setText(method.getStatusCode() + "");

        // Now, we start building the text to display.
        StringBuffer response = new StringBuffer();
```

(*continues*)

Listing 3-3 (*continued*)

```
        // First, we loop through the currently set cookies.
        Cookie[] cookies = client.getState().getCookies();
        for (int i = 0; i < cookies.length; i++)
        {
            response.append(cookies[i].getName());
            response.append("=");
            response.append(cookies[i].getValue());
            response.append("\n");
        }

        response.append("================================");
        response.append("\n");

        // Next, we get the response as a String
        response.append(method.getResponseBodyAsString());

        // Finally, we display the response.
        this.responseText.setText(response.toString());

        // Some clean-up.
        method.releaseConnection();
        method.recycle();

        // Set the cursor back
        this.setCursor(Cursor.DEFAULT_CURSOR);
}
```

Listing 3-4 shows the POST request, in this case hard-coded to map to the JSP page shown in Listing 3-2. Note that in this case, a simple POST is used—if you want to upload files, for example, you would use the `MultipartPostMethod` class instead of `PostMethod`. Also notice the use of the `releaseConnection` method—while not strictly necessary in this trivial app, you need to clean up in this fashion for better performance, and if you later want to switch to a multithreaded client (using the `MultiThreadedHttpConnectionManager`), cleaning up this way is necessary.

Listing 3-4 Swing Client POST

```
/**
 * We submit a POST request. In this example, we are submitting
 * a form where we know that a single Submit is the sole
 * contents of the form. In a "real" browser, you would have
 * parsed the sent HTML, displayed the user interface, and then
 * built the response from the displayed user elements.
 */
public void testPost()
{
    // Sometimes, the Internet is slow.
    this.setCursor(Cursor.WAIT_CURSOR);

    try
    {
        // Set up a POST retrival
        HttpMethod method =
            new PostMethod(this.urlTextField.getText());

        // Let's add the form value
        ((PostMethod)method).addParameter(
```

(*continues*)

Listing 3-4 (continued)

```
            "Submit", "Clear Cookies!");
        // Now, we send the POST
        client.executeMethod(method);

        // Here's where we handle the response. Because we've
        // hard-coded this to work with our form, we know that
        // we're trying to clear the cookies.
        StringBuffer response = new StringBuffer();
        response.append("Using form submit to clear cookies!");
        response.append("\n");
        response.append("================================");
        response.append("\n");

        // Here we get the returned response to display
        response.append(method.getResponseBodyAsString());

        // Now we display it in the Swing UI
        this.responseText.setText(response.toString());
        this.responseCodeLabel.setText(
            method.getStatusCode() + "");
    } catch (Exception e) { e.printStackTrace(); }
finally
    {   // Clean up our connection
        method.releaseConnection();
    }
        this.setCursor(Cursor.DEFAULT_CURSOR);
}
```

In the interest of completeness, the final portion of the code, shown in Listing 3-5, creates the Swing graphical user interface for the application.

Threading and Timeouts

This application executes the HTTP calls on the same thread as the Swing user interface. In practice, this means that a request to a slow or unavailable server can lead to an apparent application freeze (the user interface won't update until the response has been returned). This means that for a "real" application, you will want to run your HTTP requests on a different thread than your Swing user interface. Similarly, you may want to open multiple threads to download different resources simultaneously. To do this, create your `HttpClient` with a multi-threaded connection manager: `HttpClient client = new HttpClient(new MultiThreadedHttpConnectionManager())`. Make sure that you use a `finally` block to wrap `method.releaseConnection()` to ensure that connections are properly recycled.

Similarly, you will want to ensure that no individual connection sits idle, waiting for data from a server for too long. Simply use the `HttpClient.setTimeout()` method to specify the timeout in milliseconds.

If you are building a production Swing application and are concerned about threading, check out SwingWorker:

http://java.sun.com/products/jfc/tsc/articles/threads/update.html

Listing 3-5 Simple Swing Client Code

```java
// Swing user interface variables declaration
private javax.swing.JPanel buttonPanel;
private javax.swing.JButton clearButton;
private javax.swing.JButton goButton;
private javax.swing.JLabel responseCodeLabel;
private javax.swing.JPanel responseCodePanel;
private javax.swing.JTextArea responseText;
private javax.swing.JScrollPane responseTextPanel;
private javax.swing.JPanel topPanel;
private javax.swing.JTextField urlTextField;

/** Initializes the Swing user interface. */
private void initComponents()
{
    topPanel = new javax.swing.JPanel();
    urlTextField = new javax.swing.JTextField();
    buttonPanel = new javax.swing.JPanel();
    goButton = new javax.swing.JButton();
    clearButton = new javax.swing.JButton();
    responseCodePanel = new javax.swing.JPanel();
    responseCodeLabel = new javax.swing.JLabel();
    responseTextPanel = new javax.swing.JScrollPane();
    responseText = new javax.swing.JTextArea();

    setTitle("SwingHTTPClient");
    addWindowListener(new java.awt.event.WindowAdapter()
    {
        public void windowClosing(
            java.awt.event.WindowEvent evt)
        {
            System.exit(0);
        }
    });

    topPanel.setLayout(new java.awt.BorderLayout());
    urlTextField.setFont(new java.awt.Font("SansSerif", 1, 12));
    urlTextField.setText(
        "http://localhost:8080/ch03/index.jsp");
    topPanel.add(urlTextField, java.awt.BorderLayout.CENTER);
    buttonPanel.setLayout(new java.awt.BorderLayout());
    goButton.setText("Load");
    goButton
        .addActionListener(new java.awt.event.ActionListener()
    {
        public void actionPerformed(
            java.awt.event.ActionEvent evt)
        {
            testCookies();
        }
    });
    buttonPanel.add(goButton, java.awt.BorderLayout.WEST);
    clearButton.setText("Clear");
```

(continues)

Listing 3-5 (*continued*)

```
        clearButton
            .addActionListener(new java.awt.event.ActionListener()
        {
            public void actionPerformed(
                java.awt.event.ActionEvent evt)
            {
                testPost();
            }
        });

        buttonPanel.add(clearButton, java.awt.BorderLayout.EAST);
        topPanel.add(buttonPanel, java.awt.BorderLayout.EAST);
        getContentPane().add(topPanel, java.awt.BorderLayout.NORTH);
        responseCodePanel.setLayout(new java.awt.BorderLayout());
        responseCodePanel.setBorder(
            new javax.swing.border.EtchedBorder());
        responseCodePanel.setEnabled(false);
        responseCodeLabel.setText("Result");
        responseCodePanel.add(responseCodeLabel,
            java.awt.BorderLayout.CENTER);

        getContentPane().add(responseCodePanel,
            java.awt.BorderLayout.SOUTH);

        responseTextPanel.setViewportView(responseText);

        getContentPane().add(responseTextPanel,
            java.awt.BorderLayout.CENTER);

        java.awt.Dimension screenSize =
java.awt.Toolkit.getDefaultToolkit().getScreenSize();
        setBounds((screenSize.width - 400) / 2,
            (screenSize.height - 300) / 2, 400, 300);
    }
    public static void main(String args[])
    {
        new SwingClient().show();
    }
}
```

SUMMARY

In this chapter, you've seen how a complex library can easily be used to handle something beyond the abilities of the default JDK. Working with cookies and handling both GET and POST requests are fundamental building blocks for the Internet.

In the next chapter, you'll look at components for dealing with other fundamental building blocks, such as FTP and NNTP.

Project Ideas

Write a proxy server, recording the data sent between the browser and a web server. Save this data and then see if you can repeat the interactions with HttpClient. Would this be useful for testing web applications?

Most application developers work with GET and POST requests. Find a web server that supports the full range of HTTP requests and write an interactive application that supports the full range of HTTP request types.

Add some logic to parse the returned HTTP. Can you find URLs in the HTTP? If you can find the URLs, is it worth trying to preload the underlying data, perhaps by running HttpClient in the background as a proxy server? Alternatively, is this a reasonable approach to building a spider application to crawl through a website?

CHAPTER **4**

Net

In the previous chapters, you've looked extensively at HTTP and HTML—two of the most fundamental standards behind the Internet. The major protocols behind email (POP3, SMTP, IMAP, MIME) are all supported by JavaMail (http://java.sun.com/products/javamail/). This leaves a tremendous number of other protocols, however.

The Jakarta Commons Net package covers a huge number of the other standard Internet protocols, including Finger, Whois, TFTP, Telnet, FTP, NNTP, and some miscellaneous protocols such as Time, Echo, and BSD R. POP3 and SMTP are also supported, but JavaMail (http://java.sun.com/products/javamail/) provides a more mainstream, higher-level wrapper for these protocols.

- **Finger**—http://www.faqs.org/rfcs/rfc742.html. A simple status inquiry.
- **Whois**—http://www.faqs.org/rfcs/rfc954.html. A lookup mechanism, allowing users to find information about registered users (in particular, used by domain name registries, such as Network Solutions, http://www.networksolutions.com/en_US/whois/index.jhtml).
- **TFTP**—http://www.faqs.org/rfcs/rfc991.html. A very simple file transfer protocol with no access control. Sometimes found on local networks as part of a network boot process.
- **Telnet**—http://www.faqs.org/rfcs/rfc854.html. A generic two-way protocol, most commonly used for remote shell access, but also acting as the underlying infrastructure of other standards (such as FTP).
- **FTP**—http://www.faqs.org/rfcs/rfc959.html. A popular, more sophisticated file transfer protocol than TFTP.
- **NNTP**—http://www.faqs.org/rfcs/rfc977.html. Network News Transfer Protocol, most popularly known as the underlying protocol behind USENET. If you aren't familiar with USENET, check the Google interface available at http://www.google.com/grphp.

☞ **BSD "R" Commands**—A set of commands intended to provide remote services without a login (including rexec, rcmd/rshell, and rlogin). For more information (including a discussion of the security implications), see http://www.busan.edu/~nic/networking/firewall/ch08_04.htm.

> **Warning:** It should be noted that virtually no security is built into any of these protocols. Those that offer username/password authentication transfer login information in the clear. If you are interested in secure alternatives, you may want to consider a virtual private network or the use of an SSH tunneling system such as OpenSSH (http://www.openssh.org/).

This chapter will first look at the overall architecture of the Net package and then delve more deeply into the FTP and NNTP clients.

NET OVERVIEW

Probably the most fundamental thing to understand about the Net package is that it is intended to provide protocol access, not a higher-level abstraction. In practice, this means that objects tend to have methods that are highly sequential and generally more "procedural" in flavor. The following list indicates the packages of the Net package—you'll notice that they mostly correspond directly to the supported protocol list mentioned previously.

- examples
- org.apache.commons.net
- org.apache.commons.net.bsd
- org.apache.commons.net.ftp
- org.apache.commons.net.ftp.parser
- org.apache.commons.net.io
- org.apache.commons.net.nntp
- org.apache.commons.net.pop3
- org.apache.commons.net.smtp
- org.apache.commons.net.telnet
- org.apache.commons.net.tftp
- org.apache.commons.net.util

Let's look at one of these packages in a bit more depth. Figure 4-1 shows the ftp package classes. The key classes are FTPClient (a representation of the connection with methods to perform standard FTP connectivity), and FTPFile (which wraps directory and file list information). Most of the FTPClient methods are quite literal, issuing commands across a single connection—for example, methods such as FTPClient.deleteFile(java.lang.String pathname) or FTPClient makeDirectory(java.lang.String pathname).

Net Overview

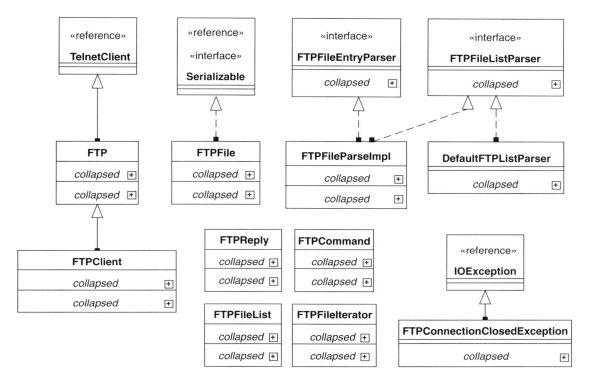

Figure 4-1   FTP class diagram.

Origins of Commons Net

According to the Apache Jakarta Commons Net web site, the package was originally developed as a commercial suite, NetComponents:

"NetComponents was originally a commercial product, but after ORO dissolved, it was continued to be made available for those who found it useful. However, no updates have been made since version 1.3.8, released in 1998. Now that certain contract obligations have expired, it is possible to make the source code freely available under the Apache Software License."

It's fortunate that even though ORO dissolved, the time and energy to convert this to an Apache Jakarta project was made. It should be noted that the comment to the effect that "no changes have been made" is incorrect, as browsing the reports of the project shows that it is still under active development as of this writing.

The usage of the Net package classes is fairly straight forward: a connection is established, the initial reply code is read, information is sent back and forth, and then the connection is disconnected.

> **Warning:** It is important to remember that checking for the initial reply code is *not* optional. Issuing other commands won't work until you retrieve that first reply code.

In this chapter, you'll look at two simple web applications that make use of this library, one to access an FTP server, the other to access an NNTP server. Neither implements a full "client," but they do demonstrate two approaches to accessing the server. The first, the FTP "gateway," opens a connection to the FTP server, reads the resulting data, and then closes the connection. The second, the NNTP "gateway," maintains a single connection to the NNTP server and attempts to cache data retrieved (a reasonable assumption, given the mostly read-and-post nature of NNTP).

FTP FUNCTIONALITY

Our FTP example shows how you can display the contents of remote FTP server via a web page, as shown in Figure 4-2. FTP is a relatively old, cumbersome protocol, not as well known as the standard HTTP/HTML used by web browsers. Most users wind up downloading and installing custom FTP clients to access FTP resources, although most modern browsers have some cumbersome FTP access capability built-in.

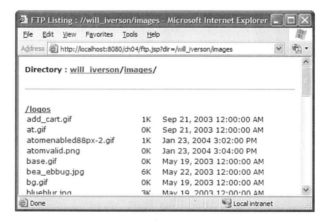

Figure 4-2 Viewing FTP directory contents.

The page is fairly simple—when the page is first visited, the default login directory is shown. When a link is clicked, the `dir` parameter is passed back to the page, and the contents of the new directory are displayed. This allows a user to easily browse the contents of an FTP server. The links at the top of the page allow a user to quickly return "up" the directory's path.

FTP IMPLEMENTATION

The code for the user interface is shown in Listing 4-1. You'll notice that the FTPConnection class does the bulk of the work, including much of the formatting of the returned listings.

Listing 4-1 FTP Web JSP User Interface

```jsp
<%@ page contentType="text/html; charset=iso-8859-1"
language="java" import="com.cascadetg.ch04.*"  %><%
String directory = request.getParameter("dir");
FTPConnection myConnection = new FTPConnection();
if(directory != null)
    myConnection.setWorkingDirectory(directory);

myConnection.connect();
%>
<!DOCTYPE html PUBLIC "-//W3C//DTD XHTML 1.0 Transitional//EN"
"http://www.w3.org/TR/xhtml1/DTD/xhtml1-transitional.dtd">
<html xmlns="http://www.w3.org/1999/xhtml">
<head>
<title>FTP Listing : /<%= myConnection.getWorkingDirectory() %></title>
<meta http-equiv="Content-Type" content="text/html; charset=iso-8859-1" />
<style type="text/css">
<!--
.filelist {
    width: 100%;
}
-->
</style>
<link href="../ch03/default.css" rel="stylesheet" type="text/css" />
</head>

<body>
<p><strong>Directory : <%=
myConnection.getHTMLFormattedWorkingDirectory("ftp.jsp")
%></strong></p>
<hr />
<p><%=myConnection.getHTMLFormattedList("ftp.jsp") %>
</p>
<p><a href="ftp.jsp">Return to default directory</a> </p>
</body>
</html>
```

The FTPConnection object used by the JSP page is fairly straightforward, as shown in Figure 4-3.

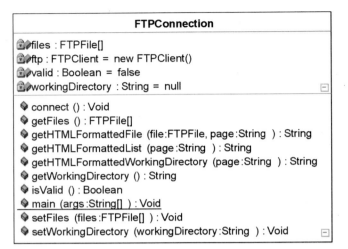

Figure 4-3 FTPConnection class.

The code for FTPConnection is shown in Listing 4-2.

Listing 4-2 FTP Connectivity Code

```
package com.cascadetg.ch04;

import java.util.Date;
import java.util.StringTokenizer;

import org.apache.commons.net.ftp.*;

public class FTPConnection
{
    /**
    * The FTP client implementation. Note that we don't preserve
    * the client between executions - doing so would significantly
    * improve performance, but would require more effort to ensure
    * synchronization. For an example of this, see the
    * NNTPConnection class.
    *
    * @see NNTPConnection
    */
    FTPClient ftp = new FTPClient();

    /** Initially, the connection is considered to be invalid */
    boolean valid = false;

    /** The file listing as returned by the connection */
    private FTPFile[] files;

    /**   We don't know the working directory. If the working
     * directory is null, we'll assume that the default directory
     * as given when the user logs in is to be used.   */
```

(*continues*)

Listing 4-2 (continued)

```java
    String workingDirectory = null;

    public boolean isValid() { return valid; }

    /**   Here, we attempt to connect to the specified working
     * directory, get the file list, close the connection, and
     * return.  */
    public void connect()
    {
        try
        {
            // Attempt the initial connection. Note that this
            // happens before we even log in - here we are just
            // trying to establish a connection.
            int reply;
            ftp.connect(NetConnectionTokens.ftp_server);

            // We have to get the reply code to continue - this is
            // required by the library.
            reply = ftp.getReplyCode();

            if (!FTPReply.isPositiveCompletion(reply))
            {
                ftp.disconnect();
                return;
            }

            // Now, we attempt to log in using the FTP username &
            // password.
            ftp.login(
                NetConnectionTokens.ftp_username,
                NetConnectionTokens.ftp_password);

            // If a working directory has been specified, we
            // attempt to
            // change to that directory
            if (this.workingDirectory != null)
                if (this.workingDirectory.length() > 0)
                    if (this.workingDirectory.compareTo("null")
                        != 0)
                        valid =
                            ftp.changeWorkingDirectory(
                                this.workingDirectory);

            // If no working directory has been specified, we try
            // to
            // find out what directory we default to and use that.
            // Also, if we've followed a link, this might be a more
            // accurate report of where we "really" are.
            this.workingDirectory = ftp.printWorkingDirectory();

            // Get the list of files from the server.
            files = ftp.listFiles();

            valid = true;

        } catch (Exception e) { e.printStackTrace();
        } finally
```

(continues)

Listing 4-2 (*continued*)

```
        {
            // Regardless of any errors, we make an effort to
            // disconnect from the server.
            if (ftp.isConnected())
            {
                try
                { ftp.disconnect();
                } catch (Exception f)
                {   // Silent failure here is fine.
                }
            }
        }
    }

    public String getWorkingDirectory() { return workingDirectory; }
    public void setWorkingDirectory(String workingDirectory)
    { this.workingDirectory = workingDirectory; }

    /** A command-line test method */
    public static void main(String[] args)
    {
        FTPConnection myConnection = new FTPConnection();
        myConnection.connect();
        FTPFile[] files = myConnection.getFiles();

        System.out.println(
            myConnection.getHTMLFormattedWorkingDirectory(
                "ftp.jsp"));
        for (int i = 0; i < files.length; i++)
        {
            System.out.println(
                myConnection.getHTMLFormattedFile(
                    files[i],
                    "ftp.jsp"));
        }
    }

    /**   Returns the current working directory nicely formatted for
     * display on an HTML page.
     *
     * @param page
     * Specify the page the links should point to
     */
    public String getHTMLFormattedWorkingDirectory(String page)
    {
        if (workingDirectory == null)
            return "";

        StringBuffer result = new StringBuffer();

        // Note the use of the built-in JDK tokenizer
        StringTokenizer tokenizer =
            new StringTokenizer(workingDirectory, "/", false);

        String built_path = "";
        String current = "";

        while (tokenizer.hasMoreTokens())
        {
            current = tokenizer.nextToken();
            built_path = built_path + "/" + current;
```

(*continues*)

Listing 4-2 (*continued*)

```java
            result.append("<a href='");
            result.append(page);
            result.append("?dir=");
            result.append(built_path);
            result.append("'>");
            result.append(current);
            result.append("</a>");
            result.append("/");
        }
        result.append("<br />");
        return result.toString();
    }

    /**  Returns the current file list nicely formatted for display
     *  on an HTML page.
     *
     * @param page
     * Specify the page the links should point to
     */
    public String getHTMLFormattedList(String page)
    {
        StringBuffer reply = new StringBuffer();
        if (files != null)
        {
            for (int i = 0; i < files.length; i++)
            {
                if (files[i].isDirectory())
                    reply.append(
                        getHTMLFormattedFile(files[i], page));
            }

            reply.append("<table class='filelist'>");
            for (int i = 0; i < files.length; i++)
            {
                if (!files[i].isDirectory())
                {
                    reply.append("<tr>");
                    reply.append(
                        getHTMLFormattedFile(files[i], page));
                    reply.append("</tr>");
                }
            }
            reply.append("</table>");
        }
        return reply.toString();
    }

    /**  Returns the current file nicely formatted for display on an
     * HTML page. Note that this is used by the
     * getHTMLFormattedList function, so this isn't actually used
     * in the JSP page.
     *
     * @param page
     * Specify the page the links should point to
     */
    public String getHTMLFormattedFile(FTPFile file, String page)
    {
        StringBuffer result = new StringBuffer();
        if (file.isDirectory())
```

(*continues*)

Listing 4-2 (*continued*)

```
    {
        result.append("<a href='");
        result.append(page);
        result.append("?dir=");
        if (workingDirectory != null)
            result.append(workingDirectory);
        result.append("/");
        result.append(file.getName());
        result.append("'><b>/");
        result.append(file.getName());
        result.append("</b></a>");
        result.append("<br />");
    } else
    {
        result.append("<td>");
        result.append(file.getName());
        result.append("</td><td>");
        result.append((file.getSize() / 1024));
        result.append("K</td><td>");
        result.append(
            new Date(file.getTimestamp().getTimeInMillis())
                .toLocaleString());
        result.append("</td>");
    }
    return result.toString();
}

public FTPFile[] getFiles() { return files; }

public void setFiles(FTPFile[] files) { this.files = files; }
}
```

This FTP connectivity code shown in Listing 4-2 suffers from a few obvious limitations—most significantly, it opens and closes the connection every time the page is requested. Although this might be adequate for extremely light usage, it would be preferable to provide some mechanism for caching the FTP data. If this was the only mechanism provided for interaction with the FTP server, as part of a content publishing framework for example, very aggressive caching might be appropriate.

Additional functionality, such as uploading files, could be added by folding in the code shown in Chapter 2, "File Upload."

NNTP Functionality

In this example, you will build a read-only web view of the latest posts made to the various `comp.lang.java.*` newsgroups.

These groups are shown in Figure 4-4.

In the next section, you'll look at a simple NNTP browser and compare the simplistic open-and-close approach of the code in Listing 4-2 with a more aggressive caching mechanism.

Clicking on the Most Recent Article link shows us an individual message post, as shown in Figure 4-5. An interface is provided to view earlier and

> **Newsgroup Organization**
>
> NNTP groups are traditionally organized according to a hierarchy, with the most general name moving from left to right. For example, comp.lang.java.* can be translated to mean "all the groups under the category Computers, Languages, Java." The most infamous section of USENET are the groups under the alt.* category. Many companies have set up their own NNTP servers, independent of USENET, allowing users to post and discuss topics of interest (for example, internal discussions, or external customers discussing product issues). It's important to keep in mind that an NNTP server can be configured to participate in exchanging one or more USENET groups, but it is by no means required.

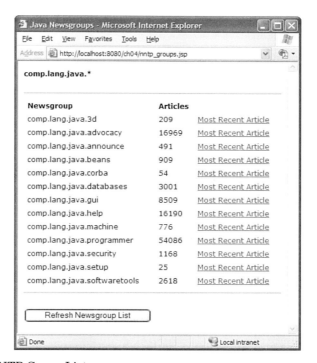

Figure 4-4 NNTP Group List.

later messages (as determined by the server), and a few of the key headers are provided.

It's easy to imagine additional functionality, such as posting new messages, displaying additional detail, or even showing a threaded view of the conversation, but this is a reasonable start.

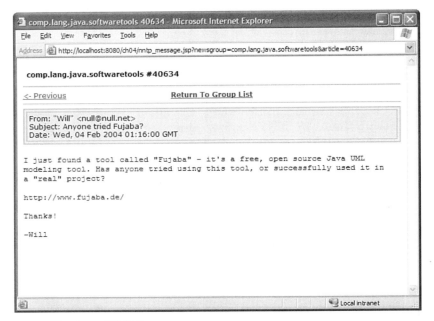

Figure 4-5 Viewing a NNTP post.

NNTP IMPLEMENTATION

There are two JSP pages used to display the NNTP client information. The code for the group list, nntp_groups.jsp (shown rendered in the browser in Figure 4-4), can be found in Listing 4-3.

Listing 4-3 NNTP Group List JSP

```
<%@ page contentType="text/html; charset=iso-8859-1"
    language="java" import="com.cascadetg.ch04.*" %>
<%
String newsgroup_pattern = "comp.lang.java.*";

NNTPConnection myNNTPConnection = new NNTPConnection();

if(request.getParameter("refresh") != null)
    myNNTPConnection.refreshNewsgroupList(newsgroup_pattern);

org.apache.commons.net.nntp.NewsgroupInfo[] newsgroups =
    myNNTPConnection.getNewsgroupList(newsgroup_pattern);
%>
<!DOCTYPE html PUBLIC "-//W3C//DTD XHTML 1.0 Transitional//EN"
"http://www.w3.org/TR/xhtml1/DTD/xhtml1-transitional.dtd">
<html xmlns="http://www.w3.org/1999/xhtml">
<head>
<title>Java Newsgroups</title>
<meta http-equiv="Content-Type" content="text/html; charset=iso-8859-1" />
<link href="../ch03/default.css" rel="stylesheet" type="text/css" />
</head>
<body>
```

(continues)

Listing 4-3 (*continued*)

```
<p><strong><%= newsgroup_pattern %></strong></p><hr />
<table width="100%"  border="0" cellspacing="3" cellpadding="3">
    <tr>
        <td><strong>Newsgroup</strong></td>
        <td><strong>Articles</strong></td>
        <td> </td>
    </tr>
<%
for(int i = 0; i < newsgroups.length; i++) { %>
    <tr>
        <td><%= newsgroups[i].getNewsgroup() %></td>
        <td><%= newsgroups[i].getArticleCount() %></td>
        <td><a href="nntp_message.jsp?newsgroup=<%=
            newsgroups[i].getNewsgroup() %>&article=<%=
            newsgroups[i].getLastArticle()
            %>">Most Recent Article</a></td>
    </tr>
<% } %>
</table><hr />
<form name="form1" id="form1" method="post" action="">
  <input name="refresh" type="submit"
      id="refresh" value="Refresh Newsgroup List" />
</form>
</body>
</html>
```

The code in Listing 4-3 relies on the underlying `org.apache.commons.net.nntp.NewsgroupInfo` class for the information about the groups. Figure 4-6 shows the methods of this class.

Figure 4-6   NewsgroupInfo class diagram.

Clicking on the link for the Most Recent Article displays the `nntp_message.jsp` page. The listing for `nntp_message.jsp` is shown in Listing 4-4.

Listing 4-4 NNTP Message Display JSP

```
<%@ page contentType="text/html; charset=iso-8859-1"
    language="java" import="com.cascadetg.ch04.*" %>
<%
NNTPConnection myNNTPConnection = new NNTPConnection();
String newsgroup = request.getParameter("newsgroup");
String article = request.getParameter("article");
String header = myNNTPConnection.getArticleHeader(newsgroup, article);
String body = myNNTPConnection.getArticleBody(newsgroup, article);
String previousArticle = myNNTPConnection.previousArticle(newsgroup,
article);
String nextArticle = myNNTPConnection.nextArticle(newsgroup, article);
%>
<!DOCTYPE html PUBLIC "-//W3C//DTD XHTML 1.0 Transitional//EN"
"http://www.w3.org/TR/xhtml1/DTD/xhtml1-transitional.dtd">
<html xmlns="http://www.w3.org/1999/xhtml">
<head>
<title><%= newsgroup %> <%= article %></title>
<meta http-equiv="Content-Type" content="text/html; charset=iso-8859-1" />
<link href="../ch03/default.css" rel="stylesheet" type="text/css" />
<style type="text/css">
<!--
.header {
    background-color: #EEEEEE;
    border: thin solid #CCCCCC;
}
.body {
    font-family: "Courier New", Courier, mono;
    font-size: small;
}
-->
</style>
</head>
<body>
<table width="100%"  border="0" cellspacing="3" cellpadding="3">
  <tr>
    <td><strong><%= newsgroup %> #<%= article %></strong></td>
  </tr>
</table>
<hr />
<table width="100%"  border="0" cellspacing="0" cellpadding="0">
  <tr>
    <td width="33%"><%
    if(previousArticle != null)
    { %>
        <a href="nntp_message.jsp?newsgroup=<%=newsgroup%>&article=<%=
            previousArticle %>">&lt;- Previous</a>
<% } %> </td>
    <td align="center"><a
        href="nntp_groups.jsp"><strong>Return To Group
List</strong></a></td>
    <td width="33%" align="right"><%
    if(nextArticle != null)
    { %>
        <a href="nntp_message.jsp?newsgroup=<%=newsgroup%>&article=<%=
            nextArticle %>">Next -&gt;</a>
```

(continues)

Listing 4-4 (*continued*)

```
<%    } %> </td>
   </tr>
</table>
<hr />
<table width="100%"  border="0" cellpadding="3"
      cellspacing="3" class="header">
   <tr>
      <td class="header"><%= header %></td>
   </tr>
</table>
<br />
<p class="body">
   <%= body %><br />
</p>
</body>
</html>
```

Now that you've seen the JSP presentation code, let's look at the underlying Java code. A diagram is shown in Figure 4-7.

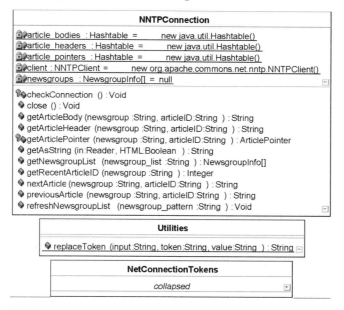

Figure 4-7 NNTP Connection example classes.

Looking at the `NNTPConnection` code shown in Listing 4-5, you'll notice that several `java.util.Hashtable` objects are used to cache the content retrieved. As NNTP is typically read-and-post, but messages are rarely deleted, this is a reasonable approach. Other NNTP clients cache data on disk or in a database.

You'll also notice the liberal use of the `synchronized` keyword to avoid contention over the use of the `NNTPClient` object—it's important for certain commands to be issued in sequence. For example, the `NNTPConnection.nextArticle()`

method issues a `client.selectNewsgroup()` call and then immediately issues `client.selectNextArticle()` and `client.selectArticle()`. If these calls were to be intermixed with other connections, the wrong data might be returned.

Listing 4-5 NNTP Connection Example

```
package com.cascadetg.ch04;

import org.apache.commons.net.nntp.*;

// http://nagoya.apache.org/bugzilla/show_bug.cgi?id=26282

public class NNTPConnection
{
    /**
     * This class attempts to improve performance over the
     * FTPConnection class by using a single static client to
     * retrieve data. It caches some of the data in-memory. You'll
     * notice that this cache code adds significant complexity,
     * however.
     */
    static org.apache.commons.net.nntp.NNTPClient client =
        new org.apache.commons.net.nntp.NNTPClient();

    /** These serve as our in-memory cache of retrieved data */
    static NewsgroupInfo[] newsgroups = null;
    static java.util.Hashtable article_bodies =
        new java.util.Hashtable();
    static java.util.Hashtable article_headers =
        new java.util.Hashtable();
    static java.util.Hashtable article_pointers =
        new java.util.Hashtable();

    /** Gets the latest newsgroup list, ignoring the cache */
    public void refreshNewsgroupList(String newsgroup_pattern)
    {
        checkConnection();
        try
        {
            synchronized (client)
            {
                newsgroups =
                    client.listNewsgroups(newsgroup_pattern);
            }
        } catch (Exception e) { e.printStackTrace(); }
    }

    /** Gets the latest articleID, given a newsgroup name */
    public int getRecentArticleID(String newsgroup)
    {
        for (int i = 0; i < newsgroups.length; i++)
        {
            if (newsgroups[i].getNewsgroup().compareTo(newsgroup)
                == 0)
                return newsgroups[i].getLastArticle();
        }
        return -1;
    }
```

(continues)

Listing 4-5 (continued)

```java
    /** Gets the list of newsgroups, from the cache if possible */
    public NewsgroupInfo[] getNewsgroupList(String newsgroup_list)
    {
        if (newsgroups == null)
            refreshNewsgroupList(newsgroup_list);

        return newsgroups;
    }
    /** Gets an article pointer given a newsgroup and articleID. */
    ArticlePointer getArticlePointer(
        String newsgroup,
        String articleID)
    {
        if (article_pointers.containsKey(newsgroup + articleID))
            return (ArticlePointer)article_pointers.get(
                newsgroup + articleID);

        checkConnection();
        ArticlePointer newPointer = new ArticlePointer();

        String result = "";
        try
        {
            synchronized (client)
            {
                client.selectNewsgroup(newsgroup);
                client.selectArticle(articleID);

                getAsString(
                    client.retrieveArticleBody(
                        articleID,
                        newPointer),
                    false);

            }
            article_pointers.put(newsgroup + articleID, newPointer);
            return newPointer;

        } catch (Exception e)
        {
            result = "Unable to retrive.";
            e.printStackTrace();
        }
        return null;
    }
    /**
     * Gets the next article given a current article. Note that
     * this method relies on the server to provide the previous and
     * next article information.
     */
    public String nextArticle(String newsgroup, String articleID)
    {
        if (articleID == null)
            return null;
        ArticlePointer myPointer = new ArticlePointer();

        checkConnection();
        try
```

(continues)

Listing 4-5 (*continued*)

```java
        {
            synchronized (client)
            {
                client.selectNewsgroup(newsgroup);
                client.selectArticle(Integer.parseInt(articleID));
                if (!client.selectNextArticle(myPointer))
                    return null;
                client.selectArticle(
                    myPointer.articleNumber,
                    myPointer);
            }
        } catch (Exception e)
        {
            e.printStackTrace();
        }
        return myPointer.articleNumber + "";
    }
    /**   See nextArticle for more information.
     */
    public String previousArticle(
        String newsgroup,
        String articleID)
    {
        if (articleID == null)
            return null;
        ArticlePointer myPointer = new ArticlePointer();

        checkConnection();
        try
        {
            synchronized (client)
            {
                client.selectNewsgroup(newsgroup);
                client.selectArticle(Integer.parseInt(articleID));
                if (!client.selectPreviousArticle(myPointer))
                    return null;
                client.selectArticle(
                    myPointer.articleNumber,
                    myPointer);
            }
        } catch (Exception e)
        {
            e.printStackTrace();
        }
        return myPointer.articleNumber + "";
    }
    /** Gets the body of an article, preferably from the cache */
    public String getArticleBody(
        String newsgroup,
        String articleID)
    {
        if (article_bodies.containsKey(newsgroup + articleID))
            return (String)article_bodies.get(
                newsgroup + articleID);

        checkConnection();
        String result = "";
        try
```

(*continues*)

Listing 4-5 (*continued*)

```java
        {
            synchronized (client)
            {
                client.selectNewsgroup(newsgroup);
                client.selectArticle(articleID);
                result =
                    getAsString(
                        client.retrieveArticleBody(articleID),
                        true);
            }
            article_bodies.put(newsgroup + articleID, result);
        } catch (Exception e)
        {
            result = "Unable to retrive.";
            e.printStackTrace();
        }
        return result;
    }
    /** Gets the header of an article, preferably from the cache */
    public String getArticleHeader(
        String newsgroup,
        String articleID)
    {
        if (article_headers.containsKey(newsgroup + articleID))
            return (String)article_headers.get(
                newsgroup + articleID);

        String result = "";
        try
        {
            checkConnection();
            synchronized (client)
            {
                client.selectNewsgroup(newsgroup);
                client.selectArticle(articleID);
                result =
                    getAsString(
                        client.retrieveArticleHeader(articleID),
                        false);
            }
            java.util.StringTokenizer myTokenizer =
                new java.util.StringTokenizer(result, "\n", true);
            result = "";
            while (myTokenizer.hasMoreTokens())
            {
                String current = myTokenizer.nextToken();
                current =
                    Utilities.replaceToken(current, "<", "&lt;");
                current =
                    Utilities.replaceToken(current, ">", "&gt;");
                if (current.startsWith("From:"))
                    result = result + current + "<br />";
```

(*continues*)

Listing 4-5 (*continued*)

```
            if (current.startsWith("Subject:"))
                result = result + current + "<br />";

            if (current.startsWith("Date:"))
                result = result + current + "<br />";
        }

        article_headers.put(newsgroup + articleID, result);
    } catch (Exception e)
    {
        result = "Unable to retrive.";
        e.printStackTrace();
    }
    return result;
}
/**   The various body & header methods return Readers, not
 * Strings. This utiltiy method converts from a Reader to a
 * String, and also performs some basic HTML formatting if
 * requested.   */
public String getAsString(java.io.Reader in, boolean HTML)
{
    if (in == null)
        return "";
    java.io.BufferedReader bufferedReader =
        new java.io.BufferedReader(in);

    StringBuffer temp = new StringBuffer();
    boolean read = true;
    String current = "";
    while (read)
    {
        try
        {
            current = bufferedReader.readLine();
        } catch (Exception e)
        { read = false; }
        if (current != null)
        {
            current = current + "\n";
            if (HTML)
            {
                current =
                    Utilities.replaceToken(
                        current, "<", "&lt;");
                current =
                    Utilities.replaceToken(
                        current, ">", "&gt;");
                temp.append(current);
                temp.append("<br />");
            } else
            { temp.append(current); }
        } else read = false;
    }
    return temp.toString();
}
/**   Verifies that the NNTP connection is valid, and attempts to
 * reestablish if not. */
```

(*continues*)

Listing 4-5 (*continued*)

```
    protected synchronized void checkConnection()
    {
        if (client.isConnected())
        {
            synchronized (client)
            {
                try
                {
                    client.stat();
                    return;
                } catch (Exception e)
                {
                    // Ok, failed, so let's try to reconnect.
                    try
                    {
                        client.disconnect();
                    } catch (Exception e1)
                    {   // No need to report this
                    }
                }
            }
        }

        try
        {
            synchronized (client)
            {
                client.connect(NetConnectionTokens.nntp_server);
                client.getReplyCode();
                client.authenticate(
                    NetConnectionTokens.nntp_username,
                    NetConnectionTokens.nntp_password);
            }
        } catch (Exception e)
        {
            System.err.println("Unable to connect to NNTP server!");
            e.printStackTrace();
        }
    }

    public synchronized void close()
    {
        try
        {
            synchronized (client)
            { client.logout(); }
        } catch (Exception e)
        {   // Silent failure.
        }
        try
        {
            synchronized (client)
            { client.disconnect(); }
        } catch (Exception e) { // Silent failure.
        }

    }
}
```

In a "real" NNTP client application, one can think of all sorts of additional features, such as preloading and sorting the headers on another thread, perhaps providing a threaded view of the messages, and interweaving the replies (for more information on NNTP message threading, see `http://nagoya.apache.org/bugzilla/show_bug.cgi?id=26282`).

> **Tip:** If you are interested in setting up your own NNTP server, you may want to investigate James, `http://james.apache.org/`, a Java-based SMTP, POP3, and NNTP server.

SUMMARY

In this chapter, two approaches for dealing with the Jakarta Commons libraries were presented. It's easy to envision much more sophisticated approaches, with complex clients performing specialized operations. For example, an FTP client could synchronize between a remote server and a local file system, or an NNTP client might generate automated status posts.

As you can see, resource management quickly becomes important when working with these protocols. A connection to a service is an important resource, as is the data that is transmitted. In the next chapter, a library that provides additional scalability and availability for database connectivity through the use of a database connection pool will be examined.

> **Project Ideas**
>
> Use Net components in conjunction with the FileUpload package (described in Chapter 2) to allow users to post files to an FTP server via a browser.
>
> Build web browser interfaces to the various protocols. Some of these (such as Telnet) imply state to be presented to the user; others (such as Finger) do not. How does this affect building a web interface?
>
> Try using TFTP and ZeroConf (also known as Rendezvous) to build a simple file local network sharing application.

CHAPTER 5

Pool

Not all Java objects are created equal. For example, some take considerably longer to create than others—an object that establishes a secure network connection can take several seconds to properly initialize. Other objects might consume significant resources. In order to minimize the creation of these objects, you may want to maintain a pool of objects—a little bit of bookkeeping to keep track of a group of objects, checked out and returned as needed. The Apache Jakarta Commons Pool package provides interfaces and implementation to make that task much easier.

Although some people might think that an object pool is easy to write, by using the Pool package, a wide suite of built-in, well-tested behaviors is provided for free. For example, you can use the Commons package to create a pool that will only allocate a maximum of ten objects and then block on future allocations until an object is returned or create up to fifty objects, with the pool automatically shrinking when the garbage collector needs the memory. By implementing a single interface and using the right combination of Apache Pool interfaces and implementations, you can configure a wide suite of pools, suitable for a broad range of uses.

> **Avoid Preoptimization**
>
> Maintaining an object pool simply to minimize the overhead of JVM-level object creation is generally not worth the bother. Modern JVM implementations are quite good at optimizing object creation. If the objects are expensive to create, however, it may be worth creating a pool.

It's worth noting that one of the most popular uses of a pool is to manage database connectivity. This is popular enough to warrant a specific Commons package, DBCP, which is based on the Pool suite described in this chapter. DBCP is described in the next chapter. In addition, Java 5.0 (also known as JDK 1.5) includes built-in support for ThreadPools and other useful operations, as described at http://java.sun.com/j2se/1.5.0/docs/guide/concurrency/index.html.

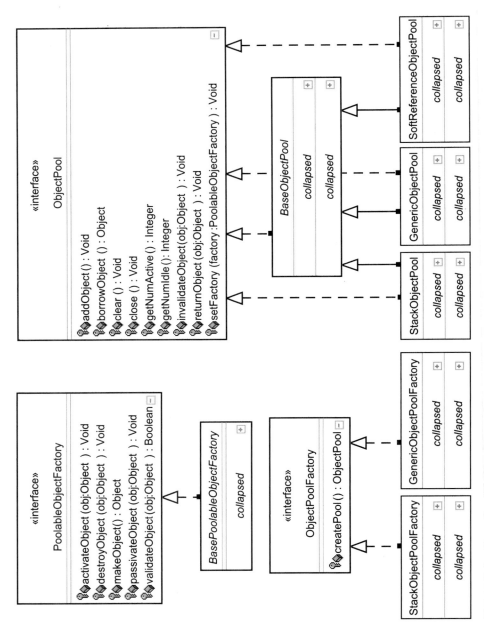

Figure 5-1 Generic pool class hierarchy.

INTERFACES AND IMPLEMENTATION

The Pool library provides both a suite of interfaces and a set of concrete implementations. This allows a developer to maintain compatibility with a wide variety of applications, while also adding new functionality as needed. In turn, the Pool library contains two hierarchies—one for a generic pool, and one for keyed pools. The hierarchy for generic pools is shown in Figure 5-1.

The semantics for an object pool are fairly straightforward—you must first implement the interface `org.apache.commons.pool.PoolableObjectFactory` (a no-operation abstract class, `org.apache.commons.pool.BasePoolableObjectFactory`, can be subclassed if preferred). At a minimum, you will need to provide an implementation of the `makeObject()` method, to define how and what should be created.

Next, you will need to create an `ObjectPool`. You can create an `ObjectPool` by using an `ObjectPoolFactory` or simply by allocating it using `new`, passing your `PoolableObjectFactory` implementation in to the constructor. Depending on the `ObjectPool` implementation you use, your object pool will have different behavior. The `GenericObjectPool` uses a first in, first out behavior, suitable for situations in which you want to ensure that all of the objects are used frequently. The `StackObjectPool`, on the other hand, uses a last in, first out behavior. A useful alternative to the `StackObjectPool` is the `SoftReferenceObjectPool`, which allows garbage collection of unused objects.

The `KeyedObjectPool` hierarchy, as shown in Figure 5-2, is similar to the `GenericPool`, but with the addition of a key value. This allows you to maintain a single pool with the elements retrievable by key. The default implementations allow one or more objects per key, but you could provide an implementation that restricts use to a single object per key.

THREAD POOL EXAMPLE

Java features a powerful, rich set of services for working with multiple threads. In this example, we will use the Pool suite to manage experimentation with the built-in Java threading facilities.

As shown in Figure 5-3, a `WorkerThreadFactory` can be used to provide new test thread objects. Our main application code, `PoolTest`, creates a suite of test threads, testing how long it takes to complete the test run in different combinations of threads and thread runs.

By changing the behavior of the `WorkerThread.run()` method, we can change the load placed on the system by each thread, and by changing the values of the `PoolTest.runTest()` method, we can determine different results when different thread loads are placed on the system. For example, by comparing the impact of 1,000 threads running once against a single thread running the same task 1,000 times, we start to understand the overhead of parallel execution on a single system compared to serial execution.

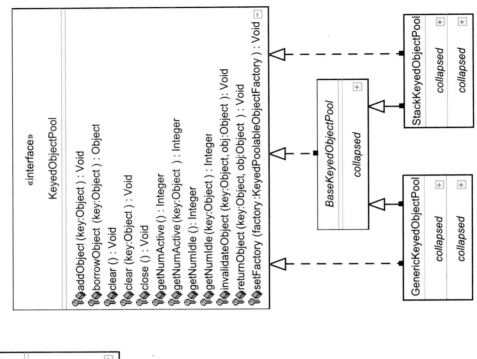
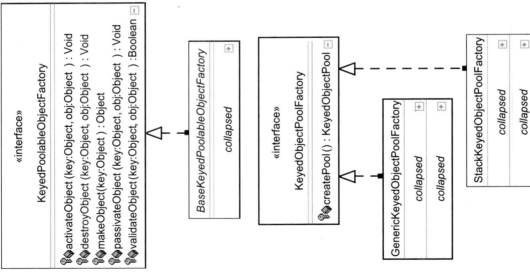

Figure 5-2 Keyed pool class hierarchy.

Thread Pool Example

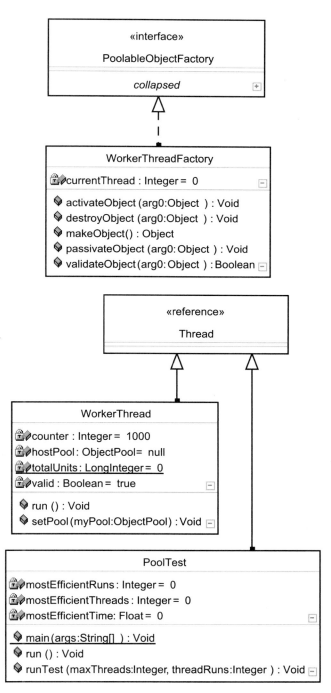

Figure 5-3 Thread pool example classes.

Listing 5-1 shows the main class for this example. Pay particular attention to the configuration of the `GenericObjectPool` object in the `runTest()` method—notice that several important configuration methods are used to set the operation of the pool. You'll also notice that in this example, `runTest()` borrows objects from the pool but doesn't return them—the `WorkerThread` objects return themselves to the pool when execution is complete.

Listing 5-1 Thread Test Runner

```
package com.cascadetg.ch05;

import org.apache.commons.pool.impl.GenericObjectPool;

public class PoolTest extends Thread
{
    /** This main method simply creates a new PoolTest thread
     * and starts it. */
    public static void main(String[] args)
    {
        new PoolTest().start();
    }

    /** The run() method (called when the PoolTest thread starts)
     * merely executes a series of test in serial fashion.
     */
    public void run()
    {
        runTest(30, 30);
        runTest(100, 100);
        runTest(1000, 1000);

        runTest(1000, 2000);
        runTest(1, 3000);
        runTest(10, 3000);
        runTest(30, 3000);
        runTest(1000, 3000);

        System.out.println("Most efficient @" + mostEfficientTime);
        System.out.println(
            "(" + mostEfficientThreads + "/"
                + mostEfficientRuns + ")");

        System.out.println("Done.");

    }

    /** Used to keep track of the most efficient run */
    int mostEfficientThreads = 0;
    int mostEfficientRuns = 0;
    float mostEfficientTime = 0;

    /** This method actually runs the test.  The higher the
     * maxThreads value, the more threads can be created to run in
     * parallel.  The threadRuns indicates the total number of
     * threads that will be created.
     *
     * @param maxThreads Used to specify the maximum number
```

(continues)

Listing 5-1 (*continued*)

```
 * of threads to be created by the object pool.
 *
 * @param threadRuns The number of executions of the thread
 * to be run.
 */
public void runTest(int maxThreads, int threadRuns)
{
    System.out.println(
        "Starting " + maxThreads + "/" + threadRuns);

    // Create an instance of our WorkerThreadFactory.
    WorkerThreadFactory myFactory = new WorkerThreadFactory();

    // Here, we create a generic object pool, passing in our
    // WorkerThreadFactory.
    GenericObjectPool myPool =
        new GenericObjectPool(myFactory);

    // Here, we configure the behavior of our pool.
    // Note the use of maxThreads to configure the number of
    // threads we want to allocate, and the behavior of the
    // threads.
    myPool.setMaxActive(maxThreads);
    myPool.setWhenExhaustedAction(
        GenericObjectPool.WHEN_EXHAUSTED_BLOCK);
    myPool.setTestOnReturn(true);

    // Gather the current timing info, and start making
    // threads.  Note that this will block if there is no
    // thread available.
    long currentTime = System.currentTimeMillis();
    for (int i = 0; i < threadRuns; i++)
    {
        try
        {
            WorkerThread myThread =
                (WorkerThread)myPool.borrowObject();
            myThread.setPool(myPool);
            myThread.start();
        } catch (Exception e)
        {
            e.printStackTrace();
        }
    }

    // Now, make sure that all of the threads we kicked off
    // have a chance to finish up what they are doing.
    while (myPool.getNumActive() > 0) { yield(); }

    // Let's do some reporting of the results.
    long time = System.currentTimeMillis() - currentTime;
    System.out.println(
        "Total created threads:"
            + myFactory.currentThread);
    System.out.println("Seconds Elapsed: " + (time / 1000f));
    System.out.println(
        "Completed:            " + WorkerThread.totalUnits);

    float efficiency = WorkerThread.totalUnits / (time / 1000f);
```

(*continues*)

Listing 5-1 (*continued*)

```
        System.out.println("units/second:        " + efficiency);

        // If this is our most efficient run, we should note that.
        if (efficiency > mostEfficientTime)
        {
            mostEfficientTime = efficiency;
            mostEfficientThreads = maxThreads;
            mostEfficientRuns = threadRuns;
        }
        System.out.println();

        // Reset the work done by the threads for the next test.
        WorkerThread.totalUnits = 0;
    }
}
```

OBJECT FACTORY EXAMPLE

The object factory, shown in Listing 5-2, implements the `PoolableObjectFactory` interface. The two key methods implemented are `makeObject()` and `validateObject()`. The factory always returns `false` for an invalid object because when a thread enters a finished state, it cannot be reused. Because the pool is configured to always test on return (as shown in Listing 5-1), this means that the `WorkerThread` will be removed when completed.

Listing 5-2 Thread Factory

```java
package com.cascadetg.ch05;

import org.apache.commons.pool.PoolableObjectFactory;

public class WorkerThreadFactory implements PoolableObjectFactory
{
    /** Keeps track of the currently created thread. */
    public int currentThread = 0;

    /**  Create and name the thread.  Naming the thread is very
     * helpful when trying to debug multi-threaded applications.
     */
    public Object makeObject() throws Exception
    {
        WorkerThread temp = new WorkerThread();
        temp.setName("Worker Thread #" + currentThread++);
        return temp;
    }

    /** We aren't reusing threads, so we always return false here,
     * causing the pool to remove this thread from the pool and
     * create a new object using the makeObject() method.
     */
    public boolean validateObject(Object arg0) { return false; }

    public void destroyObject(Object arg0) throws Exception   { }
```

(*continues*)

Listing 5-2 (*continued*)

```
    public void activateObject(Object arg0) throws Exception { }
    public void passivateObject(Object arg0) throws Exception { }
}
```

WORKER THREAD

Listing 5-3 shows our worker thread. The default implementation merely counts to 1,000, yielding every count. This is overly aggressive, but it does allow the system to remain highly responsive to other threads during execution. It's easy to imagine changing the behavior of this worker thread to do something more computationally complex—for example, when used in conjunction with the networking capabilities shown in Chapter 4, "Net" and this chapter, parallel execution could well be much faster and easier.

The implementation shown in Listing 5-3 drops out of the `run()` method when complete, rendering the thread no longer reusable. It would be possible to create a reusable `WorkerThread`—instead of completing and dropping out of the `run()` method, the thread could instead have two states—a busy state and an idle state, with the thread returning itself to the pool when switching from the busy state to idle.

Listing 5-3 Worker Thread

```
package com.cascadetg.ch05;

import org.apache.commons.pool.ObjectPool;

public class WorkerThread extends Thread
{
    // The total amount of work done by the threads.
    static public long totalUnits = 0;
    // The number of times the thread should look over a counter
    // (this is our definition of work)
    private int counter = 1000;

    // When the thread is done, it returns itself to the pool.
    private ObjectPool hostPool = null;
    // Used to indicate that a thread, when completed, is no longer
    // useful.
    public boolean valid = true;

    public void setPool(ObjectPool myPool)
    {
        hostPool = myPool;
    }

    public void run()
    {
        // Loop over a counter, and yield each time to allow other
        // threads to execute.  In a "real" app, you wouldn't need
        // to yield anywhere near this often.
        for (int i = 0; i < counter; i++)
```

(*continues*)

Listing 5-3 (*continued*)

```
        {
            totalUnits++;
            yield();
        }
        try
        {
            // We synchronize on the pool to avoid possible
            // threading problems, and return our object.
            synchronized (hostPool)
            {
                this.valid = false;
                hostPool.returnObject(this);
            }
        } catch (Exception e)
        { e.printStackTrace(); }
    }
}
```

Finally, Listing 5-4 shows an example of the output of this application. Paying close attention to the output, we can see that in this particular case, a non-parallel approach has the best timing. This is to be expected in a CPU-dependent, single system environment, but in environments involving potentially slow resources (such as network access), the results may be quite different.

Listing 5-4 Sample Output

```
Starting 30/30
Total created threads:30
Seconds Elapsed: 0.191
Completed:         30000
units/second:      157068.06

Starting 100/100
Total created threads:100
Seconds Elapsed: 0.801
Completed:         100000
units/second:      124843.945

Starting 1000/1000
Total created threads:1000
Seconds Elapsed: 9.794
Completed:         1000000
units/second:      102103.33

Starting 1000/2000
Total created threads:2000
Seconds Elapsed: 19.127
Completed:         2000000
units/second:      104564.23

Starting 1/3000
Total created threads:3000
Seconds Elapsed: 5.398
Completed:         3000000
units/second:      555761.44
```

(*continues*)

Listing 5-4 (*continued*)

```
Starting 10/3000
Total created threads:3000
Seconds Elapsed: 6.85
Completed:             3000000
units/second:          437956.22

Starting 30/3000
Total created threads:3000
Seconds Elapsed: 7.641
Completed:             3000000
units/second:          392618.78

Starting 1000/3000
Total created threads:3000
Seconds Elapsed: 28.471
Completed:             3000000
units/second:          105370.375

Most efficient @ 555761.44
(1/3000)
Done.
```

SUMMARY

This chapter shows how to use an implementation of a common pattern—the use of a pool. Pools typically serve one of two roles—either as a logical representation of a pool, or as a performance enhancement by way of a cache implementation. If a pool represents a logical pool, you should feel free to use the pattern immediately—for example, an application for reserving hotel rooms might use a pool to track the available rooms. If a pool represents a cache of some sort, it should be added to an application later rather than sooner to avoid premature optimization.

Pools are commonly used as a performance enhancement for managing connections to a database. The next chapter will look at a specific pool designed for managing database-specific resources.

Project Ideas

Build an application that uses the Pool package to wrap Net NNTP connections (as described in Chapter 4). Add a user interface to allow a user to browse the NNTP articles on one thread and then a configurable number of other threads to download articles in the background.

Build a test harness that tests the size and options available for different pools against the factories. Given this information and other data available to a running Java application (such as the current memory available), would it be possible to build a self-tuning pool?

CHAPTER **6**

DBCP (Database Connection Pool)

Opening a connection to a database is a relatively expensive operation. To avoid having to frequently open database connections, many applications rely on a database connection pool—a group of connections to the database, rotated between the various components of an application as needed. The Apache Jakarta Commons Database Connection Pool (DBCP) provides a rich set of functionality for connection pooling.

> **Note:** Most modern application servers include built-in database connection pooling functionality. If you are building an application that you intend to host in an application server, consult your server documentation for more information on the preferred connection pool mechanism.

DBCP offers a variety of mechanisms for managing your database connection pool. As shown in Figure 6-1, the pool library mimics many aspects of the normal JDBC interfaces. The best option for your application will likely depend on the environment and your existing application code (if any).

If you have an existing application that accesses a database directly (for example, a Swing application that opens JDBC connections directly to a database[1]), you may wish to take advantage of DBCP's `PoolingDriver` class—you can register a pool as a driver, and as long as your application code can easily be converted to using a new set of JDBC connection parameters, you can quickly add database connection pooling. Depending on the classes and configuration chosen, a wide suite of possible options is available.

---

1. Perhaps even a bundled in-process Java database, such as hsqldb (`http://hsqldb.sourceforge.net/`) or Apache Derby (`http://incubator.apache.org/derby/`).

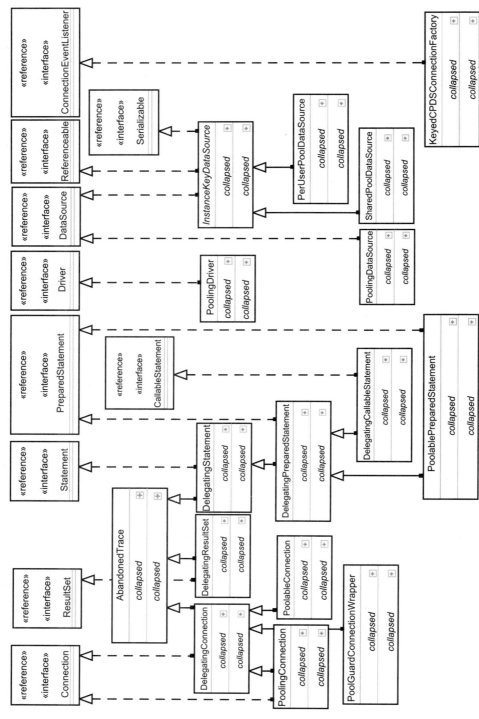

Figure 6-1 DBCP and JDBC interfaces.

> **Note:** While the Apache DBCP code includes reference to logging, this functionality is deprecated (and the current implementation lacks certain key features). Future releases of Apache Commons DBCP may include pluggable mechanisms (for example, event listeners) for more sophisticated notification of pool behavior.

Most web applications, however, rely on a `javax.sql.DataSource` for their database connectivity, typically obtained via a JNDI lookup. The `DataSource` configuration in this case is managed by the application server configuration. For example, Tomcat allows you to configure JDBC connection pools as shown at http://jakarta.apache.org/tomcat/tomcat-5.0-doc/jndi-resources-howto.html. If you are using Tomcat as the provider of your `DataSource` objects, you're using the Commons DBCP package, even though you may never need to know (or care) about the underlying implementation.

STANDALONE DATASOURCES

Under certain circumstances, however, you may not have the option of deploying (or testing) application code within the context of your application server, but you might still want to rely on a pooled `javax.sql.DataSource` for your connectivity. Here, we will look at an example of executing an application that makes use of a custom `DataSource`—and test to see just how much of a performance improvement pooling a series of database connections affords an application. Figure 6-2 shows our two classes—a series of worker threads, executing a test SQL string, and a test harness to create the shared `DataSource`.

Client Connectivity

As shown in Listing 6-1, our worker thread is given a connection at creation, runs the test SQL, and then carefully returns the connection. There is no reference to a `DataSource` or any notion of how the connection is obtained—the thread merely runs the code and terminates. In many ways, this is similar to the activity of a typical web application as might be found in a JSP, servlet, or when using EJB's Bean-Managed Persistence.

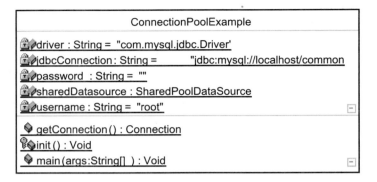
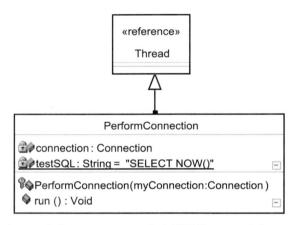

Figure 6-2 Testing pooled versus non-pooled JDBC connectivity.

Listing 6-1 Simple Database Connectivity

```
package com.cascadetg.ch06;

import java.sql.Connection;

import java.sql.ResultSet;
import java.sql.SQLException;
import java.sql.Statement;

public class PerformConnection extends Thread
{
    // The test SQL we are sending to the database.
    private static final String testSQL = "SELECT NOW()";

    Connection connection;

    // Note that by providing this constructor, the compiler will not
    // generate a no-op default constructor for us.
    PerformConnection(Connection myConnection)
```

(*continues*)

Listing 6-1 (continued)

```
    {
        this.connection = myConnection;
    }

    public void run()
    {
        Connection myConnection = connection;
        Statement myStatement = null;
        ResultSet myResult = null;
        try
        {
            // There's no advantage to creating a prepared
            // statement for a simple SQL statement such as NOW()
            myStatement = myConnection.createStatement();
            myResult = myStatement.executeQuery(testSQL);

            // Get the resulting data back, and loop through it
            // to simulate the data retrieval.
            int numcols = myResult.getMetaData().getColumnCount();
            while (myResult.next())
            {
                for (int i = 1; i <= numcols; i++)
                { myResult.getString(i); }
            }
        } catch (SQLException e)
        {
            e.printStackTrace();
        } finally
        {
            // We want to be agressive about ensuring that our
            // connection is properly cleaned up and returned to
            // our pool.
            try { myResult.close(); } catch (Exception e) { }
            try { myStatement.close(); } catch (Exception e) { }
            try { myConnection.close(); } catch (Exception e) { }
        }
    }
}
```

Building the DataSource

The code shown in Listing 6-2 shows how a pooled DataSource can be set up and configured. Pay attention to configuration details specified in the init() method, such as the maximum size of the pool.

Listing 6-2 Simple Database Connectivity

```
package com.cascadetg.ch06;

import java.sql.DriverManager;
import java.sql.Connection;
import java.sql.SQLException;

// commons-dbcp.jar
import org.apache.commons.dbcp.cpdsadapter.DriverAdapterCPDS;
```

(continues)

Listing 6-2 (*continued*)

```java
//Note that the SharedPoolDataSource relies on the
//commons-collection.jar, so you will need that on your classpath
//as well.
import org.apache.commons.dbcp.datasources.SharedPoolDataSource;

public class ConnectionPoolExample
{
    // You'll want to change these strings for the database you're
    // using.  This example was performed using a default
    // installation of the MySQL database (www.mysql.com)
    private static final String driver = "com.mysql.jdbc.Driver";
    private static final String username = "root";
    private static final String password = "";
    private static final String jdbcConnection =
        "jdbc:mysql://localhost/commons";

    private static SharedPoolDataSource sharedDatasource;

    static void init()
    {
        DriverAdapterCPDS myConnectionPoolDatasource =
            new DriverAdapterCPDS();
        try
        { myConnectionPoolDatasource.setDriver(driver);
        } catch (Exception e) { }
        myConnectionPoolDatasource.setUrl(jdbcConnection);
        myConnectionPoolDatasource.setUser(username);
        myConnectionPoolDatasource.setPassword(password);

        sharedDatasource = new SharedPoolDataSource();
        sharedDatasource.setConnectionPoolDataSource(
            myConnectionPoolDatasource);

        sharedDatasource.setMaxActive(10);
        sharedDatasource.setMaxWait(50);
    }

    public static Connection getConnection() throws SQLException
    { return sharedDatasource.getConnection(); }

    public static void main(String[] args)
    {
        init();
        try
        {
            // First we fill up the pool before starting our timings
            for (int x = 0; x < 15; x++)
            {
                Connection conn = getConnection();
                new PerformConnection(conn).start();
            }

            long currentTiming = System.currentTimeMillis();

            // Perform the SQL operation many times.  Notice that
            // we are kicking these off as simultaneous threads,
            // closer to the behavior one might expect in a
            // multi-threaded environment such as a web application
            for (int x = 0; x < 1000; x++)
```

(*continues*)

Listing 6-2 (*continued*)

```
        {
            Connection conn = getConnection();
            new PerformConnection(conn).start();
        }
        while (sharedDatasource.getNumActive() > 0)
        {   // Need to wait until all of the connections
            // have completed.
        }
        float timing =
            (System.currentTimeMillis() - currentTiming)
                / 1000f;
        System.out.println("Seconds with pool : " + timing);
        currentTiming = System.currentTimeMillis();

        // Now, we do the same number of tests, this time
        // opening and closing the connection using the driver
        // directly.
        for (int x = 0; x < 1000; x++)
        {
            Connection conn =
                DriverManager.getConnection(
                    jdbcConnection, username, password);
            new PerformConnection(conn).run();
        }
        while (sharedDatasource.getNumActive() > 0)
        {   // Need to wait until all of the connections
            // have completed.
        }
        timing =
            (System.currentTimeMillis() - currentTiming) / 1000f;
        System.out.println("Seconds without pool : " + timing);

        // Display some pool statistics
        System.out.println(
            "NumActive: " + sharedDatasource.getNumActive());
        System.out.println(
            "NumIdle: " + sharedDatasource.getNumIdle());
    } catch (Exception e) { e.printStackTrace(); }
    }
}
```

Even though the code in Listing 6-2 uses an `org.apache.commons.dbcp.datasources.SharedPoolDataSource`, if needed that object could have been cast or passed as a `javax.sql.DataSource`.

When run, this application reports the timings. An example of the output on my system, connecting to a local MySQL database, is shown in Listing 6-3. Notice that even though the pool was configured to allow up to ten possible connections, only eight are actually used—this is because the connections are returned to the pool fast enough by our client code that only eight connections are ever opened. It's easy to imagine certain lengthy client operations that might take longer to return, causing the connection pool to grow to the maximum possible size.

Listing 6-3 Sample Pooling vs. No Pooling Timings

```
Seconds with pool : 1.542
Seconds without pool : 6.219
NumActive: 0
NumIdle: 8
```

As can be seen in Listing 6-3, the use of connection pooling allows the application to run the test suite in roughly one-quarter the time—not bad, considering no modifications to the client code were necessary to take advantage of the pool.

LEGACY JDBC DRIVER

It's common to inherit a bit of code written with neither DataSources nor connection pooling of any sort in mind at all. For a variety of reasons, it may not be feasible to change your existing program logic (beyond editing the JDBC connection strings). Fortunately, DBCP supports the notion of a PoolingDriver—an implementation of a JDBC driver that implements a connection pool behind the scenes. As long as your application code opens and closes connections properly, you can add connection pooling at any time.

Listing 6-4 shows how a bit of legacy code can be adapted to support a connection pool. As you can see, you will still need to add a bit of code to initialize the connection pool (as shown in the registerPoolingDriver() method) to your legacy application's initialization process.

Listing 6-4 Legacy JDBC Application Connection Pooling

```
package com.cascadetg.ch06;

import org.apache.commons.pool.ObjectPool;
import org.apache.commons.pool.impl.GenericObjectPool;

import org.apache.commons.dbcp.*;

import java.sql.DriverManager;
import java.sql.Driver;
import java.sql.Connection;
import java.sql.Statement;
import java.sql.ResultSet;

import java.util.Properties;

public class LegacyJDBCExample
{
    public static void main(String[] args)
    {
        registerPoolingDriver();
        legacyJDBCCode();
    }
```

(continues)

Listing 6-4 (*continued*)

```java
/** This method represents a bit of legacy code.  It's assumed that
 * in your "real" legacy code, you have at least broken out or can
 * easily change the Driver and JDBC URL.  The legacy username and
 * password are ignored when connecting to the new pool.
 */
public static void legacyJDBCCode()
{
    // Note the commented out "old driver" and "old JDBC URL"

    //String legacyDriver = "com.mysql.jdbc.Driver";
    String legacyDriver =
        "org.apache.commons.dbcp.PoolingDriver";
    //String legacyJdbcConnection =
    // "jdbc:mysql://localhost/commons";
    String legacyJdbcConnection =
        "jdbc:apache:commons:dbcp:example";

    // The legacy username and password are ignored
    String legacyUsername = "ralph";
    String legacyPassword = "bingo";

    Connection myConnection = null;

    try
    {
        Driver myDriver =
            (Driver)Class.forName(driver).newInstance();

        // The connection is obtained as before, but now the
        // connection comes from the pool.
        myConnection =
            DriverManager.getConnection(
                legacyJdbcConnection, legacyUsername,
                legacyPassword);

        Statement myStatement = myConnection.createStatement();

        String testSQL = "SELECT NOW()";
        ResultSet myResults = myStatement.executeQuery(testSQL);
        while (myResults.next())
        { System.out.println(myResults.getString(1)); }
        myResults.close();
        myStatement.close();

    } catch (Exception e)
    { e.printStackTrace();
    } finally
    {
        if (myConnection != null)
            try
            {   // When closed, the connection is returned
                // to the pool.  If your legacy code doesn't
                // do this, eventually the pool will starve -
                // although you are likely already running into
                // problems.
                myConnection.close();
            } catch (Exception x) { }
    }
}
```

(*continues*)

Listing 6-4 (*continued*)

```java
        // These are the real database connectivity strings,
        // used by the pool.
        private static final String driver = "com.mysql.jdbc.Driver";
        private static final String username = "root";
        private static final String password = "";
        private static final String jdbcConnection =
            "jdbc:mysql://localhost/commons";

        public static void registerPoolingDriver()
        {
            // An object pool is used to maintain the connections. Any
            // pool may be used - for more information, see chapter 6
            ObjectPool connectionPool = new GenericObjectPool(null);

            // The connection pool factory can pass properties on
            // as needed.  The obvious candidates are username and
            // password, others will depend on your database, driver,
            // etc.
            Properties myDriverConnectionProps = new Properties();
            myDriverConnectionProps.put("username", username);
            myDriverConnectionProps.put("password", password);

            // The factory is used by the driver to create new
            // JDBC connections, based on the driver provided.
            ConnectionFactory connectionFactory = null;
            try
            {
                Class.forName(driver);
                Driver myDriver =
                    (Driver)Class.forName(driver).newInstance();

                connectionFactory = new DriverConnectionFactory(
                        myDriver, jdbcConnection, myDriverConnectionProps);

                // The PoolableConnectionFactory wraps the actual
                // Connections created by the ConnectionFactory
                // with pooling driver classes that implement the
                // pooling functionality.
                PoolableConnectionFactory poolableConnectionFactory =
                    new PoolableConnectionFactory(
                        connectionFactory, connectionPool,
                        null, null, false, true);

                // Next, attach our pooling driver as a registered driver
                Class.forName("org.apache.commons.dbcp.PoolingDriver");
                PoolingDriver driver =
                    (PoolingDriver)DriverManager.getDriver(
                        "jdbc:apache:commons:dbcp:");

                // Associate the identifier example with this connection
                // pool. We might register two different pools for
                // different database connectivity options.
                driver.registerPool("example", connectionPool);

            } catch (Exception e) { e.printStackTrace(); }
        }
    }
```

SUMMARY

This chapter shows how to use a custom pool as a performance enhancement for managing connections to a database. Interestingly, this can be done explicitly as a pool, or implicitly by injecting the pool at the driver level. While the Pool package, described in Chapter 5, "Pool," can be used to build generic pools, the DBCP is custom-built to address the common task of connecting to a database.

Project Ideas

Given a Swing application that accesses a database in some fashion, add a user interface element that displays the number of database connections currently in use (perhaps a "throbber" similar to the network connection user interface widget in a web browser).

Given a trivial SQL statement, write a utility to check the performance of DBCP versus opening and closing connections explicitly via JDBC. If you have an application container (such as Apache Jakarta Tomcat) that provides a connection pool (perhaps obtainable via JNDI), how does the performance compare?

CHAPTER **7**

BeanUtils

One of the most popular patterns in Java is the JavaBeans component model (http://java.sun.com/products/javabeans/). Originally designed to allow visual design tools to generate AWT user interfaces, the JavaBeans specification provides additional guidelines on top of the basic contracts implied by a given Java class.

The JavaBeans specification provides mechanisms for methods of a Java class to be visible to a builder tool, organized into properties, methods, and events. A property is available via accessor methods, such as `String getFirstName()` and `void setFirstName()`. Methods are ordinary Java methods. Events define standard methods for allowing one component to notify one or more components of an arbitrary event. Visual development tools use these various systems to enable visual construction of user interfaces: a button is dragged onto a panel, the properties are set (such as the label and size), and events are wired (for example, clicking on the button closes the window).

For server-side development, the most popular aspects of the JavaBeans specification are the constructor and property patterns. Specifically, a standard JavaBean must have a no-argument constructor and get/set accessor methods corresponding to the various properties. For example, the simple JavaBean shown in Listing 7-1 has two `String` properties (first name, last name) and a single `int` property (clearance).

Listing 7-1 Simple JavaBean

```
package com.cascadetg.ch07;

public class User
{
    // Private variables
    private String firstName;

    private String lastName;

    private int clearance;
```

(*continues*)

Listing 7-1 (*continued*)

```
    // Accessor methods
    public String getFirstName() { return firstName; }
    public void setFirstName(String firstName)
    { this.firstName = firstName; }

    public String getLastName() { return lastName; }
    public void setLastName(String lastName)
    { this.lastName = lastName; }

    public int getClearance() { return clearance; }
    public void setClearance(int clearance)
    { this.clearance = clearance; }
}
```

While the JavaBeans specification describes rules for how components should be written and the expected behavior of the tools, no implementation is provided. Generally speaking, it is assumed that the low-level `java.lang.reflect.*` package will be used to obtain information about the Java classes, and the tool will generate code as needed.

Over time, it has become clear that frameworks, not just visual design tools, can take advantage of the JavaBeans patterns. For example, the object/relational bridge framework Hibernate uses JavaBean patterns to help work with relational databases in a more natural fashion.

Hibernate and FormBean

Hibernate, an object/relational database integration technology, uses the JavaBeans component model as its key foundation. By combining JavaBeans with XML mapping files, a Java developer can work with complex relational databases quickly and easily. The inspiration for this chapter came from the idea that the JavaBeans model can be leveraged not just for persistence, but also for automation of user interface generation.

For more information on the object/relational framework Hibernate, see my book, *Hibernate: A J2EE Developer's Guide to Database Integration* (ISBN: 0321268199, Addison-Wesley Professional).

While it is possible to use the low-level reflection package to deal with JavaBeans, it is easier to use the Jakarta Commons BeanUtils package.

For anyone given to thinking in terms of broader architectural design and framework development, it is easy to think of other areas in which the BeanUtils package may be useful. Obviously, this package would be of interest to anyone interested in building visual development tools. Similarly, dependency injection, dynamic configuration, and runtime binding of application elements such as the user interface and other systems are all potentially of interest.

In this chapter we will look at how to use the Jakarta Commons BeanUtils package to build a simple framework for converting objects based on the JavaBeans standard to HTML forms and back.

Understanding BeanUtils

In many ways, BeanUtils can be considered a metadata wrapper that makes it as easy to work with a JavaBean as a Map. The properties are the keys, and property values can be set by simply setting the property as a value. For example:

```
myUser.setName("Bob");
```

... can instead be written:

```
BeanUtils.setProperty(myUser, "name", "Bob");
```

Similarly, an array of the properties available for `myUser` can be simply retrieved:

```
DynaProperty[] properties = WrapDynaClass.
createDynaClass(myUser.class).getDynaProperties();
```

This offers two key advantages: it allows you to decouple components of your application, and it allows you to build frameworks and tools to take advantage of the JavaBeans framework.

As shown in Figure 7-1, the BeanUtils package draws a distinction between a `DynaClass`, which describes a class, and a `DynaBean`, which describes a particular object instance. This notion can actually be extended a bit—a `DynaClass` can be used as a wrapper for a JDBC `ResultSet`, for example (in which the properties correspond to the returned results), and individual records can be returned as `DynaBeans`.

One aspect of the BeanUtils package worth calling out is the notion of a `Converter`. This provides a generic way to retrieve and set values across a suite of properties using String values, regardless of the type of the property. For example, you may want to set a property with a type of int using a String such as "2". The Converter package takes care of these details for you.

The following types are supported by built-in converters:

- BigDecimal
- BigInteger
- Boolean
- Byte
- Character
- Class
- Double
- File
- Float
- Integer
- Long
- Short
- SqlDate
- SqlTime
- SqlTimestamp
- String
- URL
- Abstract array
- Boolean array
- Byte array
- Character array
- Double array
- Float array
- Integer array
- Long array
- Short array
- String array

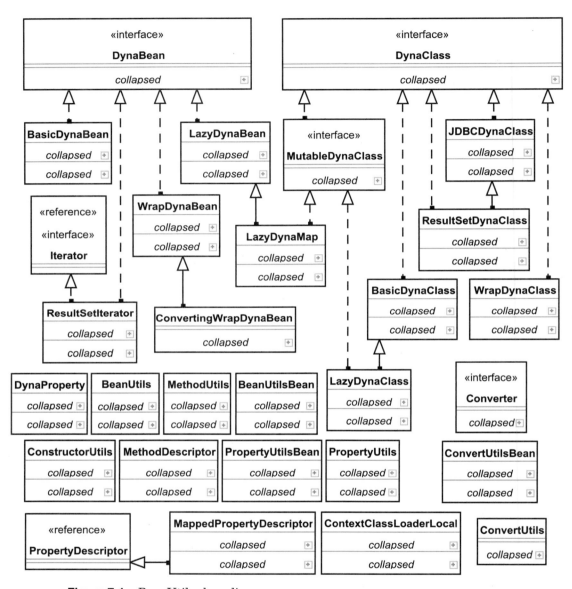

Figure 7-1 BeanUtils class diagram.

USING BEANUTILS TO GENERATE FORMS

Given the information already present in a JavaBean, the sample application will use BeanUtils to create a new library based on a new class, FormBean. FormBean generates an HTML form directly from the JavaBean information as rendered by BeanUtils. Each property results in a single label and a single text field. The label is generated automatically from the property name (for example, getFirstName is automatically labeled First Name). When the form is submitted, FormBean will attempt to set the JavaBean properties using the submitted values.

Although FormBean is not a complete framework (for example, array-based properties are not supported), it does illustrate the power of JavaBeans in conjunction with BeanUtils.

Sample JavaBeans

This example is based on the simple JavaBean shown in Listing 7-1. Note the three properties: two of type string, one of type int.

In order to demonstrate the lifecycle as handled by FormBean, the application needs to have some mechanism for storing a value. Listing 7-2 shows how the application tracks the user.

Listing 7-2 Tracking the User

```
package com.cascadetg.ch07;

public class UserManager
{
    static private User user = new User();

    static public User getUser() { return user; }

    static public void setUser(User in) { user = in; }
}
```

Presenting the Form

Given the User JavaBean, FormBean generates a form, as shown in Figure 7-2.

If a user enters incorrect data for the required property type, FormBean automatically generates and reports the error, as shown in Figure 7-3.

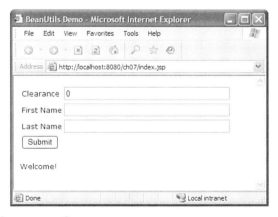

Figure 7-2 Initial FormBean form.

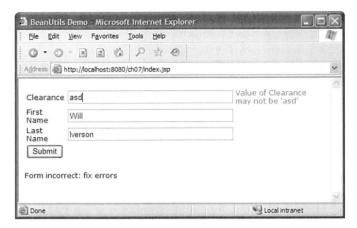

Figure 7-3 Handling a `FormBean` form error.

After the user corrects any errors and resubmits the form, `FormBean` is used to accept the submission, as shown in Figure 7-4.

Figure 7-4 Corrected `FormBean` form.

The entire JSP file to generate and handle this form is shown in Listing 7-3. Note the `.error` style defined to highlight the errors.

Listing 7-3 `FormBean` JSP

```
<%@ page language="java" im-
port="com.cascadetg.ch07.*,org.apache.commons.beanutils.*" errorPage="" %>
<%
    FormBean myFormBean = new FormBean(User.class, UserManager.getUser());
    String notification = "Welcome!";
    if(request.getParameter("Submit") != null)
```

(continues)

Listing 7-3 (continued)

```
    {
        if(myFormBean.updateValue(request))
            notification = "Form accepted!";
        else
            notification = "Form incorrect: fix errors";
    }
%>
<html>
<head><title>BeanUtils Demo</title>
<style type="text/css">
<!--
.error { color: #FF0000; }
-->
</style>
<link href="../ch03/default.css" rel="stylesheet" type="text/css">
</head>
<body>
<table>
<form name="form1" method="post" action="">
<%= myFormBean.toHTMLForm()%>
<tr><td colspan="3"><input type="submit" name="Submit" value="Submit">
</td></tr>
</form>
</table>
<p><%= notification %></p>
</body>
</html>
```

Even a simple form with minimal update and validation logic would be painful to implement by hand with JSP. For a web application with dozens of such forms, a lot of tedious work could be eliminated through the use of a framework like `FormBean`.

FormBean

The initialization of the `FormBean` is shown in Listing 7-4. As you can see, the `FormBean` uses the class and optionally an instance to configure the form. If no instance is passed in, `FormBean` will attempt to instantiate one. Either way, the `FormBean` keeps track of both the original class and instance, and then it wraps the class in a `DynaClass` and the instance in a `DynaBean` (using `WrapDynaClass`).

Listing 7-4 `FormBean` Initialization

```
package com.cascadetg.ch07;

import java.util.HashMap;
import java.util.Map;

import javax.servlet.http.HttpServletRequest;

import org.apache.commons.beanutils.BeanUtils;

import org.apache.commons.beanutils.DynaBean;
import org.apache.commons.beanutils.DynaClass;
import org.apache.commons.beanutils.DynaProperty;
```

(continues)

Listing 7-4 (*continued*)

```java
import org.apache.commons.beanutils.WrapDynaBean;
import org.apache.commons.beanutils.WrapDynaClass;

public class FormBean
{
    private HashMap errors = new HashMap();

    // The class refers to the compiled version of the class
    private Class baseClass;
    private DynaClass dynaClass;

    // The object refers to the runtime (in-memory) version
    private Object baseObject;
    private DynaBean dynaObject;

    private DynaProperty[] properties;

    // Used to help format the resulting text boxes
    private int displayStringLength = 40;
    private int maxStringLength = 100;

    /** For creation forms */
    public FormBean(Class myClass)
    {
        baseClass = myClass;
        dynaClass = WrapDynaClass.createDynaClass(baseClass);
        properties = dynaClass.getDynaProperties();
        try
        {
            baseObject = myClass.newInstance();
            dynaObject = new WrapDynaBean(baseObject);
        } catch (Exception e)
        {
            System.err
                    .println("FATAL ERROR: Unable to instantiate "
                            + dynaClass.getName());
            e.printStackTrace();
        }
    }

    /** For update forms */
    public FormBean(Class myClass, Object myObject)
    {
        baseObject = myObject;
        dynaObject = new WrapDynaBean(baseObject);
        baseClass = myClass;
        dynaClass = WrapDynaClass.createDynaClass(baseClass);
        properties = dynaClass.getDynaProperties();
    }
```

Given the class and an instance, `FormBean` has the information it needs to create a form. As shown in Listing 7-5, `FormBean` loops through the properties to generate the label and the input form and to set the default values for the form based on the object instance. Note that errors are collected in a `java.util.Map`, with the key being the property and the value being the error message.

Listing 7-5 `FormBean` Form Generation

```java
/** Converts the object into a simple HTML form. */
public String toHTMLForm()
{
    StringBuffer output = new StringBuffer();

    for (int i = 0; i < properties.length; i++)
    {
        String currentProperty = properties[i].getName();
        if (currentProperty.compareTo("class") != 0)
        {
            // Start the row
            output.append("<tr>");

            // The cell for the label
            output.append("<td>");
            output.append(FormBeanUtils
                    .formatName(currentProperty));
            output.append("</td>");

            // The cell for the input form element
            output.append("<td>");
            output.append("<input ");
            FormBeanUtils.appendAttribute(output, "name",
                    currentProperty);

            // The cell for the current value, if there is
            // one
            if (this.dynaObject.get(currentProperty) != null)
            {
                FormBeanUtils.appendAttribute(output,
                        "value", this.dynaObject.get(
                                currentProperty).toString());
            }

            // Finish the input cell
            FormBeanUtils.appendAttribute(output, "size",
                    displayStringLength + "");
            FormBeanUtils.appendAttribute(output,
                    "maxlength", maxStringLength + "");
            output.append(">");
            output.append("</td>");

            // This cell displays any errors for this
            // property
            output.append("<td class='error'>");
            if (errors.containsKey(currentProperty))
            {
                output.append(errors.get(currentProperty)
                        .toString());
            }
            output.append(" </td>");

            // Finish up this row
            output.append("</tr>");
        }
    }

    return output.toString();
}
```

Listing 7-6 shows how a submitted form is handled. Note that the logic is expressed in terms of a `Map` (not explicitly tied in to the servlet model), allowing the `FormBean` to be tested outside of the context of a container. The `BeanUtils` class is used to attempt to set the values of the bean using the string submitted by the user. A `try/catch` block wraps the conversion attempt, and failures are logged to a `Map` for later display to the user.

Listing 7-6 `FormBean` Update Request

```java
/**
 * Returns true if all of the values pass validation.
 * Otherwise, returns false (the user should therefore be
 * prompted to correct the errors).
 *
 * The incoming Map should contain a set of values, where the
 * incoming values are a single key String and the values are
 * String[] objects.
 */
public boolean updateValue(Map in)
{
    // Initialize the converters - we want format exceptions.
    FormBeanUtils.initConverters();

    boolean isGoodUpdate = true;

    for (int i = 0; i < properties.length; i++)
    {
        String key = properties[i].getName();
        Object value = in.get(key);
        try
        {
            BeanUtils.setProperty(baseObject, key, value);
        } catch (Exception e)
        {
            if (value != null)
            {
                errors.put(key, "Value of "
                        + FormBeanUtils.formatName(key)
                        + " may not be '"
                        + ((String[]) value)[0].toString()
                        + "'");
            } else
                errors.put(key, "Value may not be null");
            isGoodUpdate = false;
        }
    }

    return isGoodUpdate;
}
/**
 * Returns true if all of the values pass validation.
 * Otherwise, returns false (the user should therefore be
 * prompted to correct the errors).
 */
public boolean updateValue(HttpServletRequest request)
{
    Map in = request.getParameterMap();
    return this.updateValue(in);
}
```

Listing 7-7 demonstrates how the `FormBean` was developed—outside of a servlet container.

Listing 7-7 `FormBean`

```java
    /**
     * Note that this particular design allows you to test your
     * bean programmatically, outside of the context of a web
     * application server.
     */
    public static void main(String[] args)
    {
        FormBean myFormBean = new FormBean(User.class);
        System.out.println(myFormBean.toHTMLForm());

        User myUser = new User();
        myUser.setClearance(5);
        myUser.setFirstName("Bob");
        myUser.setLastName("Smith");

        myFormBean = new FormBean(User.class, new WrapDynaBean(myUser));
        System.out.println(myFormBean.toHTMLForm());

        Map myMap = new HashMap();
        myMap.put("firstName", new String[] { "Ralph"});
        myMap.put("lastName", new String[] { "Bingo"});
        myMap.put("clearance", new String[] { "5"});
        myFormBean.updateValue(myMap);
        System.out.println(myFormBean.toHTMLForm());

        myMap.remove("clearance");
        myMap.put("clearance", new String[] { "invalid"});
        myFormBean.updateValue(myMap);
        System.out.println(myFormBean.toHTMLForm());
    }
}
```

FormBeanUtils

A few utility methods are needed to support the `FormBean`, as shown in Listing 7-8. The `formatName` method is used to generate proper English labels from JavaBean properties. The `appendAttribute` method is used to ease the generation of HTML-style attribute values. Most importantly, the `initConverters` method is used to cause the `BeanUtils` property setter to throw an exception in the event of a failed conversion attempt. By default, `BeanUtils` will silently fail if a conversion attempt fails. By installing the converter as shown, failed attempts to convert a `String` to an `int` or `Integer` value will generate an exception. If you wish to support additional property types and generate errors for failed conversions, you can install additional converters. The BeanUtils package includes converters for all core Java types (as listed earlier in this chapter), and you can create your own customer converters as well.

Listing 7-8 `FormBean` Utilities

```java
package com.cascadetg.ch07;

import org.apache.commons.beanutils.ConvertUtils;
import org.apache.commons.beanutils.Converter;
import org.apache.commons.beanutils.converters.IntegerConverter;

public class FormBeanUtils
{
    /**
     * A utility function, takes a standard JavaBean property
     * name and converts it to a nice US English spacing.
     *
     * For example, firstName = First Name    */
    public static String formatName(String in)
    {
        String result = new String();

        for (int i = 0; i < in.length(); i++)
        {
            if (Character.isUpperCase(in.charAt(i)))
            { result = result + (" "); }
            result = result + (in.charAt(i) + "");
        }

        String result2 = new String();

        for (int i = 0; i < result.length(); i++)
        {
            if (Character.isDigit(result.charAt(i)))
            { result2 = result2 + (" "); }
            result2 = result2 + (result.charAt(i) + "");
        }

        char titleChar = result2.charAt(0);
        String result3 = Character.toUpperCase(titleChar) + "";

        result3 = result3
                + (result2.substring(1, result2.length()));

        return result3;
    }

    /**
     * A utility method, used to add an attribute in the form
     * attribute='value' with a space afterward.
     */
    public static void appendAttribute(StringBuffer in,
            String attribute, String value)
    {
        in.append(attribute);
        in.append("='");
        in.append(value);
        in.append("' ");
    }

    static private boolean convertersInitialized = false;

    static public void initConverters()
```

(*continues*)

Listing 7-8 (*continued*)

```
    {
        if (!convertersInitialized)
        {
            // No-args constructor gets the version that throws
            // exceptions
            Converter myConverter = new IntegerConverter();

            // Convert the primitive values
            ConvertUtils.register(myConverter, Integer.TYPE);

            // Convert the object version
            ConvertUtils.register(myConverter, Integer.class);
            convertersInitialized = true;
        }
    }
}
```

SUMMARY

This chapter shows how to leverage the JavaBeans pattern to provide richer application frameworks. This allows you to think of your application in terms of components and reusable frameworks, instead of a hard-coded monolith. By decomposing your application, it becomes easier to build, reuse, and test individual components.

It's easy to imagine building complex graphs of JavaBean objects, with complex access code required in certain situations involving collections. In the next chapter, JXPath is shown as a tool to assist in dealing with complex object graphs.

Project Ideas

Build a framework to test JavaBeans by inspecting the various properties, setting the properties, and calling a method on the JavaBeans. How much configuration is required beyond that which can be detected from the JavaBean type information?

Write an application to compare the performance of BeanUtils and Java's built-in reflection capabilities. Does the performance of one approach or another vary if different bits of information are cached?

If you find the idea of FormBean intriguing but are interested in a more complete solution, check out BeanView (http://beanview.attainware.com/). As of this writing, I have posted the source for a more complete framework, developed as an outgrowth of writing this chapter. My expectation is to remove the form generation and rendering components and instead rely on JavaServer Faces (http://java.sun.com/j2ee/javaserverfaces/) as a more robust framework. Feedback and comments are appreciated.

CHAPTER 8

JXPath

JXPath allows you to traverse complex graphs of objects quickly and tersely, using the W3C standard XPath syntax (http://www.w3.org/TR/xpath, and a tutorial is available at http://www.w3schools.com/xpath/). Although XPath was originally designed to provide a standardized mechanism for dealing with complex XML documents, JXPath extends the XPath syntax to support dealing with a wide variety of complex Java data types.

To understand the use of JXPath, start by considering a simple hierarchical structure of people. These people are described by Java objects based on the `Person` class, as shown in Figure 8-1. Notice that each Person has a gender at a minimum and optionally a mother, father, and children.

Given a Person object, consider the typical Java code needed to retrieve a male grandchild of a specific child, as shown in Listing 8-1. The code involves several loops and `if` statements to find the desired target—difficult to write and debug.

Listing 8-1 Normal Complex Java Object Retrieval

```
Person bob = FamilyFactory.getPerson();

Iterator children = bob.getChildren().iterator();
while (children.hasNext())
{
    Person child = (Person)children.next();
    if (child.firstName.compareTo("Jon") == 0)
    {
        Iterator grandchildren =
            child.getChildren().iterator();
        while (grandchildren.hasNext())
        {
            Person grandchild =
                (Person)grandchildren.next();
            if (grandchild.getGender()
                .compareTo(Person.FEMALE) == 0)
                    System.out.println(grandchild);
        }
    }
}
```

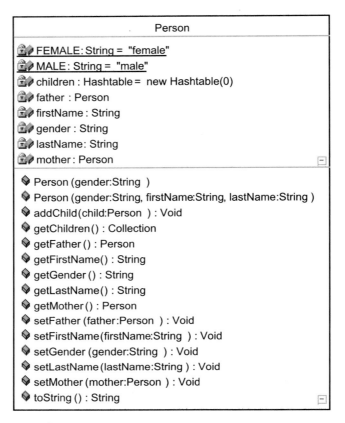

Figure 8-1 Person class.

The JXPath-based code shown in Listing 8-2 produces output identical to the code shown in Listing 8-1 but is significantly shorter.

Listing 8-2 JXPath Complex Java Object Retrieval

```
Person bob = FamilyFactory.getPerson();
JXPathContext context = JXPathContext.newContext(bob);
String searchTerm =
     "children[firstName='Jon']/children[gender='female']";
System.out.println(context.getValue(searchTerm));
```

Obviously, the code in Listing 8-2 is much easier to write and work with, assuming you are familiar with the XPath syntax (in Listing 8-2, the `searchTerm` string). In this chapter, we'll look at how to use JXPath to retrieve objects from a potentially very complex object graph.

SETTING UP THE EXAMPLE OBJECT GRAPH

Let's look at an example set of relationships, as shown by Figure 8-2. In English, it's possible to describe particular relationships between Bob Smith and the other people as expressed from Bob Smith's perspective. For example, we would say that Nancy Swenson is Bob's maternal grandmother, or that Zeppo and Mocha are Bob's grandchildren.

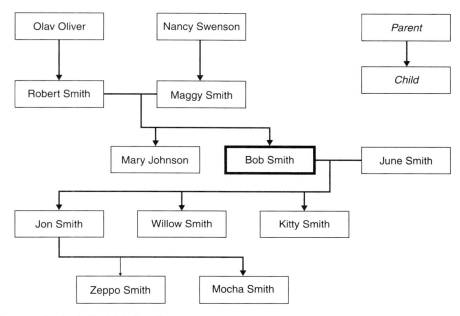

Figure 8-2 Bob Smith's family tree.

In Java, we can represent all of these people (and their relationships) with a set of Java objects of class Person, as shown in Listing 8-3. Notice that when an object specifies a father or mother, the relationship is made bidirectional (the mother or father has the referring object marked as a child).

Listing 8-3 Person Class

```
package com.cascadetg.ch08;

import java.util.Hashtable;

public class Person
{

    String firstName;
    String lastName;
```

(continues)

Listing 8-3 (*continued*)

```
    Person mother;
    Person father;
    Hashtable children = new Hashtable(0);
    String gender;

    public static final String MALE = "male";
    public static final String FEMALE = "female";

    public Person(String gender) {this.gender = gender;}

    public Person(String gender, String firstName, String lastName)
    {
        this.firstName = firstName;
        this.lastName = lastName;
        this.gender = gender;
    }

    public String toString()
    { return this.lastName + ", " + this.firstName; }

    public java.util.Collection getChildren()
    { return children.values(); }

    public void addChild(Person child)
    { this.children.put(child.toString(), child); }

    public Person getFather() { return father; }

    public void setFather(Person father)
    {
        this.father = father;
        father.addChild(this);
    }

    public String getFirstName() { return firstName; }
    public void setFirstName(String firstName)
    { this.firstName = firstName; }

    public String getLastName() { return lastName; }
    public void setLastName(String lastName)
    { this.lastName = lastName; }

    public Person getMother() { return mother; }
    public void setMother(Person mother)
    {
        this.mother = mother;
        mother.addChild(this);
    }

    public String getGender(){ return gender; }
    public void setGender(String gender) { this.gender = gender; }
}
```

Given the Person class shown in Listing 8-3, the code in Listing 8-4 creates a suite of Person objects, initializing an object hierarchy to match the family graph shown in Figure 8-2.

Listing 8-4 Initializing Bob's Family

```
package com.cascadetg.ch08;

public class FamilyFactory
{
    static Person startPerson = null;

    public static Person getPerson() { return startPerson; }

    public static void initFamily()
    {
        if (startPerson != null)
            return;

        // Bob is the "heart" of the family
        Person bobSmith = new Person(Person.MALE, "Bob", "Smith");
        startPerson = bobSmith;

        // Bob's father
        Person robertSmith =
            new Person(Person.MALE, "Robert", "Smith");
        bobSmith.setFather(robertSmith);

        // Bob's mother
        Person maggySmith =
            new Person(Person.FEMALE, "Maggy", "Smith");
        bobSmith.setMother(maggySmith);

        // Bob's sister, married
        Person maryJohnson =
            new Person(Person.FEMALE, "Mary", "Johnson");
        maryJohnson.setMother(maggySmith);
        maryJohnson.setFather(robertSmith);

        // Bob's mother's mother
        Person nancySwenson =
            new Person(Person.FEMALE, "Nancy", "Swenson");
        maggySmith.setMother(nancySwenson);

        // Bob's father's father
        Person olavOliver =
            new Person(Person.MALE, "Olav", "Oliver");
        robertSmith.setFather(olavOliver);

        // Bob's first wife
        Person juneSmith =
            new Person(Person.FEMALE, "June", "Smith");

        // Bob's three children
        Person kittySmith =
            new Person(Person.FEMALE, "Kitty", "Smith");
        kittySmith.setFather(bobSmith);
        kittySmith.setMother(juneSmith);

        Person willowSmith =
            new Person(Person.FEMALE, "Willow", "Smith");
        willowSmith.setFather(bobSmith);
        willowSmith.setMother(juneSmith);
```

(continues)

Listing 8-4 (*continued*)

```
        Person jonSmith = new Person(Person.MALE, "Jon", "Smith");
        jonSmith.setFather(bobSmith);
        jonSmith.setMother(juneSmith);

        // Bob's grandchildren
        Person zeppoSmith =
            new Person(Person.MALE, "Zeppo", "Smith");
        zeppoSmith.setFather(jonSmith);

        Person mochaSmith =
            new Person(Person.FEMALE, "Mocha", "Smith");
        mochaSmith.setFather(jonSmith);
    }
}
```

EXPLORING THE HIERARCHY

Given a suite of objects to explore, we need a mechanism for using JXPath to experiment with the XPath syntax.

XPath is essentially a new query language, allowing you to specify queries for a hierarchical structure. It can be difficult to understand XPath when you are first starting out. To make this easier, we'll create an interactive Swing client to test our various XPath queries against Bob's family, starting with Bob. As shown in Figure 8-3, XPath queries can be entered in the text field at the top, and pressing return or clicking the Execute button will cause the results of the query to be displayed in the text area below.

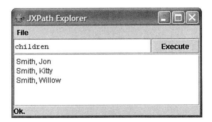

Figure 8-3 JXPath Explorer interface.

Listing 8-5 shows the code for the interactive Swing client. The code uses Bob Smith as the default context for your XPath queries—all of the queries are made starting from the Bob Smith object. Note that the actual JXPath execution is performed in the `executeButtonActionPerformed` method. In addition, keep in mind that JXPath is returning the actual Person object, not just a String, but also that the Person objects define an implementation of the `toString()` method, as shown in Listing 8-3.

Listing 8-5 Interactive JXPath Swing Client

```
package com.cascadetg.ch08;

import java.awt.Color;

public class JXPathExplorer extends javax.swing.JFrame
{

    public JXPathExplorer() { initComponents(); }

    private void initComponents()
    {
        mainScrollPane = new javax.swing.JScrollPane();
        resultsTextPane = new javax.swing.JTextPane();
        errorLabel = new javax.swing.JLabel();
        queryPanel = new javax.swing.JPanel();
        queryField = new javax.swing.JTextField();
        executeButton = new javax.swing.JButton();
        appMenuBar = new javax.swing.JMenuBar();
        fileMenu = new javax.swing.JMenu();

        setTitle("JXPath Explorer");
        setName("mainFrame");
        addWindowListener(new java.awt.event.WindowAdapter()
        {
            public void windowClosing(
                java.awt.event.WindowEvent evt)
            {
                exitForm(evt);
            }
        });

        mainScrollPane.setViewportView(resultsTextPane);

        getContentPane().add(
            mainScrollPane,
            java.awt.BorderLayout.CENTER);

        errorLabel.setText("Ready.");
        getContentPane().add(
            errorLabel,
            java.awt.BorderLayout.SOUTH);

        queryPanel.setLayout(new java.awt.BorderLayout());

        queryField.setFont(new java.awt.Font("DialogInput", 0, 12));
        queryField.setText("Enter query here");
        queryField
            .addActionListener(new java.awt.event.ActionListener()
        {
            public void actionPerformed(
                java.awt.event.ActionEvent evt)
            {
                queryFieldActionPerformed(evt);
            }
        });

        queryPanel.add(queryField, java.awt.BorderLayout.CENTER);
```

(continues)

Listing 8-5 (*continued*)

```
        executeButton.setText("Execute");
        executeButton
            .addActionListener(new java.awt.event.ActionListener()
        {
            public void actionPerformed(
                java.awt.event.ActionEvent evt)
            {
                executeButtonActionPerformed(evt);
            }
        });

        queryPanel.add(executeButton, java.awt.BorderLayout.EAST);

        getContentPane().add(
            queryPanel,
            java.awt.BorderLayout.NORTH);

        fileMenu.setText("File");
        appMenuBar.add(fileMenu);

        setJMenuBar(appMenuBar);

        java.awt.Dimension screenSize =
            java.awt.Toolkit.getDefaultToolkit().getScreenSize();
        setBounds(
            (screenSize.width - 400) / 2,
            (screenSize.height - 300) / 2,
            400,
            300);
    }
    private void executeButtonActionPerformed(
        java.awt.event.ActionEvent evt)
    {
        org.apache.commons.jxpath.JXPathContext context;
        try
        {
            this.errorLabel.setText("Working...");
            this.errorLabel.setForeground(Color.BLUE);
            this.update(this.getGraphics());

            Person bob = FamilyFactory.getPerson();
            context =
                org.apache.commons.jxpath.JXPathContext.newContext(
                    bob);

            java.util.Iterator bar =
                context.iterate(this.queryField.getText());

            StringBuffer output = new StringBuffer();

            while (bar.hasNext())
            {
                output.append(bar.next());
                output.append("\n");
            }

            this.resultsTextPane.setText(output.toString());
            this.errorLabel.setText("Ok.");
            this.errorLabel.setForeground(Color.BLACK);
            this.queryField.selectAll();
```

(*continues*)

Listing 8-5 (*continued*)

```
        } catch (Throwable e)
        {
            String message = e.getMessage();
            if (e instanceof OutOfMemoryError)
            {
                message = "Too many results - out of memory!";
                context = null;
                System.gc();
            }
            if (message.length() == 0)
                message = "Unknown error - check log for exception";

            this.errorLabel.setText(message);
            this.errorLabel.setForeground(Color.RED);
            this.queryField.selectAll();
            e.printStackTrace();
        }
    }

    private void queryFieldActionPerformed(
        java.awt.event.ActionEvent evt)
    { executeButtonActionPerformed(evt); }

    private void exitForm(java.awt.event.WindowEvent evt)
    { System.exit(0); }

    public static void main(String args[])
    { new JXPathExplorer().show(); }

    // Variables declaration
    private javax.swing.JMenuBar appMenuBar;
    private javax.swing.JLabel errorLabel;
    private javax.swing.JButton executeButton;
    private javax.swing.JMenu fileMenu;
    private javax.swing.JScrollPane mainScrollPane;
    private javax.swing.JTextField queryField;
    private javax.swing.JPanel queryPanel;
    private javax.swing.JTextPane resultsTextPane;
    // End of variables declaration
}
```

XPATH AND JXPATH SYNTAX

After you've gotten the Swing client working, you're ready to experiment with some basic XPath queries. For this example, JXPath translates your queries into Java using JavaBean-based patterns (such as the `getProperty()` methods). For example, to obtain Bob's mother, the `bob.getMother()` method is called. So, to obtain his grandmother using a `mother/mother` query, the call would effectively be `bob.getMother().getMother()`.

Basic XPath

Here are some additional examples of basic XPath syntax and the results.

```
mother/mother
```

This query simply returns Bob's grandmother.

```
father/father
```

Returns Bob's grandfather.

```
mother|father
```

Returns Bob's parents. Note the use of the vertical bar (|) to indicate that both properties should be retrieved.

```
children
```

Returns all of Bob's children by calling the Bob object's `getChildren()` method.

Complex XPath

In addition to basic queries, JXPath supports a full suite of XPath queries as described at `http://www.w3.org/TR/xpath`. It's beyond the scope of this text to describe the full range of possible XPath queries, but you should be aware that XPath supports a variety of specialized query tokens. Some examples include:

```
child::*
```

Returns the following values:

```
Smith, Jon
Smith, Kitty
Smith, Willow
Smith, Robert
Bob
male
Smith
Smith, Maggy
```

As can be seen, the expression `child::*` refers to all of the possible child attributes—not just the children as defined by our Java code, but rather the child values as expressed by object properties, including all of the children, the mother, the father, and the other properties of the Bob object. This illustrates an important concept—the notion that child and parent have particular meanings in XPath based on the object graph traversal, which may or may not be conceptually the same as the parent/child relationship for your application.

```
descendant::*
```

This query will actually result in an out-of-memory error, as it will attempt to load all of the descendants of all of the objects. Unfortunately, attempting to load all of the descendant properties of Bob leads to an infinitely recursive loop for our particular object graph. One of the Bob object's attributes is his father. His father, in turn, has the Bob object as a child, and so JXPath will attempt to continue loading Bob, his father, Bob, his father, and so on until all the available memory is exhausted. If this were used to represent a finite graph, for example, an XML document, this query would operate correctly.

```
count(children)
```

Returns the string 3.0. This query is an example of an XPath function, used in conjunction with a node query (called a node-set in XPath).

```
20 mod 6
```

Returns the string 2.0. Another XPath function. XPath does have some support for basic string and numeric functions, but these operations are often simpler, easier, and more powerful when expressed in the native programming language.

```
concat('foo', 'bar')
```

Returns foobar. This is another example of an XPath function.

JXPath Extensions

JXPath defines a few additional extensions to the XPath syntax. The most notable extensions are the ability to call arbitrary Java code, as shown in the following. Notice that the fully qualified class name is used in the query.

```
com.cascadetg.ch08.Person.new('male', 'Indigo', 'Smith')
```

Returns Smith, Indigo (the newly created object). The new term is used to indicate the class constructor for the object.

```
com.cascadetg.ch08.FamilyFactory.getPerson()
```

Calls the static method to return Smith, Bob.

```
com.cascadetg.ch08.FamilyFactory.getPerson()/children
```

Returns the values:

```
Smith, Jon
Smith, Kitty
Smith, Willow
```

This shows that you can mix the results of a Java method call with JXPath's XPath queries.

```
getFirstName(/)
```

Returns Bob. Note that the first argument of the method is the object that the method should be called upon—there is no implicit this prefacing the method call. In this case, we are using the / operator, which is a reference to the base Bob object.

```
setFirstName(/, 'Sam')
```

This query doesn't return anything, but instead modifies the base Bob object's first name, changing the value to Sam. This shows how JXPath can be used to modify an object. Following this up with a simple / query to obtain the Bob (now Sam) object, we can see that the name has been successfully changed.

For more information on other JXPath extensions to the XPath language, see http://jakarta.apache.org/commons/jxpath/users-guide.html.

SUPPORTED DATA TYPES

Having shown how JXPath can be used to navigate complex hierarchies (as represented by JavaBeans), it is useful to note that JXPath can be used with a wide array of potential object types. These include:

- JavaBeans
- Arrays
- Collections
- Maps (with String keys only)
- DOM & JDOM
- DynaBeans (see Chapter 7 for more information on DynaBeans)
- XML Documents (via a built-in JXPath Container)

Perhaps most interestingly, it's possible to mix these different object types as you traverse an object graph. For example, your JavaBean may make reference to an array of JDOM objects—which could be accessed with a single XPath query.

Performance and JXPath

Any specialized solution for a specific data type is likely to beat the performance of JXPath because JXPath is designed to work flexibly with a variety of heterogeneous object graphs (e.g., XML, DOM, JavaBeans, etc.). For example, if you wish to focus on XML only, you will likely see better performance using a technology such as Xalan's CachedXPathAPI, http://xml.apache.org/xalan-j/. Similarly, although an XPath query may be much more terse than the same Java code, the JXPath implementation needs to use Java reflection and other technologies to obtain information at run-time that would otherwise be added by the compiler.

If performance is a concern (for example, if you are working with a large server application), you may want to consider a strategy in which you cache compiled expressions (see http://jakarta.apache.org/commons/jxpath/apidocs/org/apache/commons/jxpath/CompiledExpression.html). Note that the default implementation of JXPath does perform some minimal compiled expression caching.

SUMMARY

This chapter shows that complex graphs of objects can easily be navigated with a relatively terse syntax. This can be especially useful when dealing with data in a variety of types.

As you build complex applications, stitching together complex graphs of objects, obtaining debugging information can sometimes be difficult (especially on production systems). To address these concerns, the next chapter covers Logging.

Project Ideas

How hard is it to map JXPath queries to SQL? Would it be possible to programmatically transform a JXPath query into a SQL query?

What are some additional data types that JXPath could support? For example, can a JDBC ResultSet be represented as a JXPath data type? How would the JXPath syntax map to the ResultSet?

Write a performance test application to compare JXPath access, reflection, and direct method access.

CHAPTER **9**

Logging

There is life beyond `System.out.println()`.

As applications become more sophisticated, it's important to have a mechanism for managing what can eventually become a torrent of informative and debugging information issued to the console. Over time, different systems have been developed for printing messages based on the severity or importance of the message. For example, Java defines two output streams—`System.out` for normal messages and `System.err` for warning messages.

Over time, a variety of toolkits have appeared to provide more sophisticated solutions, including Log4j (`http://logging.apache.org/log4j/docs/`) and the introduction of a logging toolkit in JDK 1.4 (`http://java.sun.com/j2se/1.4.2/docs/guide/util/logging/`). These logging toolkits support a variety of levels of detail for logging events, with independently configurable options for recording these events. Unfortunately, by writing directly to a specific logging package, you risk tying your application to a toolkit that may lack needed functionality. To provide for better maintainability and flexibility, the Apache Commons Logging project allows you to separate your choice of logging toolkit from your application code and provides a minimalist default logging system (if, for example, you are running on a pre-JDK 1.4 Java virtual machine and don't have Log4j installed).

TRACE LEVELS

At the heart of most logging packages is the notion of different levels of messages. By sorting your application's messages into these different levels, you can provide different levels of detail. Depending on the specific logging toolkit in use, you might route certain messages to `System.out` or to a file on disk and simply ignore others.

Logging defines several different logging levels, as shown in Table 9-1, in order of severity.

Table 9-1 Logging Levels

Logging Level	Meaning	Corresponding JDK 1.4 Level
fatal	Severe errors that cause premature termination. Expect these to be immediately visible on a status console.	SEVERE
error	Other runtime errors or unexpected conditions. Expect these to be immediately visible on a status console.	SEVERE
warn	Use of deprecated APIs, poor use of an API, and other runtime situations that are undesirable or unexpected but that don't necessarily represent an application failure. Expect these to be immediately visible on a status console.	WARNING
info	Interesting runtime events (startup/shutdown). Expect these to be immediately visible on a console, so be conservative and keep them to a minimum.	INFO
debug	Detailed information on the flow of the system. Expect these to be written to logs only.	FINE
trace	Even more detailed information than a debug trace. Expect these to be written to logs only.	FINEST

USING LOGGING

To use the Logging package, you'll first add a line to each class you want to log as a reference to the logging package. So, for a class `MyClass`, you would add the line:

```
private static Log log = LogFactory.getLog(MyClass.class);
```

You'll then make a call to the `log` whenever you want to make a log entry. The method name is simply the log level you want to make, with a message and an optional `Throwable` (`Throwable` is the superclass for all errors and exceptions in the Java language).

It's important to keep in mind that different logging toolkits have different capabilities for reporting, independent of the Logging API. Listing 9-1 shows the use of the Logging API. Assuming you are using JDK 1.4 or later, Listing 9-1 will use the JDK 1.4 logging package to log some messages to the console and some messages to disk.

Listing 9-1 Logging Example

```
package com.cascadetg.ch09;

import org.apache.commons.logging.Log;
import org.apache.commons.logging.LogFactory;
```

(continues)

Listing 9-1 (continued)

```java
import org.apache.commons.logging.impl.Jdk14Logger;

public class LogGenerator
{
    // Note that you pass in an instance of this class to the
    // log generator.  This allows you to find the messages
    // generated by this class.
    private static Log log = LogFactory.getLog(LogGenerator.class);

    public static void configJDKLogger()
    {
        try
        {
            ((Jdk14Logger)log).getLogger().setLevel(
                java.util.logging.Level.ALL);

            ((Jdk14Logger)log).getLogger().addHandler(
                (java.util.logging.FileHandler)Class
                    .forName("java.util.logging.FileHandler")
                    .newInstance());

            System.out.println("Added JDK 1.4 file handler");
        } catch (Exception e)
        {
            System.out.println("Unable to load JDK 1.4 logging.");
            e.printStackTrace();
        }
    }

    public static void main(String[] args)
    {
        configJDKLogger();
        System.setErr(System.out);

        System.out.println();
        System.out.println("Test fatal log");

        try
        {
            String foo = null;
            int x = 0 / (new Integer(foo)).intValue();
        } catch (Exception e)
        {
            log.fatal(e.getMessage(), e);
        }

        System.out.println();
        System.out.println("Test error log");

        try
        {
            Object foo = null;
            foo.toString();
        } catch (Exception e)
        {
            log.error(e.getMessage(), e);
        }

        System.out.println();
        System.out.println("Test warn log");
```

(continues)

Listing 9-1 (*continued*)

```
            try
            {
                Class.forName("com.cascadetg.NonexistantClass");
            } catch (Exception e)
            {
                log.warn("Can't find a non-existant class!");
            }

            System.out.println();
            System.out.println("Test info log");

            log.info("Starting app!");
            log.info("Quitting app!");

            System.out.println();
            System.out.println("Test debug log");

            if (1 > 2)
            {
                log.debug("1 > 2 evaluated true");
                if (10 % 2 == 0)
                    log.debug("10 % 2 is 0");
                else
                    log.debug("10 % 2 is not 0");
            } else
            {
                log.debug("1 > 2 evaluated false");
            }

            System.out.println();
            System.out.println("Test trace log");

            log.trace("Calling trace method.");
            log.trace("Calling trace method.");
            log.trace("Calling trace method.");
            log.trace("Calling trace method.");
            log.trace("Calling trace method.");

            System.out.println();
            System.out.println("Log test complete.");

    }
}
```

LOGGING OUTPUT

Running the code as shown in Listing 9-1 will produce two different output streams. First, `System.out` (normally, the console) will produce the output as shown in Listing 9-2.

Listing 9-2 Logging Example

```
Added JDK 1.4 file handler

Test fatal log
Mar 22, 2004 9:04:06 PM com.cascadetg.ch09.LogGenerator main
SEVERE: null
```

(*continues*)

Listing 9-2 (continued)

```
java.lang.NumberFormatException: null
    at java.lang.Integer.parseInt(Unknown Source)
    at java.lang.Integer.<init>(Unknown Source)
    at com.cascadetg.ch09.LogGenerator.main(LogGenerator.java:44)

Test error log
Mar 22, 2004 9:04:06 PM com.cascadetg.ch09.LogGenerator main
SEVERE: null
java.lang.NullPointerException
    at com.cascadetg.ch09.LogGenerator.main(LogGenerator.java:56)

Test warn log
Mar 22, 2004 9:04:06 PM com.cascadetg.ch09.LogGenerator main
WARNING: Can't find a non-existant class!

Test info log
Mar 22, 2004 9:04:06 PM com.cascadetg.ch09.LogGenerator main
INFO: Starting app!
Mar 22, 2004 9:04:06 PM com.cascadetg.ch09.LogGenerator main
INFO: Quitting app!

Test debug log

Test trace log

Log test complete.
```

You'll notice that the output written to `System.out` does not contain all of the messages—the debug and trace level information is not sent to the console. Instead, the remaining data is written to disk. By default, JDK 1.4 will write to a file called `java0.log` in your home directory (~ on UNIX systems, or `C:\Documents and Settings\User Name` on Windows 2000/XP).

The default file output for JDK 1.4 is an XML file, as shown in Listing 9-3 (only one record is shown for brevity).

Listing 9-3 Detailed XML Logging Output

```xml
<?xml version="1.0" encoding="windows-1252" standalone="no"?>
<!DOCTYPE log SYSTEM "logger.dtd">
<log>
<record>
  <date>2004-03-22T21:04:06</date>
  <millis>1080018246773</millis>
  <sequence>0</sequence>
  <logger>com.cascadetg.ch09.LogGenerator</logger>
  <level>SEVERE</level>
  <class>com.cascadetg.ch09.LogGenerator</class>
  <method>main</method>
  <thread>10</thread>
  <message>null</message>
  <exception>
    <message>java.lang.NumberFormatException: null</message>
    <frame>
      <class>java.lang.Integer</class>
      <method>parseInt</method>
    </frame>
```

(continues)

Listing 9-3 (*continued*)

```
    <frame>
      <class>java.lang.Integer</class>
      <method>&lt;init&gt;</method>
    </frame>
    <frame>
      <class>com.cascadetg.ch09.LogGenerator</class>
      <method>main</method>
      <line>44</line>
    </frame>
  </exception>
</record>
<record>
...
</record>
</log>
```

To view the XML file in a validating browser or parser, you'll need a DTD file (or else just delete the `<!DOCTYPE log SYSTEM "logger.dtd">` declaration at the top of the file). You can find the contents of this file at http://java.sun.com /j2se/1.4.2/docs/guide/util/logging/overview.html#3.0—simply copy the text of the DTD into a file called `logger.dtd` and place it in the same directory as the log file. Figure 9-1 shows the resulting log file.

Figure 9-1 XML logging output in a browser.

As you can see, the generated XML file contains all of the data from the application's run, including debug and trace data. These log files can quickly become large, but JDK 1.4 includes provisions for automatically closing and rotating files as needed.

It's easy to imagine combining these resulting log files with more sophisticated XML parsing and retrieval tools, such as JXPath and XPath, as described in Chapter 8, "JXPath."

As a final note, significant effort is made to minimize the impact of logging statements on the performance of your application code. Assuming you follow proper rules for Java execution flow (in particular, avoiding the use of exceptions as a form of program flow control), your logging statements should have minimal impact on your application's performance.

SUMMARY

By using the Logging package, robust configurable logging can be added to your applications. Depending on your needs, this can be used to debug your application while under development, to debug your application in production, to record performance information, or even as a mechanism for generating access or other usage log files.

Logging is an example of a function that is commonly used across a wide variety of applications. In the next chapter, an even more general set of commonly used utilities will be presented.

Project Ideas

Use the Logging interface to build an application that generates a wide variety of log data. Compare the performance, configurability, and details provided by log4j to the default Java logging implementation. How do various types of logging affect application performance?

Write a tool, perhaps using SAX, DOM, XSLT, or JDOM, to process large XML log files. What sort of useful metrics can be generated, perhaps as a summary HTML document?

CHAPTER **10**

Lang

Almost every development project winds up with a lot of strange little utility functions, often buried in a class named something like "Utils." Common examples include a utility function for escaping a bit of HTML or SQL, or a quick class to make it easier to return a `Date` object formatted to a particular locale. The Lang package is essentially a fifty-odd set of these utilities.

The difficult thing about the Lang package is not any particular complexity, but rather simply remembering what functionality is present. In this chapter, we provide a general overview of the Lang package. It may seem easy to write your own utility methods, but those thirty minute one-offs can start to add up—and other developers familiar with the Lang package will immediately know where to find and how to use those utility routines.

The Lang package is split up into six main packages:

`org.apache.commons.lang`	A wide variety of miscellaneous routines.
`org.apache.commons.lang.builder`	Assists in creating consistent `equals(Object)`, `toString()`, `hashCode()`, and `compareTo(Object)` methods.
`org.apache.commons.lang.enum`	Support for type-safe Java enums.
`org.apache.commons.lang.exception`	Provides JDK 1.4 style nested exceptions on earlier versions of the JDK.
`org.apache.commons.lang.math`	Fractions, ranges, random numbers, and some additional math-related utilities.
`org.apache.commons.lang.time`	Formatting, stopwatch, and a variety of other time-related utilities.

BASE LANG CLASSES

Unfortunately, the functionality in the base `org.apache.commons.lang` classes does not easily sort into any particular logical groups. Therefore, this section touches on each class in alphabetical order.

ArrayUtils

The `ArrayUtils` class affords the following basic functionality: a set of immutable empty arrays corresponding to all of the various primitive types and their corresponding object types, clone operations for primitive arrays, and methods to check if an array contains a particular value. For example, the code:

```
boolean contains = false;
for(int i = 0; i < myArray.length; i++)
    if(myArray[i] == searchVal) contains = true;
```

. . . can be replaced with a simple:

```
boolean contains = ArrayUtils.contains(myArray, searchVal);
```

In addition, `indexOf` methods will return the index of the search value (or -1 if the search value is not found). The `lastIndexOf` methods work backwards. The `double` versions of `contains`, `indexOf`, and `lastIndexOf` methods even allow for a search range tolerance.

An `isEquals` method with support for multidimensional arrays is provided. A set of `reverse` methods is provided to reorder arrays. The `toMap` method converts an object array to a `java.util.Map` instance. Finally, `toObject` and `toPrimitive` methods allow for easy conversion of arrays from the primitive version to object versions. For example:

```
long[] vals = {1, 2, 3};
Long valObjects = ArrayUtils.toObject(vals);
```

BitField

A wide suite of operations for operating on bits. Unlike many of the other operations in the base Lang package, a `BitField` is an actual class, not a collection of static methods.

A `BitField` is created with an `int` mask, specifying the number of bits of interest. Further operations may be performed using provided methods, such as clearing and setting particular bits.

BooleanUtils

Methods for working with boolean values—in particular, operations for converting values to and from boolean values. For example, this:

```
boolean isOk = true;
String result;
```

```
if(isOk)
    result = "ready";
else
    result = "not ready";
```

... can be replaced simply with:

```
String result = BooleanUtils.toString(isOk, "ready", "not ready");
```

Generally speaking, `BooleanUtils` can be grouped into a set of methods to convert values to `Boolean` or `boolean` or from a `boolean`/`Boolean` to integers or `String` objects. Additional methods are provided specifically for converting strings such as "on," "off," "true," "false," "yes," and "no" to and from `boolean`/`Boolean` values.

Finally, `xor` methods are provided for `Boolean`/`boolean` arrays.

CharRange, CharSet, and CharSetUtils

A `CharRange` represents a contiguous range of characters. The `CharSet` class uses the `CharRange` class to express various ASCII ranges such as alphabetic and numeric characters.

For character sets that happen to afford logical sorting of characters into ranges (such as ASCII), these classes provide helpful containment checks. The full range of Unicode characters supported by Java is much larger than ASCII, however, and so many applications will likely need to describe their own `CharRange` sets, perhaps in conjunction with the data available from the `java.lang.Character`.

You can use `CharRange` and `CharSet` values (either the predefined values or custom values) in conjunction with the `CharSetUtils` class to perform certain useful operations, such as counting the number of characters, deleting characters present in a String based on sets passed in, or even squeezing repeated characters as shown:

```
String in = "abc123def";

String chars = CharSetUtils.delete(in, CharSet.ASCII_NUMERIC
        .toString());

String nums = CharSetUtils.keep(in, CharSet.ASCII_NUMERIC
        .toString());

System.out.println(chars);  // prints abcdef
System.out.println(nums);   // prints 123

String extras = "bookkeeping";

extras = CharSetUtils.squeeze(extras, CharSet.ASCII_ALPHA
        .toString());

System.out.println(extras);   // prints bokeping
```

ClassUtils

In addition to `BeanUtils`, the Lang `ClassUtils` package provides additional functionality for working with classes. The utilities in this package do not use the functionality in the `java.lang.reflect.*` package—they use only the information available directly from `java.lang.Class` and where possible from the class name (for example, the class name string is parsed to retrieve package information in lieu of reflection).

The methods `convertClassesToClassNames` and `convertClassNamesToClasses` convert a `List` of classes to class names and back. The methods `getAllInterfaces` and `getAllSuperclasses` return `List` objects. Although it's hard to think of a relevant situation for applications other than development tools, an `isInnerClass` method is provided. Several different signatures are provided to `getPackageName` and `getShortClassName`. Perhaps one of the most useful is the `isAssignable` method, allowing you to check if you can cast a value before actually performing the operation (which is useful if you want to check if an assignment is valid without incurring the risk of a `ClassCastException`).

ObjectUtils and ObjectUtils.Null

The `ObjectUtils` class principally provides extra semantic control over `null` values. For example, `defaultIfNull`, `equals`, and `toString` implementations all handle `null` values gracefully. The `appendIdentityToString` allows you to retrieve the identity value normally returned by the `Object.toString` implementation even if the object has overridden `toString`.

Perhaps the most interesting part of `ObjectUtils` is the addition of an `ObjectUtils.Null` class to serve as a placeholder for `null` in instances when `null` has an additional meaning. Ironically, the addition of type-safe collections to JDK 1.5 will likely mean that this class is increasingly less useful, which is probably for the best in many situations.

RandomStringUtils

The various implementations of `random` in this class allow you to easily create random string values according to a wide range of configurable options.

```
System.out.println(RandomStringUtils.randomAscii(16));
// Prints ]_uKDOL*md):fDTT

System.out.println(RandomStringUtils.randomAlphabetic(16));
// Prints ygatjcqBbYbCwVBt

System.out.println(RandomStringUtils.randomNumeric(16));
// Prints 6731467475431887

char[] availChars = {'A', 'B', 'C', 'D'};
System.out.println(RandomStringUtils.random(16, availChars));
// Prints ADDADCCCDDDDCCBC
```

Base Lang Classes

Note that an additional `RandomUtils` package is provided in the Lang `math` package, which is described later.

SerializationUtils

This class provides a few methods to assist with the use of Java serialization. The functionality available includes a generic deep clone operation, allowing a graph of objects to be serialized with a single method call. In addition, serialization and deserialization methods are provided, which wrap the various exceptions as well as the closing of the stream.

StringEscapeUtils

This class is perhaps one of the most immediately useful for many web applications. Routines are provided to escape and unescape strings for Java, JavaScript, HTML, XML, and SQL. This is useful to guard against attempts by unscrupulous users to inject code into your application (for example, JavaScript in a bit of text to be displayed on a web page, or even an attempt to inject SQL into a form in an attempt to hijack a database).

Here is a comparison of the various escape routines in action:

```
String HTML = "<B>$ to \u00A3 Rate</B>";
String Java = "\"It's on my \t tab\"";
String SQL = "Ain't bad";

// Original values
System.out.println(HTML);
System.out.println(Java);
System.out.println(SQL);

System.out.println();

// Conversion examples
System.out.println(StringEscapeUtils.escapeHtml(HTML));
System.out.println(StringEscapeUtils.escapeXml(HTML));
System.out.println(StringEscapeUtils.escapeJava(Java));
System.out.println(StringEscapeUtils.escapeJavaScript(Java));
System.out.println(StringEscapeUtils.escapeSql(SQL));
```

. . . produces the output:

```
<B>$ to £ Rate</B>
"It's on my      tab"
Ain't bad

&lt;B&gt;$ to &pound; Rate&lt;/B&gt;
&lt;B&gt;$ to &#163; Rate&lt;/B&gt;
\"It's on my \t tab\"
\"It\'s on my \t tab\"
Ain''t bad
```

StringUtils

The `StringUtils` class contains a variety of `null`-safe miscellaneous methods. All of the methods will gracefully handle `null` values, simply returning `null` if `null` is passed as an argument.

isAlpha isBlank isEmpty isNumeric isWhitespace contains containsOnly containsNone equals	The various `is` methods check if the entire `String` evaluates to true for the mentioned condition. The `contains` methods check against a set of characters passed as an argument.
indexOf indexOfAny indexOfAnyBut lastIndexOf lastIndexOfAny lastIndexOfAnyBut countMatches	Various methods to search `Strings`.
left mid right substring substringAfter substringBefore substringBetween trim	Methods to trim `Strings` in various ways.
center leftPad repeat rightPad strip	Methods that assist the presentation of `Strings`, particularly useful for console applications.
split join	`split` serves as a more convenient wrapper to the `StringTokenizer`. `join` serves as an easy way to fuse an array or `Iterator` into a single `String`.

replace replaceChars replaceOnce delete overlay	Manipulate one String with another.
uppercase lowerCase swapCase capitalize uncapitalize	Manipulate the case of a String.
defaultString	Wrapper to automatically protect against null values.
chomp chop	chomp removes the last bit of new line information from a String. chop removes the last character of a String.
reverse reverseDelimited	Reverse a String.
difference	Returns the differing characters between two String objects.
abbreviate	Abbreviates a String, terminating with an ellipsis if necessary.
getLevensteinDistance	Number of changes needed to change one String into another.

Most of these methods are self-explanatory. The getLevensteinDistance is perhaps the most unusual—it calculates the number of changes need to convert a String from one value to another. Below are examples of the use of the two most interesting methods:

```
String longLine = "This is a long bit of text.";

System.out.println(StringUtils.abbreviate(longLine, 15));
System.out.println(StringUtils.abbreviate(longLine, 100));

String start = "time";
String end = "fine";
System.out.println(StringUtils.getLevensteinDistance(start, end));
```

This code produces the following output:

```
This is a lo...
This is a long bit of text.
2
```

SystemUtils

The `SystemUtils` class provides two basic bits of functionality—a set of static variable values corresponding to the various standard system properties, such as `file.encoding`, `file.separator`, `java.class.path`, etc., and a suite of `boolean` values corresponding to a wide variety of possible platform checks a user might want to perform (e.g., `IS_OS_MAC_OSX`).

An additional version check method is provided to detect the Java version, allowing for easy basic system conformance checks. For example:

```
System.out.println(SystemUtils.isJavaVersionAtLeast(1.3f));
```

... returns the value `true` on a JDK 1.4 system.

Validate

Validation essentially serves as a mechanism for evaluating conditions and throwing an exception if the condition is not true. Most significantly, the various assertions will generate exceptions and will run on a variety of platforms.

```
Validate.isTrue( i > 0, "The value must be greater than zero: ", i);
Validate.notNull( surname, "The surname must not be null");
```

A suite of static methods is used to assert that values and expressions evaluate to true; otherwise an exception is thrown. An advantage of the `Validate` class is that it allows you to easily set a message string on the thrown exception. This makes `Validate` more useful for validating user-generated data, as opposed to developer-managed interactions.

On JDK 1.4 or later systems, for development-level contracts, you may want to use assertions instead. For more information, see http://java.sun.com/j2se/1.4.2/docs/guide/lang/assert.html. If you have adopted JUnit (http://www.junit.org/) as a test framework, you may want to use that assertion facility instead (http://www.junit.org/junit/javadoc/3.8.1/junit/framework/Assert.html).

WordUtils

The `WordUtils` class in many ways serves as an extension of the already large `StringUtils` class. It works with whitespace-delimited words, mainly performing various capitalization operations. The `capitalize` method works only on the first letter of each word, whereas the `capitalizeFully` method works on all of the alphabetical characters. The `uncapitalize` method only works on a single character (there is no `unCapitalizeFully` method). This class also offers a `wrap` function, useful for console applications. For example, the code:

```
String sample = "this is a GREAT System! ";

System.out.println(WordUtils.capitalize(sample));
System.out.println(WordUtils.capitalizeFully(sample));
```

```
System.out.println(WordUtils.uncapitalize(sample));
System.out.println(WordUtils.swapCase(sample));

sample = sample + sample + sample + sample + sample;
System.out.println(WordUtils.wrap(sample, 45));
```

. . . produces the result:

```
This Is A GREAT System!
This Is A Great System!
this is a gREAT system!
THIS IS A great sYSTEM!
this is a GREAT System! this is a GREAT
System! this is a GREAT System! this is a
GREAT System! this is a GREAT System!
```

BUILDER

Perhaps slightly misnamed, this package assists in the creation of `Object.equals`, `Object.toString`, `Object.hashCode`, and `Comparable.compareTo` methods. Generally speaking, each class (`CompareToBuilder`, `EqualsBuilder`, `HashCodeBuilder`, `ReflectionToStringBuilder`, and `ToStringBuilder`) allows you to construct an implementation via either select properties or via a reflection-based comparison. They can be used to quickly construct implementations.

The `StandardToStringStyle` and `ToStringStyle` classes can be used to create formatting rules, which can then be used to control the output of the new `toString` implementation.

For example, the code:

```
Object foo = new Object()
{
    public String[] arrayExample =
    { "One", "Two", "Three"};

    public String foo = "sample";

    public String toString()
    {
        return new ReflectionToStringBuilder(this).toString();
    }
};

System.out.println(foo.toString());
```

. . . produces the output:

```
com.cascadetg.ch10.StringExample$1@1a8c4e7[arrayExample={One,Two,Three},
foo=sample]
```

ENUM

The `Enum` package provides additional support for strongly typed enumerations. The package requires you to create a subclass of `Enum`, which then allows you to use the `EnumUtils` class to interrogate the `Enum` implementation. Unfortunately, to implement an `Enum`, several supporting methods must be included. Although a classic C-style `enum` is a useful pattern, in practice it's hard to imagine using this `Enum` package.

If you are able to use Java 2 5.0 (also known as JDK 1.5), you can use the built-in `enum` support as described at `http://java.sun.com/j2se/1.5.0/docs/guide/language/enums.html`.

EXCEPTION

The `Exception` package provides support for JDK 1.4-style nested Exceptions on pre-JDK 1.4 systems.

MATH

The class `Range` and subclasses `DoubleRange`, `FloatRange`, `IntRange`, `LongRange`, and `NumberRange` are used to store inclusive ranges of numbers. These range classes can be interrogated for containment, minimums, and maximums.

The `Fraction` class allows you to work with fractions accurately. Fractions are stored as you might write them. For example, the code:

```
Fraction myFraction = Fraction.getFraction(2, 3, 5);
System.out.println(myFraction.floatValue());

Fraction secondFraction = Fraction.getFraction(1, 1, 3);
System.out.println(secondFraction.floatValue());

myFraction = myFraction.add(secondFraction);
System.out.println(myFraction.floatValue());

System.out.print(myFraction.getProperWhole() + " ");
System.out.print(myFraction.getProperNumerator() + "/");
System.out.println(myFraction.getDenominator());
```

... outputs the values:

```
2.6
1.3333334
3.9333334
3 14/15
```

Note that the `float` values are represented by a rounded-off value, whereas the `Fraction` is stored precisely. The `Fraction` class allows you to parse a string in the standard format x y/z (such as 3 14/15) into a `Fraction`.

The `JVMRandom` and `RandomUtils` classes provide wrappers to return various primitive values from the `Math.random` method. `RandomUtils` caches the `Random` object, with each method returning a new value from the same system-wide seed, whereas multiple `JVMRandom` objects can be created if multiple random number seeds are desired.

The `NumberUtils` class provides static constants for various 0 and 1 values, utility checks to verify that a `String` is actually a number, `max` and `min` checks for a wide variety of types including arrays, and methods to automatically convert strings directly to `int` values.

TIME

The `Time` package has four classes: `DateFormatUtils`, `DateUtils`, `FastDateFormat`, and `StopWatch`. Both `DateFormatUtils` and `FastDateFormat` serve to make it easier to render dates into strings. `FastDateFormat` is a quick, thread-safe implementation of a date and time formatter. `DateFormatUtils` includes several `FastDateFormat` objects, preconfigured for different uses, including different ISO8601 formats as well as an SMTP format.

The `StopWatch` class allows you to perform timings much like a stopwatch—it allows you to start a timer, perform a split, stop, reset, and so on. Note that the `StopWatch` class is really only a holder for time values from `System.currentTimeMillis()`—there is no notion of a scheduler or execution thread. Interestingly, the code:

```
StopWatch testWatch = new StopWatch();
try {
    testWatch.start();
    Thread.sleep(1000);
    testWatch.stop();
    System.out.println(testWatch.getTime());
    } catch (Exception e)   { e.printStackTrace(); }
```

... returns a value of 1001.

SUMMARY

Although the Lang package offers a wide suite of packages, it can be hard to keep track of the various capabilities. This chapter provides an overview, but for more detail on the base classes and the time package, see Appendix A.

Almost every Java application can benefit from the Lang package. Similarly, many programs can benefit from the Collections package, described in the next chapter.

Project Ideas

Write a Swing user interface to wrap the conversion capabilities of `StringEscapeUtils`. Compare this with writing a command-line interface for the same capabilities, perhaps using the CLI package described in Chapter 13, "CLI (Command Line Interface)." What are the tradeoffs of this approach?

Create a clock application using the various date and time formats as described in the `Time` package.

CHAPTER **11**

Collections

The term "collections" refers to the notion of objects that contain or manage other objects. Most developers are familiar with the basic collections, including the classic array (such as `String[]`) or the built-in Java classes (such as `java.util.Hashtable`). The introduction of a rich Java Collections Framework in Java 2 (JDK 1.2) brought a standardized implementation of classes for expressing more complex relationships. The Apache Jakarta Commons Collections project adds even more capability, as described in this chapter.

Table 11-1 compares some of the key differences between basic collection types. When possible, you should try to rely on the interfaces shown, not on the underlying implementation. For example, even if you have marked a HashMap as typed, sorted, and unmodifiable, you should still interface with it as a `java.util.Map` whenever possible:

```
java.util.Map myMap = new java.util.HashMap();
```

For more information on the built-in JDK 1.4 collections, see `http://java.sun.com/j2se/1.4.2/docs/guide/collections/reference.html`. Note that this chapter does not duplicate information included in the default JDK documentation—for example, the `Stack` and `SortedMap` interfaces are concepts covered as part of the standard Java collection interface.

Table 11-1 Collection Features

	Interface	Duplicates	Keys	Indexed	Ordered
Array	*Object[]*	Yes	No	Yes	Yes
Bag	org.apache.commons.collections.Bag	Yes	No	No	No
List	java.util.List	Yes	No	Yes	Yes
Map	java.util.Map	No	Yes	No	Optional
Primitive Array	*primitive[]*	Yes	No	Yes	Yes
Set	java.util.Set	No	No	No	Optional

The meaning of each column heading in Table 11-1 is as follows:

- **Interface:** The expected Java interface for this collection type.
- **Duplicates:** Are duplicate elements allowed?
- **Keys:** Are elements accessible by a key value (e.g., java.util.Hashtable)?
- **Indexed:** Is the order of the elements maintained by a column in the database?
- **Ordered:** Are the results returned as a sorted collection?

COLLECTIONS CONCEPTS

It can be difficult to get a handle on the Collections package due to the sheer number of classes and interfaces provided (as shown in Figure 11-1), some of which are new or unfamiliar to many Java developers. Despite this initial overwhelming complexity, these classes can be broken down into several core concepts, each of which is presented in this chapter. The various utility classes are used to help generate the appropriate combinations of various items. For example, a typed, sorted bag can be returned from the appropriate static BagUtils.

Generating Output

The various examples in this chapter make use of a method echo(). This method is simply a utility method that writes the contents of the collection to System.out.

Bag

A Bag is an unordered collection that may contain duplicate elements. The Bag maintains counts for the duplicate items, managing each count and performing operations against this count. The Commons Bag hierarchy is shown in Figure 11-2.

For example, imagine a Bag containing the objects a, a, b, and c. Calling getCount(Object) passing in the a object would return 2. Calling uniqueSet() would return a, b, and c. This is an important consideration with the Bag interface, as multiple calls to add an object will increment that object count. The remove(Object) method removes the object completely from the Bag, regardless of the current count. To decrement the count, remove(Object, int) is used, with the second parameter indicating the number of items to be removed.

For example, the code:

```
org.apache.commons.collections.Bag myBag
    = new org.apache.commons.collections.bag.HashBag();
myBag.add("Test1", 3);
myBag.add("Test2");
```

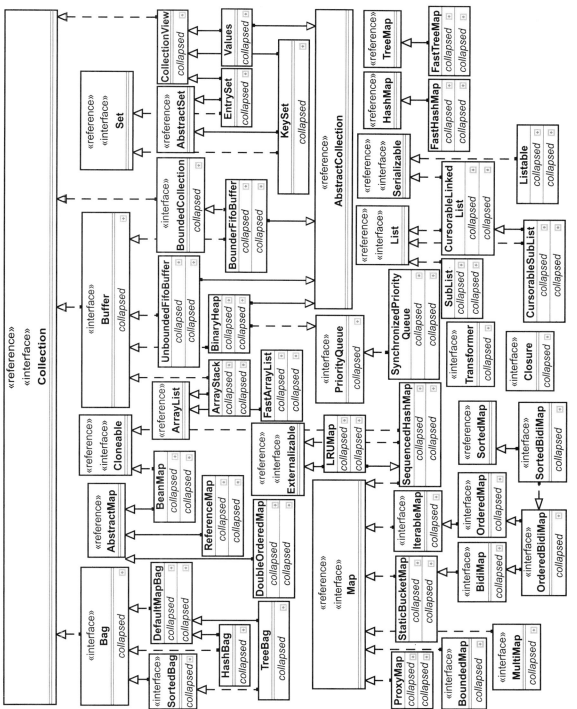

Figure 11-1 Collection class overview.

```
echo(myBag);

System.out.println();

myBag.remove("Test1");

echo(myBag);
```

... produces the output:

```
Test2
Test1
Test1
Test1

Test2
```

> **Warning:** The `Bag` interface changes the interpretation of the Collection methods. This change in behavior can be a rude shock if you are not precisely familiar with the changes. Although changed methods are marked in the javadoc as being in violation, the changes are all related to the notion of `Bag`'s count tracking behavior.

Note that some of the following classes are not actually subclasses but are instead intended to serve as wrappers for a `Bag` to add additional behavior. For example, the `TypedBag` class allows you to add type checking to a `Bag`.

Related Classes: `AbstractBagDecorator`, `AbstractMapBag`, `AbstractSortedBagDecorator`, `Bag` `BagUtils`, `DefaultMapBag`, `HashBag`, `PredicatedBag`, `PredicatedSortedBag`, `SortedBag`, `SynchronizedBag`, `SynchronizedSortedBag`, `TransformedBag`, `TransformedSortedBag`, `TreeBag`, `TypedBag`, `TypedSortedBag`, `UnmodifiableBag`, `UnmodifiableSortedBag`

Bean

The `BeanMap` class allows you to wrap and present a JavaBean as a `java.util.Map`. The various properties of the JavaBean are treated as keys, with the property values exposed as `Map` properties.

For more information on JavaBeans, see `BeanUtils`.

For example, the code:

```
java.awt.Button myButton = new java.awt.Button();

java.util.Map myMap = new
org.apache.commons.collections.BeanMap(
        myButton);
myMap.put("label", "hello");
```

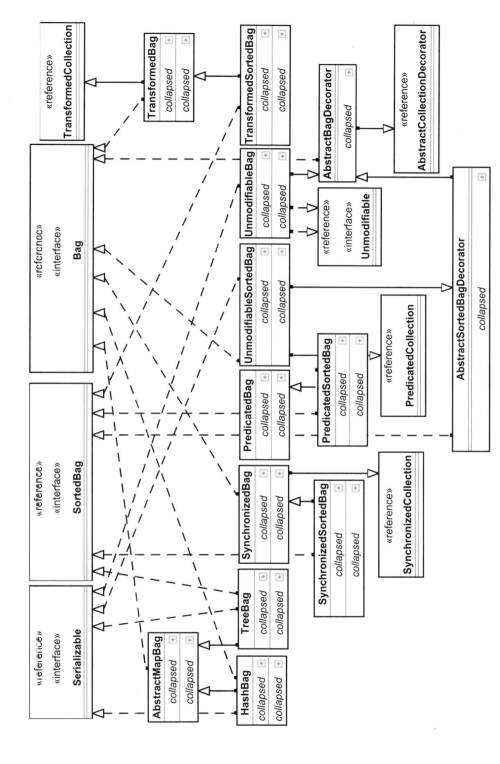

Figure 11-2 Bag classes.

```
java.util.Set myKeys = myMap.keySet();
System.out.println("Keys:");
echo(myKeys);

System.out.println();

System.out.println("Values:");
echo(myMap.values());
```

... produces the output:

```
Keys:
accessibleContext
focusable
actionListeners
label
enabled
actionCommand
visible
background
name
foreground
font

Values:
java.awt.Button$AccessibleAWTButton@17fa65e
true
[Ljava.awt.event.ActionListener;@18385e3
hello
true
hello
true
null
button0
null
null
```

Related Classes: `BeanMap`

BidiMap

The `BidiMap` classes allow for bidirectional use of map. The default `Map` interface allows you to retrieve a value from a map with the key, but not the other way around (it is necessary to iterate through the keys and values to identify the value from the key, unless there is some other contract in play). The Commons BidiMap hierarchy is shown in Figure 11-3.

The code:

```
org.apache.commons.collections.BidiMap myBidiMap = new
org.apache.commons.collections.bidimap.TreeBidiMap();

myBidiMap.put("Example", "1");
myBidiMap.put("Another", "2");
```

Collections Concepts

```
// Note easy (and fast) access to key from value
System.out.println(myBidiMap.getKey("1"));
System.out.println(myBidiMap.get("Another"));

echo(myBidiMap);

System.out.println("Notice the now missing Example key:");
myBidiMap.put("Another", "1");

echo(myBidiMap);
```

... produces the output:

```
Example
2
Another=2
Example=1
Notice the now missing Example key:
Another=1
```

> **Warning:** `BidiMap` enforces a strict 1:1 relationship between the keys and values. If one side of the key/value pair exists when a new key/value pair is added, the existing key/value pair will be removed. For example, if an A/B key/value pair exists, adding either A/C or C/B will cause the A/B value pair to be removed.

Related Classes: `AbstractBidiMapDecorator`, `AbstractDualBidiMap`, `AbstractOrderedBidiMapDecorator`, `AbstractSortedBidiMapDecorator`, `BidiMap`, `DualHashBidiMap`, `DualTreeBidiMap`, `OrderedBidiMap`, `SortedBidiMap`, `TreeBidiMap`, `UnmodifiableBidiMap`, `UnmodifiableOrderedBidiMap`, `UnmodifiableSortedBidiMap`

Blocking

Used to decorate another `Buffer` class to make the `get()` and `remove()` methods block if the `Buffer` is empty. Note that this class extends `SynchronizedBuffer` and is thread-safe.

Related Classes: `BlockingBuffer`

Bounded

The various `Bounded` collections are used to indicate that a maximum number of elements are allowed in the collection. An exception is thrown if an attempt is made to add an element to a full collection.

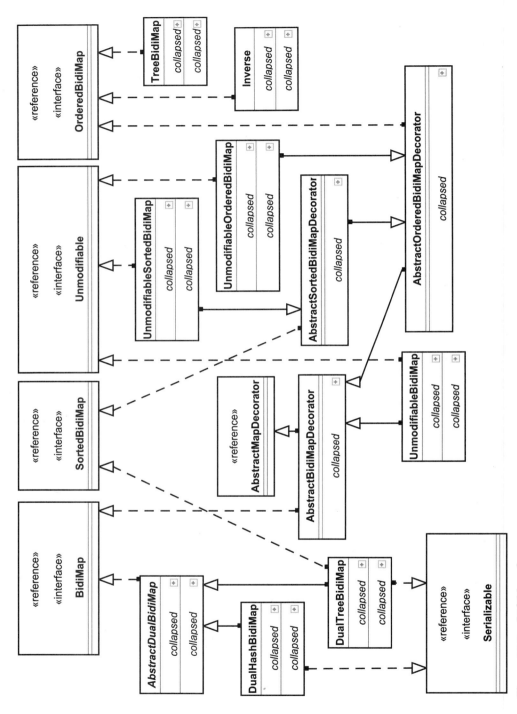

Figure 11-3 BidiMap classes.

The code:

```
java.util.Map myMap = new java.util.HashMap();
myMap.put("One", "1");
myMap.put("Two", "2");
myMap.put("Three", "3");

myMap = org.apache.commons.collections.map.FixedSizeMap
        .decorate(myMap);
try
{
    myMap.put("Four", "4");
} catch (Exception e)
{
    System.out.println(e.getMessage());
}
```

... produces the output:

```
Cannot put new key/value pair - Map is fixed size
```

Related Classes: `BoundedCollection`, `BoundedFifoBuffer`, `BoundedMap`, `UnmodifiableBoundedCollection`

Buffer

A buffer is used to describe a collection that expects to remove objects in a specific order. Last-in-first-out (LIFO) buffer (`ArrayStack`), first-in-first-out (FIFO) buffer (`UnboundedFifoBuffer`), and `java.util.Comparator`-based (`PriorityBuffer`) implementations are provided, among others. The Commons Buffer hierarchy is shown in Figure 11-4.

Related Classes: `AbstractBufferDecorator`, `BlockingBuffer`, `BoundedFifoBuffer`, `BoundedFifoBuffer`, `Buffer`, `BufferOverflowException`, `BufferUnderflowException`, `BufferUtils`, `CircularFifoBuffer`, `PredicatedBuffer`, `PriorityBuffer`, `SynchronizedBuffer`, `TransformedBuffer`, `TypedBuffer`, `UnboundedFifoBuffer`, `UnboundedFifoBuffer`, `UnmodifiableBuffer`

Circular

`CircularFifoBuffer` is a first-in-first-out buffer with a fixed size that replaces the least recently added element if full. It is both a bounded collection and a buffer.

Related Classes: `CircularFifoBuffer`

Closure

A closure simply provides a simple interface with a single `void execute(java.lang.Object input)` method. The only failure signal is a thrown exception, implying that a closure method is not expected to fail. A closure is useful in conjunction with a transformer.

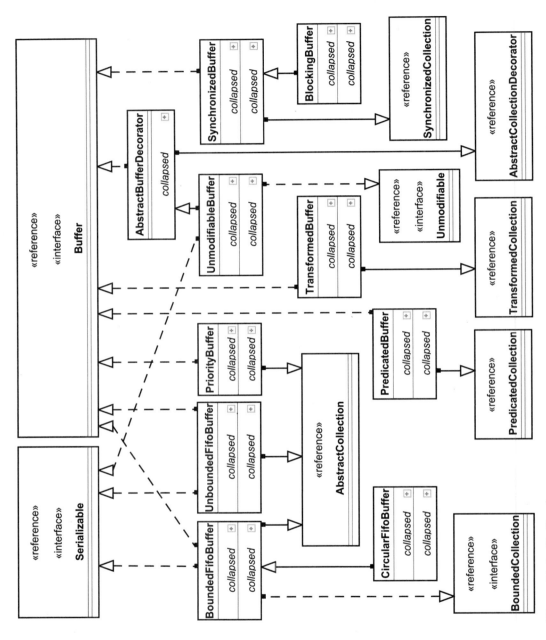

Figure 11-4 Buffer classes.

See the Functor entry for more information.
For example, the code:

```
org.apache.commons.collections.Closure myEchoClosure = new
org.apache.commons.collections.Closure()
{
    public void execute(Object in)
    {
        System.out.println(in.toString());
    }
};

org.apache.commons.collections.Closure mySizeClosure = new
org.apache.commons.collections.Closure()
{
    public void execute(Object in)
    {
        System.out.println(in.toString()
            .length());
    }
};

java.util.Map myMap = new java.util.HashMap();

myMap = org.apache.commons.collections.map.TransformedMap
        .decorate(
            myMap,
            org.apache.commons.collections.functors.ClosureTransformer
                .getInstance(myEchoClosure),
            org.apache.commons.collections.functors.ClosureTransformer
                .getInstance(mySizeClosure));

myMap.put("Hello", "World");
myMap.put("Apple", "Orange");
myMap.put("One", "Example of a String");
```

... generates the output:

```
Hello
5
Apple
6
One
19
```

You'll notice in this example that the closures are used to echo values when elements are added to the `Map`. The first closure writes the value of the object to `System.out`, and the second closure writes the length of the `String` representation.

Related Classes: `ChainedClosure, Closure, ClosureTransformer, ClosureUtils, ExceptionClosure, ForClosure, IfClosure, NOPClosure, SwitchClosure, TransformerClosure, WhileClosure`

Collating

A `CollatingIterator` can be used to sort an `Iterator` according to a particular `Comparator`. Even more powerful, a `CollatingIterator` can seamlessly weave together two or more `Iterators` as a single `Iterator` using the comparator provided.

The code:

```
java.util.SortedMap myMap = new java.util.TreeMap();
myMap.put("Hello", "World");
myMap.put("Apple", "Orange");
myMap.put("One", "Example of a String");

java.util.SortedSet mySet = new java.util.TreeSet();
mySet.add("Example");
mySet.add("Bingo");

org.apache.commons.collections.iterators.CollatingIterator
myIterator = new
org.apache.commons.collections.iterators.CollatingIterator();
myIterator.setComparator(java.text.Collator
        .getInstance());
myIterator.addIterator(myMap.keySet()
        .iterator());
myIterator.addIterator(mySet.iterator());

while (myIterator.hasNext())
    System.out.println(myIterator.next());
```

. . . produces the output:

```
Apple
Bingo
Example
Hello
One
```

Note that the iterators supplied to the `CollatingIterator` are already sorted. Although `CollatingIterator` can be used to weave together an arbitrary number of iterators into a single iterator, it will only produce properly sorted results if the supplied iterators are already sorted.

Related Classes: `CollatingIterator`

Comparator

The built-in JDK comparator functionality is used to provide a relative order for two objects. This order is given an integer value. For example, the order between "A" and "D" might be expressed as 3, and "D" and "A" as -3. The `Collections` package makes heavy use of the `Comparator` interface, and it provides a rich set of additional comparators, including comparators for handling null values, reversing a comparator, and chaining comparators (for example, combining the natural comparator with the null comparator).

Related Classes: `BooleanComparator`, `ComparableComparator`, `ComparatorChain`, `ComparatorUtils`, `FixedOrderComparator`, `NullComparator`, `ReverseComparator`, `TransformingComparator`

Composite

This allows you to join a set of collections and provide them as a single, unified view. For example, given a map of cats and a map of dogs, you may want to present them as a single map. Changes to objects may be performed directly, but add and remove operations require the use of a custom `CompositeCollection.CollectionMutator` implementation to determine which collection will actually remove or add the object.

Related Classes: `CompositeCollection`, `CompositeMap`, `CompositeSet`

Cursorable

Typically, changes to the owning collection are not possible from an iterator. The `CursorableLinkedList` class provides an exception to this rule—modifications to the collection are possible from the iterator. As long as the `CursorableLinkedList` is operated on from a single thread, you can make modifications from either the owning collection or the iterator as needed.

For example:

```
org.apache.commons.collections.list.CursorableLinkedList
myList = new org.apache.commons.collections.list.CursorableLinkedList();
myList.add("1 (original)");
myList.add("2 (original)");
myList.add("3 (original)");
myList.add("4 (original)");
myList.add("5 (original)");
myList.add("6 (original)");

java.util.ListIterator myIterator = myList
        .listIterator();

while (myIterator.hasNext())
{
    System.out.println(myIterator.next());
    int nextIndexValue = myIterator
            .nextIndex();

    if (nextIndexValue < 5)
        myList.add((myList.size() + 1)
                + " (added)");
}
```

. . . produces the output:

```
1 (original)
2 (original)
3 (original)
```

```
4 (original)
5 (original)
6 (original)
7 (added)
8 (added)
9 (added)
10 (added)
```

Notice that changes made to the list while processing the iterator actually cause the iterator to update.

Related Classes: `CursorableLinkedList`

Factory

This is an interface corresponding to the popular design pattern. Default `Factory` implementations are provided for a variety of scenarios, including no-arg constructor classes, or even a factory for objects with a specific constructor and set of arguments.

Factory implementations are useful in conjunction with `Lazy` collections.

Related Classes: `ConstantFactory`, `ExceptionFactory`, `Factory`, `FactoryTransformer`, `FactoryUtils`, `InstantiateFactory`, `PrototypeFactory`

Fast

The various `Fast` classes are intended for use in multi-threaded environments in which the vast majority of the access is intended to be read-only. After a collection is created and the data is added, calling `setFast(true)` puts the collection in a high performance mode.

There is no advantage to using a "Fast" implementation on a single thread.

If you have a `Map` that is expected to have three or fewer elements and performance is a consideration, you may want to consider the `Flat3Map` implementation.

Related Classes: `FastArrayList`, `FastHashMap`, `FastTreeMap`

Fifo

Describes a first-in-first-out buffer. See `Buffer` for more information.

Related Classes: `BoundedFifoBuffer`, `BoundedFifoBuffer`, `CircularFifoBuffer`, `UnboundedFifoBuffer`, `UnboundedFifoBuffer`

FixedSize

Allows you to decorate a given collection to indicate that the size of the collection is fixed—any attempt to add or remove an element is prohibited. An element may be replaced, however (as this would not change the size of the collection).

Related Classes: `FixedOrderComparator`, `FixedSizeList`, `FixedSizeMap`, `FixedSizeSortedMap`

Flat3

Describes a Map highly optimized for read/write access when less than three elements are present. When more than three elements are present, this class defaults to the HashMap implementation, with a slight penalty for the extra methods.

Related Classes: `Flat3Map`

Functor

Functors describe a set of interfaces defining a single operation. For example, a closure simply provides an execute method, a predicate provides a function for boolean evaluation, a transformer provides a single method to produce an object given an object, and a factory provides a single method for creating a new object. Closures and predicates are only useful in conjunction with other classes, in particular a transformer. Custom functors are often passed as anonymous inner objects. When combined with the functors provided by the Collections package, complex operations can be wrapped and handled in conjunction with a collection.

See `Closure`, `Predicate`, `Transformer`, and `Factory` for more information.

Hash

All Java objects extend `java.lang.Object`, which defines a method `int hashCode()`. This hash code is used by various hash implementations as values for optimizing access. For a more detailed explanation of the meaning and use of a hash-based collection, see http://www.linuxgazette.com/issue57/tindale.html.

Note that the various hash collections rely on a "good" value to be returned by the `hashCode()` function. The `org.apache.commons.lang.builder.HashCodeBuilder`, part of the Lang package, can assist in creating `hashCode()` implementations.

Related Classes: `AbstractHashedMap`, `DualHashBidiMap`, `FastHashMap`, `HashBag`, `HashedMap`, `MultiHashMap`, `SequencedHashMap`

Identity

Most collections use the `Object.equals()` method to determine if two objects are equal. The identity classes use the `==` operation to determine equality instead. The `==` operation compares the object reference identity of two objects. Two objects created independently with identical data may or may not have the same object reference identity, depending on the situation and compiler.

Generally speaking, the `==` operation is useful for lower-level object comparisons more concerned with the underlying thread, compiler, and class loader, whereas the `equals()` method is useful for business operations.

Related Classes: `IdentityMap`, `IdentityPredicate`, `ReferenceIdentityMap`

Lazy

The `Lazy` classes allow you to decorate a collection, defining factories that will be used to automatically create objects when a null value would otherwise be returned. For example, if the tenth element of a lazy list with a size of six was requested, the lazy list would grow the size of the list to ten, create a new object at the tenth slot, and return the new object.

For example, the code:

```
org.apache.commons.collections.Factory factory = new
org.apache.commons.collections.Factory()
{
    public Object create()
    {
        return new java.util.Date();
    }
};

java.util.Map lazy = org.apache.commons.collections.map.LazyMap
        .decorate(new java.util.HashMap(),
                factory);
String current = lazy.get("NOW").toString();
String second = lazy.get("SECOND").toString();

System.out.println(lazy.size());
```

... outputs the value 2.

Related Classes: `LazyList`, `LazyMap`, `LazySortedMap`

Linked

A linked list simply provides bidirectional access to a list, allowing for easy retrieval of objects in either order.

Related Classes: `AbstractLinkedList`, `AbstractLinkedMap`, `CursorableLinkedList`, `CursorableLinkedList`, `LinkedMap`, `NodeCachingLinkedList`

List

This is an ordered collection (also known as a sequence). The user of this interface has precise control over where in the list each element is inserted. The user can access elements by their integer index (position in the list) and search for elements in the list. A list is the next step up from a simple array. A

Collections Concepts 155

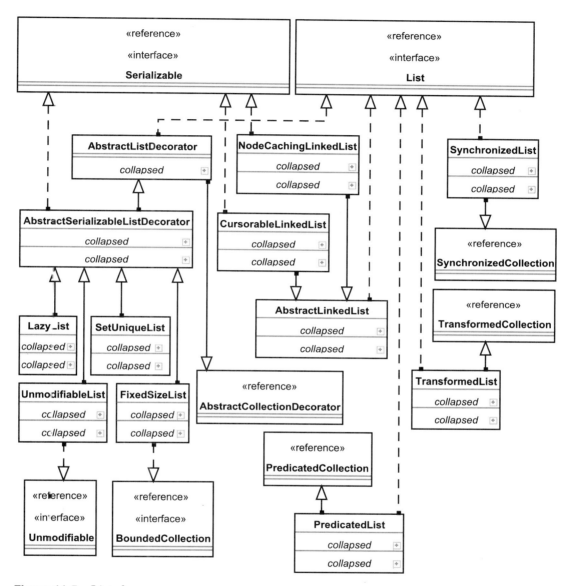

Figure 11-5 List classes.

list is particularly useful in conjunction with a transformer. The Commons List hierarchy is shown in Figure 11-5.

Related Classes: `AbstractLinkedList`, `AbstractListDecorator`, `AbstractListIteratorDecorator`, `AbstractSerializableListDecorator`, `ArrayListIterator`, `CursorableLinkedList`, `CursorableLinkedList`, `EmptyListIterator`, `FastArrayList`, `FilterListIterator`, `FixedSizeList`,

LazyList, ListIteratorWrapper, ListOrderedMap ListOrderedSet, ListUtils, NodeCachingLinkedList, ObjectArrayListIterator, PredicatedList ProxyListIterator, ResettableListIterator, SetUniqueList, SingletonListIterator, SynchronizedList, TransformedList, TreeList, TypedList, UnmodifiableList, UnmodifiableListIterator

LRU

Refers to the notion that the fixed size map maintains a notion of the frequency of use, removing the "least recently used" entry when the map is full and a new entry is submitted. Only the `put` and `get` operations affect the tracking of items—iteration and queries to verify the presence of a key or value do not affect the map.

For example, the code:

```
java.util.Map myMap = new
org.apache.commons.collections.map.LRUMap(3);
myMap.put("One", "1");
myMap.put("Two", "2");
myMap.put("Three", "3");

myMap.get("One");
myMap.get("Three");

myMap.put("Four", "4");

echo(myMap.keySet());
```

. . . produces the results:

```
One
Three
Four
```

Related Classes: LRUMap

Map

This is an object that maps keys to values. A map cannot contain duplicate keys; each key can map to at most one value. A sorted map will maintain the keys in order. One of the most popular types of collection, the vast majority of the classes in the Collection package involve maps in one way or another. The Commons Map hierarchy is shown in Figure 11-6.

Keep in mind that many of the map classes merely act as decorators for other map instances. For example, the `MapUtils.typedSortedMap(java.util.SortedMap map, java.lang.Class keyType, java.lang.Class valueType)` method allows you to take an existing HashMap, sort it using a comparator, and apply runtime type-checks to both the keys and values.

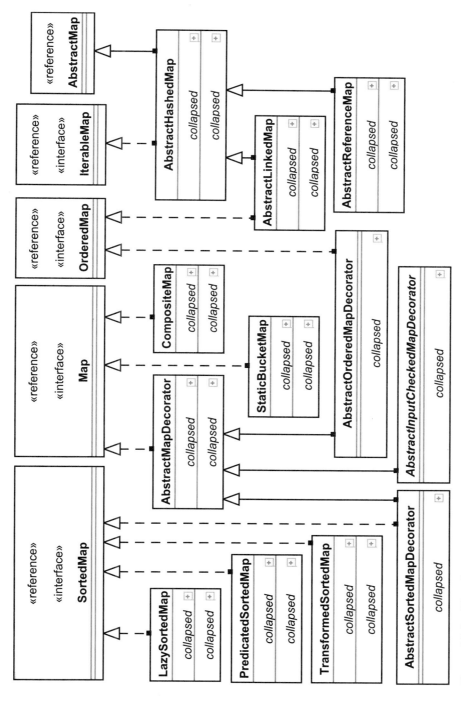

Figure 11-6 Map classes.

Multi

A `Multi` map is used to track a map of maps. In other words, each element requires two identifying key values.

For example, the code:

```
String first = "Will";
String last = "Iverson";

String phone = "(321) 555-1212";

java.util.Map myMap = new java.util.HashMap();
org.apache.commons.collections.keyvalue.MultiKey multiKey =
new org.apache.commons.collections.keyvalue.MultiKey(
        first, last);
myMap.put(multiKey, phone);

System.out.println(myMap.get(multiKey));

System.out.println();
echo(myMap);
```

... produces the result:

```
(321) 555-1212

MultiKey[Will, Iverson]=(321) 555-1212
```

Related Classes: `MultiHashMap`, `MultiKey`, `MultiKeyMap`, `MultiMap`

NodeCaching

By default, a List will use Node objects to maintain the items within. The `NodeCachingLinkedList` implementation attempts to reuse these Nodes to avoid excessive object creation and garbage collection. It is therefore particularly useful as a long-lived object that expects significant addition and removal of objects over time.

Related Classes: `NodeCachingLinkedList`

ObjectGraph

Creates a single `Iterator` to walk down a complex graph of objects. This may be an `Iterator` that in turn contains an arbitrarily deep number of nested `Iterators` and objects, or a root object with a custom transformer (which returns either objects or `Iterators` as appropriate).

For example, the code:

```
org.apache.commons.collections.Transformer myTransformer =
new org.apache.commons.collections.Transformer()
{
    public Object transform(Object input)
```

```java
        {
            if (input instanceof java.util.Collection)
            {
                return ((java.util.Collection) input)
                        .iterator();
            } else
                return input;
        }
    };

    java.util.Set firstSet = new java.util.HashSet();
    java.util.Set secondSet = new java.util.HashSet();
    java.util.Set thirdSet = new java.util.HashSet();

    firstSet.add("Orange");
    firstSet.add("Apple");
    secondSet.add("Radio");
    secondSet.add("Television");
    thirdSet.add("Fire");
    thirdSet.add("Water");
    firstSet.add(secondSet);
    firstSet.add(thirdSet);

    org.apache.commons.collections.iterators.ObjectGraphIterator myIterator =
    new org.apache.commons.collections.iterators.ObjectGraphIterator(
            firstSet, myTransformer);

    while (myIterator.hasNext())
        System.out.println(myIterator.next());
```

... produces the output:

```
Water
Fire
Apple
Radio
Television
Orange
```

Related Classes: `ObjectArrayIterator`, `ObjectArrayListIterator`, `ObjectGraphIterator`

Ordered

An ordered collection allows for both forward and backward iteration over the elements in the collection. This includes quick access to the first, last, next, and previous element.

Related Classes: `AbstractOrderedBidiMapDecorator`, `AbstractOrderedMapDecorator`, `AbstractOrderedMapIteratorDecorator`, `DoubleOrderedMap`, `EmptyOrderedIterator`, `EmptyOrderedMapIterator`, `ListOrderedMap`, `ListOrderedSet`, `OrderedBidiMap`, `OrderedIterator`, `OrderedMap`, `OrderedMapIterator`, `UnmodifiableOrderedBidiMap`, `UnmodifiableOrderedMap`, `UnmodifiableOrderedMapIterator`

Predicate

A simple interface used to perform a test—a single method, `boolean evaluate(java.lang.Object object)`. Unlike a closure, it returns true/false. For more information, see `Functor`.

Related Classes: `AllPredicate, AndPredicate, AnyPredicate, EqualPredicate, ExceptionPredicate, FalsePredicate, IdentityPredicate, InstanceofPredicate, NonePredicate, NotNullPredicate, NotPredicate, NullIsExceptionPredicate, NullIsFalsePredicate, NullIsTruePredicate, NullPredicate, OnePredicate, OrPredicate, Predicate, PredicatedBag, PredicatedBuffer, PredicatedCollection, PredicateDecorator, PredicatedList, PredicatedMap, PredicatedSet, PredicatedSortedBag, PredicatedSortedMap, PredicatedSortedSet, PredicateTransformer, PredicateUtils, TransformedPredicate, TransformerPredicate, TruePredicate, UniquePredicate`

Reference

The various reference map collections allow you to specify that entries may be removed by the garbage collector. In other words, references from this collection "don't count" when the Java virtual machine is assessing an object as still being in use for purposes of garbage collection.

Related Classes: `AbstractReferenceMap, ReferenceIdentityMap, ReferenceMap`

Set

This is a collection that contains no duplicate elements. More formally, sets contain no pair of elements *e1* and *e2* such that *e1.equals(e2)*, and at most one null element. A sorted set will maintain the elements in order. The Commons Map hierarchy is shown in Figure 11-7.

Related Classes: `AbstractSerializableSetDecorator, AbstractSetDecorator, AbstractSortedSetDecorator, CompositeSet, EntrySetMapIterator, ListOrderedSet, MapBackedSet, PredicatedSet, PredicatedSortedSet, SetUniqueList, SetUtils SynchronizedSet, SynchronizedSortedSet, TransformedSet, TransformedSortedSet, TypedSet, TypedSortedSet, UnmodifiableEntrySet, UnmodifiableSet, UnmodifiableSortedSet`

Singleton

This is a collection that may contain one and only one element. The element may be changed, but no operation that would result in zero or more than one element is allowed.

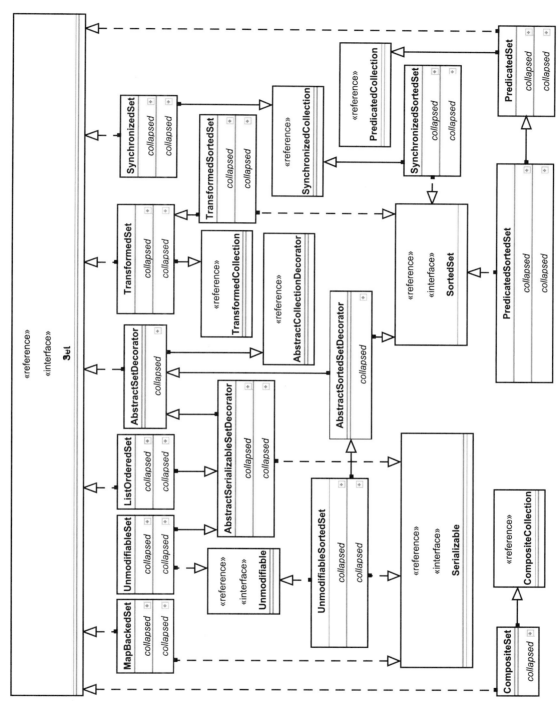

Figure 11-7 Set classes.

Related Classes: `SingletonIterator`, `SingletonListIterator`, `SingletonMap`

StaticBucket

An efficient, thread-safe Map, designed for situations in which the Map is expected to be accessed frequently by multiple threads. If you expect to only access the `put`, `get`, `remove`, and `containsKey` methods, this class will dramatically reduce thread contentions. Bulk operations, however, are not atomic, meaning that two or more threads operating on the same collection can have indeterminate results.

Related Classes: `StaticBucketMap`

Synchronized

The various `Synchronized` collection classes allow you to decorate a collection, providing synchronized implementations of the collection methods, which are then passed along to the underlying collection.

Related Classes: `SynchronizedBag`, `SynchronizedBuffer`, `SynchronizedCollection`, `SynchronizedList`, `SynchronizedPriorityQueue`, `SynchronizedSet`, `SynchronizedSortedBag`, `SynchronizedSortedSet`

Transformed/Transformer

The transformed classes allow a transform operation to be performed on objects as they are added to the collection. These classes merely decorate another implementation—they are not intended to serve as standalone implementations.

The `java.lang.Object transform(java.lang.Object input)` method of the `Transformer` interface is used to perform the operation. Note that the input object is generally expected to be unchanged, and a new output object is generated.

For an example of a transformation, see the previous entries on `Closure` and `ObjectGraph`.

Related Classes: `ChainedTransformer`, `CloneTransformer`, `ClosureTransformer`, `ConstantTransformer`, `ExceptionTransformer`, `FactoryTransformer`, `InstantiateTransformer`, `InvokerTransformer`, `MapTransformer`, `NOPTransformer`, `PredicateTransformer`, `StringValueTransformer`, `SwitchTransformer`, `TransformedBag`, `TransformedBuffer`, `TransformedCollection`, `TransformedList`, `TransformedMap`, `TransformedPredicate`, `TransformedSet`, `TransformedSortedBag`, `TransformedSortedMap`, `TransformedSortedSet`, `Transformer`, `TransformerClosure`, `TransformerPredicate`, `TransformerUtils`, `TransformingComparator`, `TransformIterator`

Typed

Decorators that allow runtime type checks to be applied to a collection. Note that the addition of generics to Java 5.0 (also known as JDK 1.5) reduces the need for these type wrappers. For more information on generics, see http://java.sun.com/j2se/1.5.0/docs/guide/language/generics.html.

For example, the code:

```
java.util.Set mySet = new java.util.HashSet();
mySet = org.apache.commons.collections.set.TypedSet
        .decorate(mySet, Integer.class);

mySet.add(new Integer(5));
mySet.add(new Integer(15));
try
{
    mySet.add(new Long(100000));
} catch (Exception e)
{
    System.out.println(e.getMessage());
}

echo(mySet);
```

... produces the result:

```
Cannot add Object '100000' - Predicate rejected it
15
5
```

Related Classes: TypedBag, TypedBuffer, TypedCollection, TypedList, TypedMap, TypedSet, TypedSortedBag, TypedSortedMap, TypedSortedSet

Unmodifiable

This is a decorator that wraps a collection as unmodifiable. For example, a configuration collection may be initialized at application launch and then shared with a variety of resources over the course of the application's life cycle, with changes to the configuration object disallowed by decorating the collection as unmodifiable.

Related Classes: UnmodifiableBag, UnmodifiableBidiMap, UnmodifiableBoundedCollection, UnmodifiableBuffer, UnmodifiableCollection, UnmodifiableEntrySet, UnmodifiableIterator, UnmodifiableList, UnmodifiableListIterator, UnmodifiableMap, UnmodifiableMapEntry, UnmodifiableMapIterator, UnmodifiableOrderedBidiMap, UnmodifiableOrderedMap, UnmodifiableOrderedMapIterator, UnmodifiableSet, UnmodifiableSortedBag, UnmodifiableSortedBidiMap, UnmodifiableSortedMap, UnmodifiableSortedSet

SUMMARY

The Collections package provides a broad suite of functionality associated with managing relationships between objects. While many introductions to object-oriented development focus on the design of objects and the class hierarchy, the proper use of relationships to bind objects together is as, if not more, important.

Project Ideas

What user interfaces are best used to present the various collection types to users? How are these interfaces impacted by the size of the collection? Is this easier or harder in Swing or HTML?

Consider applications that you have written using the collection types built in to Java. How hard would it be to add more control to the various collections using the Commons Collections package?

CHAPTER **12**

Codec

The term codec originates from the words compression/decompression (amusingly, the abbreviation is in a sense a form of compression). Popular codecs perform such functions as compressing and decompressing arbitrary data (e.g., ZIP, RAR), image-specific data (e.g., GIF, JPEG), or audio data (e.g., MP3, AIFF). Over time, the term codec has grown to include a wide variety of data translations, not all of which are useful for compression and decompression but instead serve other functions such as security, data transmission, or even spell-checking. While the JDK offers a variety of built-in handlers for dealing with popular compression formats such as ZIP, GIF, and JPG, the Apache Commons Codec project fills in other gaps in functionality.

As of this writing, the Codec includes utilities in the following areas:

- Data transmission (Base64 and Hex encoding/decoding)
- Hash encoding (MD5 and SHA, useful for passwords and file signatures)
- Phonetic encoding (useful for features such as spell-checking)

In this chapter, we will look at this functionality in a series of methods in a single class. Listing 12-1 shows the header information for the class—note the imports from the Codec package.

Listing 12-1 Imports and Class Header

```
package com.cascadetg.ch12;

import java.io.FileInputStream;
import java.io.UnsupportedEncodingException;

import org.apache.commons.codec.binary.Base64;
import org.apache.commons.codec.binary.Hex;
import org.apache.commons.codec.digest.DigestUtils;
import org.apache.commons.codec.language.DoubleMetaphone;
import org.apache.commons.codec.language.Metaphone;
import org.apache.commons.codec.language.RefinedSoundex;
import org.apache.commons.codec.language.Soundex;
import org.apache.commons.codec.net.URLCodec;
```

(continues)

Listing 12-1 (*continued*)

```
// To change the default encoding, use the command
// java -Dfile.encoding=UTF8 EncodingDemo
// when launching. Keep in mind that if you change the encoding,
// you should also change the encoding of the terminal to
// match (an option not available on all systems).

public class EncodingDemo
{
    public static void printHeader(String title)
    {
        System.out.println();
        System.out.println("================================");
        System.out.println(title);
        System.out.println("================================");
    }

    public static void main(String[] args)
    {
        fileEncodingDemo();
        encodingDemo();
        phoneticDemo();
        hashEncodingDemo();
        formURLEncodingDemo();
    }
... // Rest of code follows.
```

The imports refer to the various classes of the `Codec` package, as shown in Figure 12-1. The MD5 and SHA classes aren't part of the rest of the hierarchy but are instead broken out into a utility class. All of the interfaces provided are intended for use with either `string` or `byte[]` parameters, not the more sophisticated stream interfaces present in the JDK. This is acceptable for most uses, but it does require the entire data set to be loaded into memory before use.

CHARACTER ENCODINGS

Let us start by considering basic facts about binary data. Generally speaking, binary data consists of streams of bytes. These bytes have numerical values from 0 to 255, as composed by 8 bits (zeros or ones). The meaning of the bytes depends on the application.

Now, compare binary data with character data. At first, most English speakers think of ASCII as character data—an international standard for converting byte data (numbers from 0 to 255) to characters. However, ASCII only defines the meaning of the lower 128 values—the remaining 128 possible numbers (also known as high-bit characters) don't correspond to a specific character. On some systems, these high-bit characters are used to represent locale-specific information. For example, a French system might use high-bit characters to represent French-specific information, whereas an English system might use the high-bit characters to represent special graphics (such as the trademark symbol).

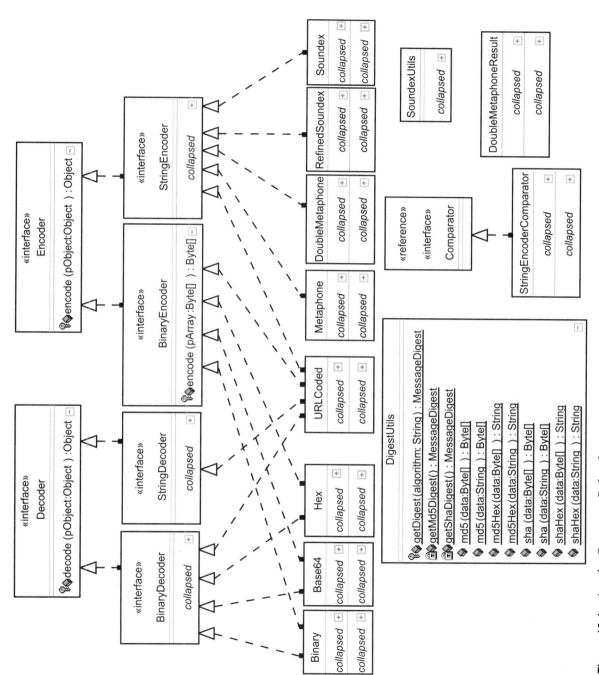

Figure 12-1 Apache Commons Codec classes.

As if high-bit characters weren't complicated enough, many languages have far more than 255 characters. To support these languages, two or even three bytes may be required to store individual characters. Therefore, to properly read and understand the character data represented by a stream of bytes, you must know the proper encoding for the data. In other words, the character encoding is a bit of information that lets your application know how to interpret the binary representation of the data as character data.

Java uses Unicode, a unified international standard for representing character data, to store character data internally. So, a `String` in Java represents a series of Unicode bytes.

Listing 12-2 shows a bit of code that illustrates the various interpretations of a bit of character data. The string `highBitCharacters` is used as our test case—this string contains a normal ASCII character and also several Unicode character points, expressed with the \u0000 format, that represent characters not common to all languages. The \u represents a Unicode escape sequence, and the 0000 represents the specific character.

Listing 12-2 Encoding Example Source

```java
public static void encodingDemo()
{
    // These strings are used to refer to specific
    // encoding types.
    String UTF8 = "UTF-8";
    String WindowsLatin1 = "Cp1252";

    // These characters are, in order, the ordinary ASCII letter X,
    // a pound sign (the UK currency), a latin capital letter C
    // with cedilla, a latin small letter e with diaeresis, and
    // registered sign (typically used to indicate a registered
    // trademark).  These characters are represented internally
    // in the JVM as Unicode.  Their output as bytes is
    // determined by the default encoding for the system, or
    // potentially by an overidden setting on a per-method basis.
    String highBitCharacters = "X\u00a3\u00c7\u00eb\u00ae";

    printHeader("Encoding Demo");

    System.out.print("Default JVM encoding: ");
    System.out.println(System.getProperty("file.encoding"));

    System.out.print("Test high bit character output: ");
    System.out.println(highBitCharacters);

    System.out.print("It takes ");
    System.out.print(highBitCharacters.getBytes().length);
    System.out.println(" bytes to store this string.");

    try
    {
        System.out.print("Windows Cp1252 Characters: ");
        String winstring =
            new String(
                highBitCharacters.getBytes(),
                WindowsLatin1);
```

(*continues*)

Listing 12-2 (*continued*)

```
            System.out.println(winstring);

            System.out.println();
            System.out.println("Everything looks fine, but some");
            System.out.println("systems automatically convert the");
            System.out.println("data.  Here, note the lossy ");
            System.out.println("conversion to ? characters:");
            System.out.println();

            System.out.print("ASCII Characters: ");
            String asciiString =
                new String(highBitCharacters.getBytes(), "ASCII");
            System.out.println(asciiString);

            System.out.println();
            System.out.println(
                "Commons Encoding supports converting");
            System.out.println("bytes to two-digit 0-f hex codes.");
            System.out.println();

            System.out.print("Hex Characters: ");
            byte[] hexresults;
            hexresults =
                new Hex().encode(highBitCharacters.getBytes());
            System.out.println(new String(hexresults));
        } catch (UnsupportedEncodingException e)
        {
            e.printStackTrace();
        }
    }
}
```

As we can see in the output shown in Listing 12-3, converting the string from Unicode code points to Cp1252 (the default encoding on a US English Windows system) works fine, but the encoding conversion to pure ASCII results in the loss of information.

Listing 12-3 Encoding Example Results

```
================================
Encoding Demo
================================
Default JVM encoding: Cp1252
Test high bit character output: X£Çë®
It takes 5 bytes to store this string.
Windows Cp1252 Characters: X£Çë®

Everything looks fine, but some
systems automatically convert the
data.  Here, note the lossy
conversion to ? characters:

ASCII Characters: X????

Commons Encoding supports converting
bytes to two-digit 0-f hex codes.

Hex Characters: 58a3c7ebae
```

This example shows us the first use of the Apache Commons project—the ability to translate a series of characters from raw byte data to a hex representation. In a hex representation, each byte is transformed to a two-letter ASCII representation, 0-f. The hex format, while potentially useful for reading and writing binary data to an ASCII representation, is not as well known or popular as the Base64 format.

BASE64 ENCODING

Having seen how character encodings can have a major impact on our data, let's look at how the Base64 Codec can be used to convert binary data to a format easily represented by ASCII characters. Many systems understand and can easily transmit binary data when encoding using Base64—in particular, Base64 encoding is commonly found when sending binary files as email attachments.

Listing 12-4 shows how a binary file (in this case, a small GIF) can be loaded and converted to 7-bit ASCII characters. Generally speaking, 7-bit ASCII characters are safe for transmission across a variety of systems—even copying and pasting from one application to another on a wide variety of systems.

Listing 12-4 Base64 File Encoding Source

```
public static void fileEncodingDemo()
{
    printHeader("Base64 File Encoding Test");

    java.io.File myFile = new java.io.File("demo.gif");
    try
    {
        if (myFile.exists());
        {
            FileInputStream myFileContents =
                new FileInputStream(myFile);

            byte[] fileContents =
                new byte[(int)myFile.length()];
            myFileContents.read(fileContents);

            String myGIF = new String(fileContents);
            System.out.println(
                "Notice the strange, non-ASCII characters...");
            System.out.println(myGIF.substring(0, 79));

            System.out.println();

            byte[] result;
            result = Base64.encodeBase64Chunked(fileContents);

            System.out.println(
                "Note all ASCII characters, and that the data ");
```

(continues)

Listing 12-4 (*continued*)

```
            System.out.println(
                "is automatically formatted to 79 characters");
            System.out.println(new String(result));
        }
    } catch (Exception e)
    {
        e.printStackTrace();
    }
}
```

When run, the application produces output as shown in Listing 12-5 (for a very small test GIF). You'll notice that instead of using the simple `encode()` method, we took advantage of a `encodeBase64Chunked()` utility method to retrieve data already broken into 76 character wide columns—easily used on even legacy 80 character column terminal displays.

Listing 12-5 Base64 File Encoding Results

```
================================
Base64 File Encoding Test
================================
Notice the strange, non-ASCII characters...
GIF89a<<unprintable characters, will vary on your terminal>>

Note all ASCII characters, and that the data
is automatically formatted to 76 characters
R0lGODlhIAAgAIAAAP///wAAACwAAAAAIAAgAAACUkyAqcuNdpycAEaKk72Zbt45HxguI1k+Z8qc
Bqu4L1zJaGbPaa6HfI/73UTCYatojCGTqiVmCfFAgaYpVWO91rIobrTqBYW/zTF2PENbtuq2pQAA
Ow==
```

URL Form Encoding

Uniform Resource Locators (URLs) are wonderful things—they allow us to point to information all over the Internet and local networks. We are all familiar with such strings as `http://www.example.com/page.jsp?id=1`. If you have done much in the way of web application development, you recognize that this string points to a specific JSP called `page.jsp` on a web server with a domain name of `www.example.com` and is sending a parameter called `id` with a value of 1. Special characters, such as `?` and `=`, are used as tokens by the server to indicate how to parse the incoming request.

Now, let's imagine that we want to use a parameter value that happens to have a `?`, `=`, or even a space character. This is allowable according to the specification using a special encoding format (www-form-urlencoded, commonly referred to as URL encoding). Make sure, however, that you are encoding the data to be sent along as a parameter, not the URL itself.

Listing 12-6 shows an example of how a complex URL parameter is encoded and then appended to the URL.

Listing 12-6 URL Parameter Encoding Source

```
public static void formURLEncodingDemo()
{
    printHeader("Form URL Encoding Demo");
    try
    {

        String badParameterValue =
            "http://www.example.org/page.jsp?foo=bar next";
        System.out.println(
            "Here is an example of a difficult ");
        System.out.println("string to use as a URL parameter:");
        System.out.println(badParameterValue);

        byte[] badURLresult =
            new URLCodec().encode(badParameterValue.getBytes());

        System.out.println();

        System.out.println("Here is the string, properly");
        System.out.println("formatted for use as a link:");
        System.out.println(
            "http://www.example.com/view.jsp?url="
              + new String(badURLresult));

        System.out.println();

    } catch (Exception e)
    {
        e.printStackTrace();
    }
}
```

As shown in Listing 12-7, the parameter passed along is another URL. This could be useful in a variety of situations—for example, our web application might verify the availability of a web site, and so a URL needs to be passed along as a parameter.

Listing 12-7 URL Parameter Encoding Results

```
================================
Form URL Encoding Demo
================================
Here is an example of a difficult
string to use as a URL parameter:
http://www.example.org/page.jsp?foo=bar next

Here is the string, properly
formatted for use as a link:
http://www.example.com/view.jsp?url=http%3A%2F%2Fwww.example.
org%2Fpage.jsp%3Ffoo%3Dbar+next
```

Hash Generation

Not all encoding systems are bidirectional. Some, such as JPEG, are inherently lossy—the conversion process discards some data in the name of compression. MD5 and SHA, on the other hand, allow you to encode a particular stream of bytes to generate a hash—a fingerprint of that stream of bytes. This hash is specifically intended to *not* allow you to decode back to the original data.

What Are SHA and MD5?

"SHA-1: The Secure Hash Algorithm (SHA) was developed by NIST and is specified in the Secure Hash Standard (SHS, FIPS 180). SHA-1 is a revision to this version and was published in 1994. It is also described in the ANSI X9.30 (part 2) standard. SHA-1 produces a 160-bit (20 byte) message digest. Although slower than MD5, this larger digest size makes it stronger against brute force attacks.

MD5: MD5 was developed by Professor Ronald L. Rivest in 1994. Its 128 bit (16 byte) message digest makes it a faster implementation than SHA-1.

In both cases, the fingerprint (message digest) is also non-reversible. . . . your data cannot be retrieved from the message digest, yet as stated earlier, the digest uniquely identifies the data."

From `http://www.secure-hash-algorithm-md5-sha-1.co.uk/`

The precise use of this functionality is up to your application. For example, for security reasons, you may not want to store user passwords in your database as clear text but rather as an MD5 hash of the password. You may want to perform an MD5 hash of a file before sending it to someone and then send the hash in another email so the recipient can verify that the file sent is the same as the file received (you will often see reference to this on the Apache Software Foundation download pages). Many applications use an MD5 hash routine to generate serial numbers for registered users.

Regardless of your particular application, Apache Codec provides a simple, easy-to-use mechanism for generating MD5 and SHA hash values. Listing 12-8 shows how both a password and a bit of text can be converted to their hash values.

Listing 12-8 MD5 and SHA Digest Generation Source

```
    public static void hashEncodingDemo()
    {
        String shakespeareText =
            "ROMEO : \n"
                + "Peace, peace, Mercutio, peace!\n"
                + "Thou talk'st of nothing.\n"
                + "\n"
```

(continues)

Listing 12-8 (continued)

```
                    + "MERCUTIO : \n"
                    + "True, I talk of dreams,\n"
                    + "Which are the children of an idle brain,\n"
                    + "Begot of nothing but vain fantasy,\n"
                    + "Which is as thin of substance as the air\n"
                    + "And more inconstant than the wind, who wooes\n"
                    + "Even now the frozen bosom of the north,\n"
                    + "And, being anger'd, puffs away from thence,\n"
                    + "Turning his face to the dew-dropping south.";

         printHeader("Hash Encoding Demo");

         String password_text = "my_password";

         System.out.println("MD5 Password Encryption:");
         String encryption_result =
              DigestUtils.md5Hex(password_text);
         System.out.println(encryption_result);
         System.out.println(encryption_result.length());
         System.out.println();

         System.out.println("MD5 Document Fingerprint:");
         encryption_result = DigestUtils.md5Hex(shakespeareText);
         System.out.println(encryption_result);
         System.out.println(encryption_result.length());
         System.out.println();

         System.out.println("SHA Password Encyption:");
         encryption_result = DigestUtils.shaHex(password_text);
         System.out.println(encryption_result);
         System.out.println(encryption_result.length());
         System.out.println();

         System.out.println("SHA Document Fingerprint:");
         encryption_result = DigestUtils.shaHex(shakespeareText);
         System.out.println(encryption_result);
         System.out.println(encryption_result.length());
    }
```

As can be seen from the results of the example, shown in Listing 12-9, MD5 generates 32-character-long hash codes. The hash is the same length for both a password less than 32 characters and a snippet of text much longer than 32 characters. SHA performs a similar function, taking a bit more time to generate a more sophisticated (and secure) 40-character hash.

Listing 12-9 MD5 and SHA Digest Generation Results

```
================================
Hash Encoding Demo
================================
MD5 Password Encryption:
a865a7e0ddbf35fa6f6a232e0893bea4
32

MD5 Document Fingerprint:
bf5dea92a8a43beee75a7d3f44b41cf4
32
```

(continues)

Listing 12-9 (*continued*)

```
SHA Password Encyption:
5eb942810a75ebc850972a89285d570d484c89c4
40

SHA Document Fingerprint:
7b810d5b8e4853c91071895117543cd1927a4604
40
```

PHONETIC ANALYSIS

In this chapter we've looked at traditional encoding methods and also hash generation, but Codec offers an additional set of classes for use in phonetic analysis.

It's beyond the scope of this text to delve into the theory behind Soundex and Metaphone phonetic analysis, but suffice to say that these algorithms provide different mechanisms for generating a phonetic key. This key is designed to be able to help answer the question, "How much does this word sound like another?"

Table 12-1 shows how different phonetic algorithms included with Codec translate words into phonetic keys. Depending on the application you are trying to build, different algorithms may be of interest. For example, a spell-checking application might use Metaphone to determine alternative words as part of a spell-checking routine, whereas a voice-recognition system might rely on the RefinedSoundEx algorithm to determine the most likely words the speaker is trying to convey. Notice that while SoundEx produces the same length key for all words, the other algorithms produce variable length keys.

Table 12-1 Phonetic Algorithm Results

Word	SoundEx	RefinedSoundEx	Metaphone	Double Metaphone
hello	H400	H070	HL	HL
fellow	F400	F2070	FL	FL
mellow	M400	M8070	ML	ML
monster	M523	M8083609	MNST	MNST
monstrous	M523	M80836903	MNST	MNST

By using these algorithms and a very large set of words, you can generate a set of keys linking the words phonetically—the fundamentals needed for a spell checker.

Listing 12-10 shows the code used to generate the terms as shown in Table 12-1.

Listing 12-10 Phonetic Key Generation Source

```java
public static void phoneticDemo()
{
    printHeader("Phonetic Demo");

    String[] words =
        { "hello", "fellow", "mellow", "monster", "monstrous" };

    System.out.println("Notice the sounds of the words, and");
    System.out.println("how the sounds are translated into 4");
    System.out.println("character character flags.");

    System.out.print("Word, SoundEx, RefinedSoundEx, ");
    System.out.println("Metaphone DoubleMetaphone");
    for (int i = 0; i < words.length; i++)
    {
        System.out.print(words[i] + ", ");
        System.out.print(new Soundex().encode(words[i]) + ", ");

        System.out.print(
            new RefinedSoundex().encode(words[i]) + ", ");

        System.out.print(
            new Metaphone().encode(words[i]) + ", ");

        System.out.print(
            new DoubleMetaphone().encode(words[i]));

        System.out.println();

    }
}
```

For more information on phonetic analysis, see the following sites:

- http://encyclopedia.thefreedictionary.com/Soundex
- http://www.archives.gov/research_room/genealogy/census/soundex.html
- http://aspell.sourceforge.net/metaphone/

SUMMARY

The Codec package contains utilities that are useful in unusual places. For example, you might use the phonetic routines to help provide corrected spellings for free text searches. You also might use the encoding of binary data to a string to help send data over the network. By adding these to your toolbox, you can provide richer services while focusing on unique aspects of your application.

Project Ideas

Write an application that parses arbitrarily large bodies of text and generates a database of phonetic data. What are the best ways to store this? How large is the generated database?

Write an application that calculates the MD5 and SHA results for large bodies of text and binary data. What are the performance tradeoffs? How large does a data set have to be before this becomes an issue?

Write a command-line application to convert files to Base64 and back again. How does this compare to converting files to `.zip` and back? When would you use Base64, and when would you use `.zip`?

CHAPTER **13**

CLI (Command-Line Interface)

The Apache Jakarta Commons CLI package is intended to assist in the creation of command-line applications. In conjunction with the `String` manipulation afforded by the Commons Lang package, aspiring developers could potentially create quite sophisticated console applications. This package takes care of the complexities of parsing incoming arguments, validating the arguments, and displaying help information.

In this chapter, a simple utility function (searching various paths for the location(s) of a particular class file) is first presented from a high level, then a command-line wrapper based on this utility using CLI is shown, and for completeness, the full implementation of the class search tool is presented.

CLASSPATHTOOL OVERVIEW

The `ClassPathTool` utility is intended to allow a user to search class path(s) for a particular Java class file, specified by name. The `ClassPathTool` is smart enough to handle two special cases—first, searching for a particular path and file, and second, looking for a matching entry in a JAR or ZIP file. This serves two purposes: first, a user can search an arbitrary directory for a desired class file hidden in an unknown JAR file (for example, if a particular class is referenced by a source file). Second, a user may want to search the current class path to determine if the expected version of the class is actually on the class path. This is increasingly common given the complexity of server-side Java development and the proliferation of popular utility libraries (such as Jakarta Commons).

The `ClassPathTool` utility, as shown in Figure 13-1, does not actually have a user interface. It is exposed as a simple JavaBean-style library, with properties available to set options and a single `getEntries()` method to perform the search as configured. There is no reason that the `ClassPathTool` utility could not have a Swing or even web user interface, but those interfaces may be prohibitive in certain server environments. Therefore, the `CommandLineDemo` class is provided as a wrapper, making use of Commons CLI.

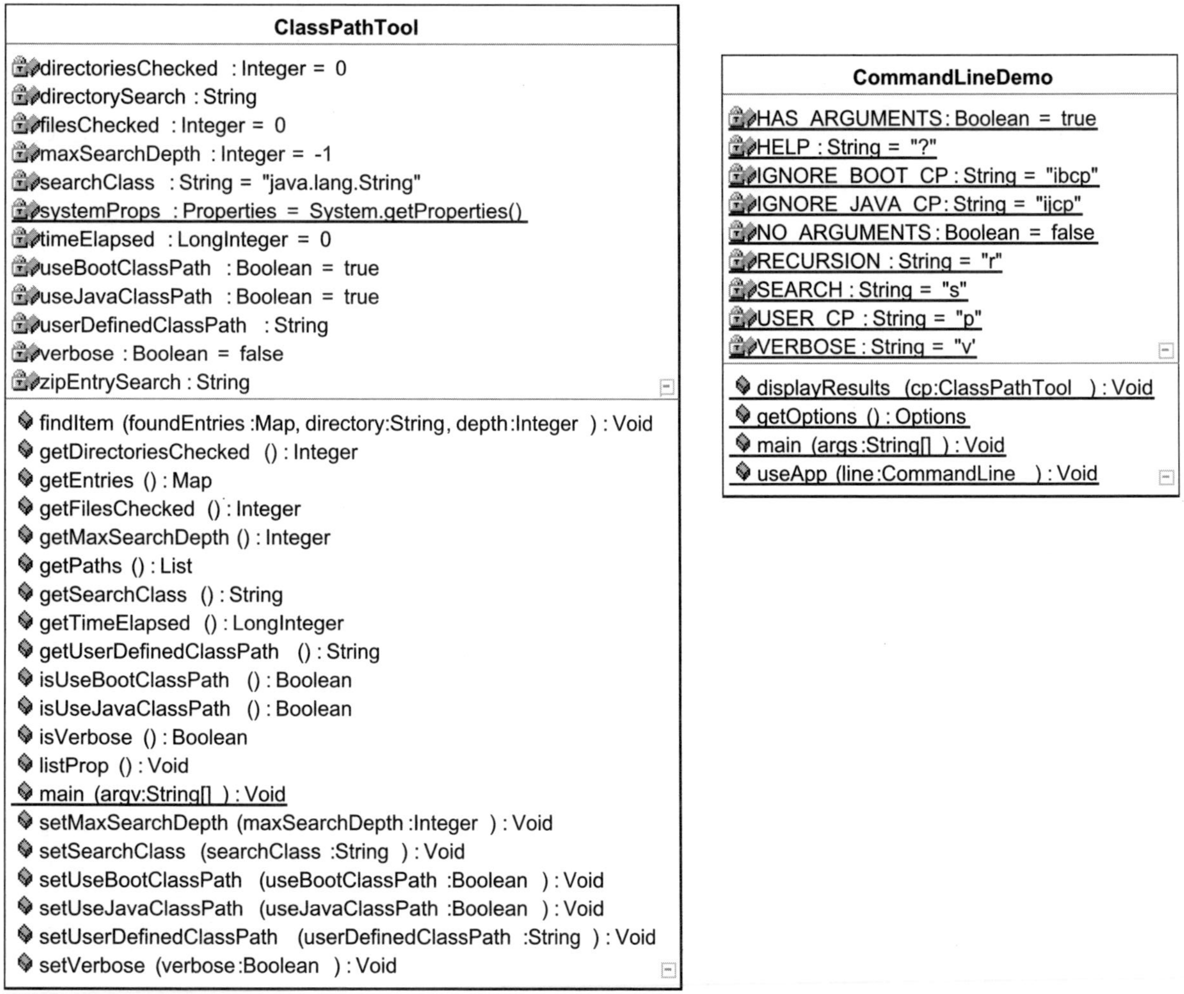

ClassPathTool

- directoriesChecked : Integer = 0
- directorySearch : String
- filesChecked : Integer = 0
- maxSearchDepth : Integer = -1
- searchClass : String = "java.lang.String"
- systemProps : Properties = System.getProperties()
- timeElapsed : LongInteger = 0
- useBootClassPath : Boolean = true
- useJavaClassPath : Boolean = true
- userDefinedClassPath : String
- verbose : Boolean = false
- zipEntrySearch : String

- findItem (foundEntries :Map, directory :String, depth :Integer) : Void
- getDirectoriesChecked () : Integer
- getEntries () : Map
- getFilesChecked () : Integer
- getMaxSearchDepth () : Integer
- getPaths () : List
- getSearchClass () : String
- getTimeElapsed () : LongInteger
- getUserDefinedClassPath () : String
- isUseBootClassPath () : Boolean
- isUseJavaClassPath () : Boolean
- isVerbose () : Boolean
- listProp () : Void
- main (argv:String[]) : Void
- setMaxSearchDepth (maxSearchDepth :Integer) : Void
- setSearchClass (searchClass :String) : Void
- setUseBootClassPath (useBootClassPath :Boolean) : Void
- setUseJavaClassPath (useJavaClassPath :Boolean) : Void
- setUserDefinedClassPath (userDefinedClassPath :String) : Void
- setVerbose (verbose:Boolean) : Void

CommandLineDemo

- HAS_ARGUMENTS : Boolean = true
- HELP : String = "?"
- IGNORE_BOOT_CP : String = "ibcp"
- IGNORE_JAVA_CP : String = "ijcp"
- NO_ARGUMENTS : Boolean = false
- RECURSION : String = "r"
- SEARCH : String = "s"
- USER_CP : String = "p"
- VERBOSE : String = "v"

- displayResults (cp:ClassPathTool) : Void
- getOptions () : Options
- main (args :String[]) : Void
- useApp (line:CommandLine) : Void

Figure 13-1 CLI example overview.

BUILDING A COMMAND-LINE INTERFACE

As shown in the preparation code of `CommandLineDemo` in Listing 13-1, the short versions of the arguments for the command-line application are provided as `String` values. These values are used in several places in the application.

As part of the initialization, the `getOptions()` method returns a configured set of CLI options. These options are used both to parse the incoming arguments as well as generate the output of the "help" documentation displayed upon request or when a user enters incorrect input. Various Option objects are used to configure the various kinds of options—for example, some options are merely off/on switches, whereas others accept an additional argument.

Listing 13-1 CLI Example Initialization

```java
package com.cascadetg.ch13;

import java.util.Iterator;
import java.util.Map;

import org.apache.commons.cli.CommandLine;
import org.apache.commons.cli.HelpFormatter;
import org.apache.commons.cli.MissingArgumentException;
import org.apache.commons.cli.Option;
import org.apache.commons.cli.Options;
import org.apache.commons.cli.PosixParser;
import org.apache.commons.cli.CommandLineParser;
import org.apache.commons.lang.SystemUtils;

public class CommandLineDemo
{

    public static final String VERBOSE = "v";
    public static final String RECURSION = "r";
    public static final String IGNORE_JAVA_CP = "ijcp";
    public static final String IGNORE_BOOT_CP = "ibcp";
    public static final String USER_CP = "p";
    public static final String SEARCH = "s";
    public static final String HELP = "?";

    public static final boolean HAS_ARGUMENTS = true;
    public static final boolean NO_ARGUMENTS = false;

    public static Options getOptions()
    {
        Options myOptions = new Options();

        Option verbose = new Option(VERBOSE, "verbose", NO_ARGUMENTS,
                "Show additional details");

        Option help = new Option(HELP, "help", NO_ARGUMENTS,
                "Show available options");
```

(continues)

Listing 13-1 (continued)

```
        Option recursive = new Option(
                RECURSION,
                "recursion",
                HAS_ARGUMENTS,
         "Search recursively in specified directories. Default (-1) is"
                + " unlimited depth. 0 for no recursion.");
        recursive.setType(Integer.class);
        recursive.setArgName("depth");

        Option ignoreJavaClassPath = new Option(IGNORE_JAVA_CP,
                "ignoreJavaCP", NO_ARGUMENTS,
                "Ignore the system Java class path setting");
        Option ignoreBootClassPath = new Option(IGNORE_BOOT_CP,
                "ignoreBootCP", NO_ARGUMENTS,
                "Ignore the Java boot class path setting");

        Option searchClass = new Option(SEARCH, "search",
                HAS_ARGUMENTS,
                "REQUIRED: The fully qualified class name to find "
                + "(e.g. java.lang.String)");
        searchClass.setArgName("classname");
        searchClass.setType(String.class);

        Option searchDirectory = new Option(USER_CP, "path",
                HAS_ARGUMENTS,
                "Set additional user defined search path[s]");
        searchDirectory.setArgName("path["
                + SystemUtils.PATH_SEPARATOR + "path...]");
        searchDirectory.setType(String.class);

        myOptions.addOption(searchClass);
        myOptions.addOption(verbose);
        myOptions.addOption(recursive);
        myOptions.addOption(ignoreJavaClassPath);
        myOptions.addOption(ignoreBootClassPath);
        myOptions.addOption(searchDirectory);
        myOptions.addOption(help);

        return myOptions;
    }
```

Listing 13-2 shows how the output is generated upon successful configuration and execution of `ClassPathTool`. The returned information is a `Map`, with the key being the path of the located directory or file and the value being the timestamp of the file.

Listing 13-2 CLI Output

```
    public static void displayResults(ClassPathTool cp)
    {
        Map foundEntries = cp.getEntries();

        if (foundEntries.size() > 0)
        {
            System.out.println();
            System.out.println("Found " + cp.getSearchClass()
                    + " at :");
```

(continues)

Listing 13-2 (continued)

```
            Iterator found = foundEntries.keySet().iterator();
            while (found.hasNext())
            {
                Object foundFile = found.next();
                System.out.print("[");
                System.out.print(foundEntries.get(foundFile));
                System.out.print("] ");
                System.out.println(foundFile.toString());
            }
            System.out.println();
            System.out.println("Files checked: "
                    + cp.filesChecked);
            System.out.println("Directories checked: "
                    + cp.directoriesChecked);
            System.out.println("Elapsed time: "
                    + cp.getTimeElapsed() / 1000 + "."
                    + cp.getTimeElapsed() % 1000 + " sec");
        } else
        {
            System.out.println("Unable to find entry.");
        }
    }
```

Listing 13-3 shows how the command-line options parsed by CLI (via the `CommandLine` object) are used to configure the `ClassPathTool` instance. Given that the `CommandLine` object performs the "heavy lifting" of parsing the input, the actual configuration and execution of `ClassPathTool` is quite straightforward.

Listing 13-3 Using CLI to Configure `ClassPathTool`

```
public static void useApp(CommandLine line) throws Exception
{
    if (!line.hasOption(SEARCH))
    {
        throw new MissingArgumentException(
                "No search class specified.");
    } else
    {
        System.out.println("Searching for "
                + line.getOptionValue(SEARCH) + "...");
    }

    ClassPathTool cp = new ClassPathTool();

    cp.setSearchClass(line.getOptionValue(SEARCH));

    if (line.hasOption(RECURSION))
    {
        cp.setMaxSearchDepth(Integer.parseInt(line
                .getOptionValue(RECURSION)));
    }
```

(continues)

Listing 13-3 (continued)

```
        if (line.hasOption(VERBOSE))
            cp.setVerbose(true);

        if (line.hasOption(IGNORE_JAVA_CP))
            cp.setUseJavaClassPath(false);
        if (line.hasOption(IGNORE_BOOT_CP))
            cp.setUseBootClassPath(false);

        if (line.hasOption(USER_CP))
            cp.setUserDefinedClassPath(line
                    .getOptionValue(USER_CP));

        displayResults(cp);
    }
```

Listing 13-4 shows the actual `main()` method and the core process behind the use of CLI. A `CommandLineParser` is created, the options defined in `getOptions` and the command-line arguments are passed to the parser, and assuming no exceptions are thrown, execution proceeds normally. If the user entered `-?` as an option or an exception is thrown, the application prints the help output and terminates. Note that the same options used to configure the parser are used to generate the help information.

Listing 13-4 Running `ClassPathTool` with CLI

```
public static void main(String[] args)
{
    try
    {
        CommandLineParser parser = new PosixParser();
        CommandLine line = parser.parse(getOptions(), args);
        if (line.hasOption("?"))
        {
            HelpFormatter formatter = new HelpFormatter();
            formatter.printHelp("CommandLineDemo",
                    getOptions());
        } else
        {   useApp(line); }
    } catch (Exception e)
    {
        System.out.println("ERROR: " + e.getClass());
        System.out.println(e.getMessage());
        HelpFormatter formatter = new HelpFormatter();
        formatter.printHelp("CommandLineDemo", getOptions());
    }
}
```

RUNNING COMMAND LINE

As shown in Figure 13-2, running the command line with no arguments results in the display of the help text, generated by the options passed to CLI.

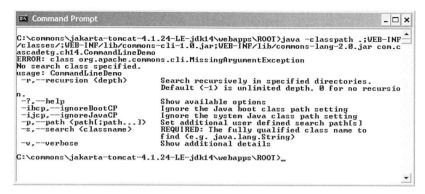

Figure 13-2   Running without arguments.

Passing in a single -s java.lang.String argument, as shown in Figure 13-3, searches the default system class path. As can be seen, the class can be found in the rt.jar file supplied with the JRE.

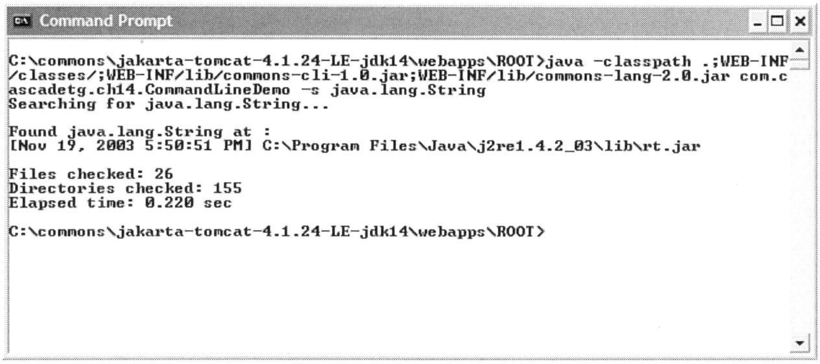

Figure 13-3   A simple search.

As shown in Figure 13-4, a more complex search can be performed by passing -s org.apache.commons.lang.StringUtils -p C:\devenv\ -r 6 as an argument. This searches for all instances of org.apache.commons.lang.StringUtils in the C:\devenv\ directory, with a maximum recursion depth of 6. As can be seen, a number of instances of the Lang library were found on my system. Some of these explicitly contain a reference to the version of the library; several do not. It's easy to imagine running this utility to search the installation of an application server to troubleshoot class path problems.

Figure 13-4 A complex search.

BEHIND THE SCENES WITH CLASSPATHTOOL

Finally, for the sake of completeness, Listing 13-5 shows the source for the class path search routines used by `ClassPathTool`. It is highly recursive, and on systems with symbolic links (such as most UNIX systems), you may want to either change the default maximum search depth or be sure to set the recursion (`-r`) to a non-negative number.

Listing 13-5 Searching for Classes

```
package com.cascadetg.ch13;

import java.io.File;
import java.util.*;
import java.util.zip.*;
```

(continues)

Listing 13-5 (continued)

```java
import org.apache.commons.lang.SystemUtils;

public class ClassPathTool
{
    // Utility values, initialized once
    static Properties systemProps = System.getProperties();

    // Class configuration
    boolean verbose = false;
    boolean useJavaClassPath = true;
    boolean useBootClassPath = true;
    String userDefinedClassPath;
    String searchClass = "java.lang.String";

    // Reporting statistics
    int filesChecked = 0;
    int directoriesChecked = 0;
    long timeElapsed = 0;

    // The maximum recursion depth to check, or -1 for infinite
    int maxSearchDepth = -1;

    // Used during search, the directory version (e.g.
    // \java\lang\String.class
    private String directorySearch;

    // Used during search, the ZIP entry version (e.g.
    // /java/lang/String.class
    private String zipEntrySearch;

    public List getPaths()
    {
        String[] paths = new String[3];
        if (useJavaClassPath)
                paths[0] = System.getProperty("java.class.path");

        if (useBootClassPath)
                paths[1] = System
                        .getProperty("sun.boot.class.path");

        paths[2] = userDefinedClassPath;

        java.util.List results = new LinkedList();
        for (int i = 0; i < 3; i++)
        {
            if (paths[i] != null)
            {
                StringTokenizer myJavaClassPathTokenizer =
new StringTokenizer(
                        paths[i], SystemUtils.PATH_SEPARATOR,
                        false);
                while (myJavaClassPathTokenizer
                    .hasMoreElements())
                        results.add(myJavaClassPathTokenizer
                            .nextElement());
            }
        }

        return results;
    }
```

(continues)

Listing 13-5 (*continued*)

```java
    public void findItem(Map foundEntries, String directory,
            int depth)
    {
        boolean pathIsZip = false;
        if (directory.endsWith(".jar")) pathIsZip = true;
        if (directory.endsWith(".zip")) pathIsZip = true;

        File myFile = new File(directory);

        if (myFile.isDirectory())
        {
            directoriesChecked++;

            File checkLoc = new File(myFile.getPath()
                    + SystemUtils.FILE_SEPARATOR
                    + directorySearch);
            if (checkLoc.exists())
            {
                foundEntries.put(checkLoc.getAbsolutePath(),
                        new java.util.Date(checkLoc
                                .lastModified())
                                .toLocaleString());
            }

            if (maxSearchDepth != 0)
            {
                File[] items = myFile.listFiles();
                for (int i = 0; i < items.length; i++)
                {
                    boolean keepRecursing = true;
                    if (maxSearchDepth != -1)
                        if (depth > maxSearchDepth)
                            keepRecursing = false;
                    if (keepRecursing)
                    {
                        findItem(foundEntries, items[i]
                                .getAbsolutePath(), (depth + 1));
                    }
                }
            }
        }

        if (pathIsZip)
        {
            ZipFile myZip = null;
            try
            {
                if (myFile.exists())
                {
                    filesChecked++;

                    myZip = new ZipFile(myFile,
                            ZipFile.OPEN_READ);
                    ZipEntry myEntry = myZip
                            .getEntry(zipEntrySearch);
                    if (myEntry != null)
                    {
                        foundEntries.put(myZip.getName(),
```

(*continues*)

Listing 13-5 (continued)

```
                                new java.util.Date(myFile
                                        .lastModified())
                                        .toLocaleString());
                }
            }
        } catch (Exception e)
        {
            System.err.print("While opening file: "
                    + directory + " ");
            if (verbose)
            {
                e.printStackTrace();
            } else
            {
                System.err.println(e.getMessage());
            }
        } finally
        {
            try
            {
                if (myZip != null) myZip.close();
            } catch (Exception e)
            {
                // Silent failure.
            }
        }
    }
}

/** Performs the search based on the current settings. */
public java.util.Map getEntries()
{
    long startTime = System.currentTimeMillis();

    HashMap foundEntries = new HashMap();
    Iterator paths = getPaths().iterator();

    directorySearch = searchClass.replace('.',
            SystemUtils.FILE_SEPARATOR.charAt(0));
    directorySearch = directorySearch + ".class";

    zipEntrySearch = searchClass.replace('.', '/');
    zipEntrySearch = zipEntrySearch + ".class";

    while (paths.hasNext())
    {
        String current = (String) paths.next();
        if (verbose)
                System.out
                        .println("Base search: " + current);
        findItem(foundEntries, current, 0);
    }

    timeElapsed = System.currentTimeMillis() - startTime;

    return foundEntries;
}
```

(continues)

Listing 13-5 (*continued*)

```java
    public void listProp()
    {
        Iterator myPropKeys = systemProps.keySet().iterator();
        while (myPropKeys.hasNext())
        {
            String key = myPropKeys.next().toString();
            System.out.print(key);
            System.out.print(":");
            System.out.println(systemProps.getProperty(key));
        }
    }

    public static void main(String[] argv)
    {
        ClassPathTool cp = new ClassPathTool();
        String input = "org.hsqldb.Database";
        cp.setUserDefinedClassPath("C:\\devenv\\");
        cp.setVerbose(false);
        cp.setMaxSearchDepth(4);

        Map foundEntries = cp.getEntries();

        System.out.println("Files checked: " + cp.filesChecked);
        System.out.println("Directories checked: "
                + cp.directoriesChecked);
        System.out.println("Elapsed time: "
                + cp.getTimeElapsed() / 1000 + "."
                + cp.getTimeElapsed() % 1000 + " sec");

        if (foundEntries.size() > 0)
        {
            System.out.println("Found in:");
            Iterator found = foundEntries.keySet().iterator();
            while (found.hasNext())
            {
                Object foundFile = found.next();
                System.out.print(foundFile.toString());
                System.out.print(" [");
                System.out.print(foundEntries.get(foundFile));
                System.out.println("]");
            }
        } else
        {
            System.out.println("Unable to find entry.");
        }
    }

    public boolean isVerbose() { return verbose; }
    public void setVerbose(boolean verbose) { this.verbose = verbose; }
    public String getUserDefinedClassPath()
    { return userDefinedClassPath; }
    public void setUserDefinedClassPath(String userDefinedClassPath)
    { this.userDefinedClassPath = userDefinedClassPath; }

    public String getSearchClass() { return searchClass; }
    public void setSearchClass(String searchClass)
    { this.searchClass = searchClass; }

    public boolean isUseBootClassPath() { return useBootClassPath; }
```

(*continues*)

Listing 13-5 (continued)

```
    public void setUseBootClassPath(boolean useBootClassPath)
    { this.useBootClassPath = useBootClassPath; }

    public boolean isUseJavaClassPath() { return useJavaClassPath; }
    public void setUseJavaClassPath(boolean useJavaClassPath)
    { this.useJavaClassPath = useJavaClassPath; }

    public int getDirectoriesChecked() { return directoriesChecked; }
    public int getFilesChecked() { return filesChecked; }

    public int getMaxSearchDepth() { return maxSearchDepth; }
    public void setMaxSearchDepth(int maxSearchDepth)
    { this.maxSearchDepth = maxSearchDepth; }

    public long getTimeElapsed() { return timeElapsed; }
}
```

Summary

While many applications provide a graphical user interface via Swing or HTML, it's not always the appropriate interface. System administrators in particular often appreciate a command-line interface, as it is easier to work into a scripting environment or via a remote login (such as SSH). By building an application using the CLI package, system administrators will find your software to be easier to use.

Project Ideas

How hard is it to convert an existing Swing application to support a command-line interface? Instead of accepting arguments via `main()`, try adding a command-line text box to a Swing application. Is this interactive application easier to use? How about speed of command entry?

CHAPTER **14**

Other Projects

In addition to the projects described in this book, a variety of Commons projects, both proper and sandbox, are available for further exploration.

ADDITIONAL COMMONS PROPER PROJECTS

The Commons proper projects not described in detail in this book are described in a bit more detail in the following. For more information on these packages, visit the `http://jakarta.apache.org/commons/` web site.

Betwixt

Services for mapping JavaBeans to XML documents, and vice versa. Intended for use when a JavaBean wants to be serialized to XML. Note that JDK 1.4 introduced long-term serialization-to-XML capability (`http://java.sun.com/j2se/1.4.2/docs/guide/beans/changes14.html`).

Chain

Provides a "Chain of Responsibility" pattern implementation for organizing complex processing flows. As of this writing, despite the status as a proper package (not sandbox), there have been no official releases.

Configuration

Tools to assist in the reading of configuration/preferences files in various formats. Allows for configuration information from Properties files, XML documents, JNDI, and JDBC data sources to be accessed in a unified manner.

Daemon

An alternative invocation mechanism for UNIX-daemon-like Java code. Specifically, this project contains native code for receiving system status notifications from the operating system for both UNIX and Windows. If you are writing server code and are interested in this project, you may also be interested in the JDesktop Integration Components (JDIC), https://jdic.dev.java.net/.

DbUtils

JDBC helper library that factors out mundane resource cleanup code for common database tasks. DbUtils is intended to remove the drudgery of raw JDBC, but it is not an object/relational database package. It is simply a helper library.

Digester

An XML-to-Java-object mapping utility commonly used for parsing XML configuration files. Intended to serve as a common framework for dealing with large configuration files; for many application developers, starting with a generic XML library (such as JDOM, http://www.jdom.org/) may be more appropriate.

Discovery

Provides tools for locating resources (including classes) by mapping service/reference names to resource names using a variety of schemes. It is only at a 0.2 release.

EL

An interpreter for the Expression Language defined by the JavaServer Pages™ specification, version 2.0. This might be useful as a scripting language to be embedded in certain applications.

IO

Collection of I/O utilities, including stream implementations, file filters, and endian classes. The `org.apache.commons.io.CopyUtils` class contains a comprehensive set of static methods for copying from a `String`, `byte[]`, `InputStream`, or `Reader` to an `OutputStream` or `Writer`. Similarly, the `org.apache.commons.io.IOUtils` class contains additional tools for safely closing streams and creating `String` and byte arrays from streams and readers. The `org.apache.commons.io.FileUtils` class contains methods for retrieving different components of a file path (directory name, file base name, file extension), methods for copying files to other files and directories, and methods for querying, deleting, and cleaning directories. Additional classes provide filters for use with `FileDialog`, or for converting the endian ordering of bytes.

Jelly

XML-based scripting and processing engine. While Jelly has found some success in projects such as Maven, the general consensus is that XML is a poor choice for a programming language—even the creator of Jelly apologized at http://radio.weblogs.com/0112098/2004/03/26.html#a472.

Jexl

An expression language that extends the Expression Language of the JSTL. Note that this package is not compatible with JSTL or JSP—it is a nonstandard expression language.

Latka

An HTTP functional testing suite for automated QA, acceptance, and regression testing. XML is used to define HTTP(S) requests and validation tests.

Launcher

Cross-platform Java application launcher. Eliminates the need for a batch or shell script to launch a Java class. Originally developed for Tomcat, it allows for complex configurations of class path and system properties.

Math

Library of lightweight, self-contained mathematics and statistics components addressing the common practical problems not immediately available in the Java programming language. This includes basic statistics and linear equation support.

Modeler

Provides mechanisms to create Model MBeans compatible with the Java Management Extensions (JMX) specification. If you wish to expose management of your application via JMX, you will likely want to investigate this package.

Primitives

Smaller, faster, and easier to work with types supporting Java primitive types, with an emphasis on collections. The provided collection of types and utilities is optimized for working with Java primitives (`boolean`, `byte`, `char`, `double`, `float`, `int`, `long`, `short`).

Validator

Simple, extendable framework to define validation methods and validation rules in an XML file. Supports internationalization of rules and error messages. Includes basic validation rules for credit card numbers, dates, email addresses, and URLs.

SANDBOX PROJECTS

The sandbox projects, generally speaking, are not as stable or popular as the proper projects. You should expect both functionality and interfaces to change. Virtually all of the sandbox projects have not released official binary or source releases—expect to use CVS to access the latest source.

Attributes

Attributes provides a runtime API to metadata attributes such as doclet tags, inspired by the Nanning and XRAI projects, as well as JSR 175 and C# attributes. Values may be specified in code using a @@ symbol, similar to Java 5.0 (aka JDK 1.5) annotations as specified by JSR 175 (http://www.jcp.org/en/jsr/detail?id=175) or XDoclet (http://xdoclet.sourceforge.net/). The Attributes package will parse your source files and generate Java source files corresponding to the attributes.

Cache

Cache provides object-caching services. As of this writing, this project has not released any official binary builds.

Clazz

Clazz focuses on introspection and class manipulation. As of this writing, this project has not released any official binary builds.

Compress

Commons Compress defines an API for working with tar, zip, and bzip2 files. The JDK offers built-in support for ZIP files, and while this project has not released any official binary builds as of this writing, you may want to investigate the CVS repository if you need access to tar or bzip2 files.

Convert

Convert aims to provide a single library dedicated to the task of converting an object of one type to another. No official binary builds have been released.

Email

Email provides a simple library for sending email from Java. It aims to simplify certain tasks on top of the JavaMail API (http://java.sun.com/products/javamail/), in particular multipart email and HTML email with embedded images. No official binary builds have been released.

Events

Events provides additional classes for firing and handling events. It focuses on the Java Collections Framework, providing decorators to other collections that fire events. No official binary builds have been released.

FeedParser

Generic FeedParser interface and concrete implementations for Atom, FOAF, OPML and RSS. No official binary builds have been released.

Functor

A functor is a function that can be manipulated as an object, or an object representing a single, generic function. While this package has not released any official binary releases, additional information on functors is available as part of the Collections package.

Id

Id is a component used to generate unique identifiers, including numeric, long, session, alphanumeric, and UUID identifiers. No official binary releases.

JJar

Jakarta JAR Archive Repository. An attempt to build a single online repository to access binaries for various projects. For example, you might want to distribute an Ant task that will automatically download a required library if it's not present. Therefore, this project does not represent a particular lump of code so much as a common point for downloading other Jakarta projects.

This project is largely considered superseded by the Apache Depot project (http://incubator.apache.org/depot/).

Mapper

Mapper is a thin abstraction layer around a project's chosen data mapping technology (a.k.a. DAO pattern). It purports to isolate an application from the underlying persistence store—it is unclear how effective this is in practice.

Messenger

Messenger is an easy to use and lightweight framework for working with JMS in the web tier. Intended to put a friendly face on JMS, it also can serve as a bridge between two different JMS engines.

Resources

Resources provides a lightweight framework for defining and looking up internationalized message strings keyed by a `java.util.Locale` and a message key.

Scaffold

Scaffold is a toolkit for building web applications. As of this writing, it consists of a variety of loosely coupled utility methods.

SQL

Commons SQL is a component for working with databases and generating DDL. It contains a simple set of beans that represent a relational database schema such as a Database, Table, Column, etc. It even allows for simple mappings of a table to objects. Most projects will likely want to adopt a more robust object/relational package.

ThreadPool

ThreadPool is a simple component for asynchronously dispatching work to another thread in a pool for simple multithreaded programming. This project has largely been superseded by the `util.concurrency` package available at http://gee.cs.oswego.edu/dl and included in Java 2 5.0 (a.k.a. JDK 1.5).

Transaction

Transaction provides a set of utility classes for transactional data structures, locks, and a transactional file system. Of particular interest is support for decorating a Map to render it capable of transactional behavior (with an optional interface to plug in to a JCA implementation and participate in distributed JTA transactions). A locking package and transactional file system wrapper are also provided.

VFS

VFS is a Virtual File System component for treating various file systems as a single logical file system. File systems supported include CIFS, FTP, local files, HTTP/HTTPS, SFTP, temporary files, WebDAV, ZIP, and JAR.

Workflow

Workflow provides a framework for building workflow management systems in XML. No official binary releases have been produced.

SUMMARY

The Apache Jakarta Commons project is a unique repository of open source Java components. As you take advantage of the Commons, keep in mind the hard work that has gone into developing and maintaining this software. The Apache license represents one of the least selfish approaches toward software in the world, and this is repaid in tremendous goodwill and respect. If you can, consider donating some of your own time to this project. Download the source via CVS, participate on the mailing lists, and contribute code. Learn, listen, and comment with grace, and you will be repaid many times over.

APPENDIX A

Lang Reference

This appendix provides a summary of the javadoc for a subset of the most commonly used portions of the Commons Lang package. This includes all of the classes in the `org.apache.commons.lang.*` package and `org.apache.commons.lang.time.*` package.

ORG.APACHE.COMMONS.LANG

ArrayUtils

Operations on arrays, primitive arrays (like `int[]`) and primitive wrapper arrays (like `Integer[]`).

BitField

Operations on bit-mapped fields.

BooleanUtils

Operations on `boolean` primitives and `Boolean` objects.

CharRange

A contiguous range of characters, optionally negated.

CharSet

A set of characters.

CharSetUtils

Operations on `CharSets`.

ClassUtils

Operates on classes without using reflection.

ObjectUtils

Operations on `Object`.

ObjectUtils.Null

Class used as a `null` placeholder where `null` has another meaning.

RandomStringUtils

Operations for random strings.

SerializationUtils

Assists with the serialization process and performs additional functionality based on serialization.

StringEscapeUtils

Escapes and unescapes strings for Java, Java Script, HTML, XML, and SQL.

StringUtils

Operations on `String` that are `null` safe.

SystemUtils

Helpers for `java.lang.System`.

Validate

Assists in validating arguments.

WordUtils

Operations on strings that contain words.

ORG.APACHE.COMMONS.LANG.ARRAYUTILS

Operations on arrays, primitive arrays (like `int[]`), and primitive wrapper arrays (like `Integer[]`).

This class tries to handle `null` input gracefully. An exception will not be thrown for a `null` array input. However, an object array that contains a `null` element may throw an exception. Each method documents its behavior.

```
public static final java.lang.Object[] EMPTY_OBJECT_ARRAY
```

An empty immutable `Object` array.

```
public static final java.lang.Class[] EMPTY_CLASS_ARRAY
```

An empty immutable `Class` array.

```
public static final java.lang.String[] EMPTY_STRING_ARRAY
```

An empty immutable `String` array.

```
public static final long[] EMPTY_LONG_ARRAY
```

An empty immutable `long` array.

```
public static final java.lang.Long[] EMPTY_LONG_OBJECT_ARRAY
```

An empty immutable `Long` array.

```
public static final int[] EMPTY_INT_ARRAY
```

An empty immutable `int` array.

```
public static final java.lang.Integer[] EMPTY_INTEGER_OBJECT_ARRAY
```

An empty immutable `Integer` array.

```
public static final short[] EMPTY_SHORT_ARRAY
```

An empty immutable `short` array.

```
public static final java.lang.Short[] EMPTY_SHORT_OBJECT_ARRAY
```

An empty immutable `Short` array.

```
public static final byte[] EMPTY_BYTE_ARRAY
```

An empty immutable `byte` array.

```
public static final java.lang.Byte[] EMPTY_BYTE_OBJECT_ARRAY
```

An empty immutable `Byte` array.

```
public static final double[] EMPTY_DOUBLE_ARRAY
```

An empty immutable `double` array.

```
public static final java.lang.Double[] EMPTY_DOUBLE_OBJECT_ARRAY
```

An empty immutable `Double` array.

```
public static final float[] EMPTY_FLOAT_ARRAY
```

An empty immutable `float` array.

```
static final java.lang.Float[] EMPTY_FLOAT_OBJECT_ARRAY
```

An empty immutable `Float` array.

```
public static final boolean[] EMPTY_BOOLEAN_ARRAY
```

An empty immutable `boolean` array.

```
public static final java.lang.Boolean[] EMPTY_BOOLEAN_OBJECT_ARRAY
```

An empty immutable `Boolean` array.

```
public static final char[] EMPTY_CHAR_ARRAY
```

An empty immutable `char` array.

```
public static final java.lang.Character[] EMPTY_CHARACTER_OBJECT_ARRAY
```

An empty immutable `Character` array.

Constructor Detail

```
public ArrayUtils()
```

ArrayUtils instances should NOT be constructed in standard programming. Instead, the class should be used as `ArrayUtils.clone(new int[] {2})`. This constructor is public to permit tools that require a JavaBean instance to operate.

Method Detail

```
public static java.lang.String toString(java.lang.Object array)
```

Outputs an array as a `String`, treating `null` as an empty array. Multi-dimensional arrays are handled correctly, including multi-dimensional primitive arrays. The format is that of Java source code, for example {a,b}.

Parameters: `array`—the array to get a `toString` for, may be `null`
Returns: a `String` representation of the array, '{}' if `null` array input

```
public static java.lang.String toString(java.lang.Object array,
java.lang.String stringIfNull)
```

Outputs an array as a `String` handling `null`s. Multi-dimensional arrays are handled correctly, including multi-dimensional primitive arrays. The format is that of Java source code, for example `{a,b}`.

> **Parameters:** `array`—the array to get a `toString` for, may be `null`
> `stringIfNull`—the `String` to return if the array is `null`
> **Returns:** a `String` representation of the array

```
public static int hashCode(java.lang.Object array)
```

Get a hashCode for an array handling multi-dimensional arrays correctly. Multi-dimensional primitive arrays are also handled correctly by this method.

> **Parameters:** `array`—the array to get a hashCode for, may be `null`
> **Returns:** a hashCode for the array, zero if `null` array input

```
public static boolean isEquals(java.lang.Object array1,
                               java.lang.Object array2)
```

Compares two arrays, using equals(), handling multi-dimensional arrays correctly. Multi-dimensional primitive arrays are also handled correctly by this method.

> **Parameters:** `array1`—the array to get a hashCode for, may be `null`
> `array2`—the array to get a hashCode for, may be `null`
> **Returns:** `true` if the arrays are equal

```
public static java.util.Map toMap(java.lang.Object[] array)
```

Converts the given array into a `Map`. Each element of the array must be either a `Map.Entry` or an array, containing at least two elements, where the first element is used as key and the second as value.

This method can be used to initialize:

```
// Create a Map mapping colors.
Map colorMap = MapUtils.toMap(new String[][] {{
{"RED", "#FF0000"}, {"GREEN", "#00FF00"}, {"BLUE", "#0000FF"}});
```

This method returns `null` if `null` array input.

> **Parameters:** `array`—an array whose elements are either a `Map.Entry` or an array containing at least two elements, may be `null`
> **Returns:** a `Map` that was created from the array
> **Throws:** `java.lang.IllegalArgumentException`—if one element of this array is itself an array containing less then two elements
> `java.lang.IllegalArgumentException`—if the array contains elements other than `Map.Entry` and an array

```
public static java.lang.Object[] clone(java.lang.Object[] array)
```

Shallow clones an array returning a typecast result and handling `null`. The objects in the array are not cloned; thus there is no special handling for multi-dimensional arrays. This method returns `null` if `null` array input.

Parameters: `array`—the array to shallow clone, may be `null`
Returns: the cloned array, `null` if `null` input

```
public static long[] clone(long[] array)
```

Clones an array returning a typecast result and handling `null`. This method returns `null` if `null` array input.

Parameters: `array`—the array to clone, may be `null`
Returns: the cloned array, `null` if `null` input

```
public static int[] clone(int[] array)
```

Clones an array returning a typecast result and handling `null`. This method returns `null` if `null` array input.

Parameters: `array`—the array to clone, may be `null`
Returns: the cloned array, `null` if `null` input

```
public static short[] clone(short[] array)
```

Clones an array returning a typecast result and handling `null`. This method returns `null` if `null` array input.

Parameters: `array`—the array to clone, may be `null`
Returns: the cloned array, `null` if `null` input

```
public static char[] clone(char[] array)
```

Clones an array returning a typecast result and handling `null`. This method returns `null` if `null` array input.

Parameters: `array`—the array to clone, may be `null`
Returns: the cloned array, `null` if `null` input

```
public static byte[] clone(byte[] array)
```

Clones an array returning a typecast result and handling `null`. This method returns `null` if `null` array input.

Parameters: `array`—the array to clone, may be `null`
Returns: the cloned array, `null` if `null` input

```
public static double[] clone(double[] array)
```

Clones an array returning a typecast result and handling `null`. This method returns `null` if `null` array input.

Parameters: `array`—the array to clone, may be `null`
Returns: the cloned array, `null` if `null` input

```
public static float[] clone(float[] array)
```

Clones an array returning a typecast result and handling `null`. This method returns `null` if `null` array input.

Parameters: `array`—the array to clone, may be `null`
Returns: the cloned array, `null` if `null` input

```
public static boolean[] clone(boolean[] array)
```

Clones an array returning a typecast result and handling `null`. This method returns `null` if `null` array input.

Parameters: `array`—the array to clone, may be `null`
Returns: the cloned array, `null` if `null` input

```
public static boolean isSameLength(java.lang.Object[] array1,
java.lang.Object[] array2)
```

Checks whether two arrays are the same length, treating `null` arrays as length 0. Any multi-dimensional aspects of the arrays are ignored.

Parameters: `array1`—the first array, may be `null`
`array2`—the second array, may be `null`
Returns: `true` if length of arrays matches, treating `null` as an empty array

```
public static boolean isSameLength(long[] array1, long[] array2)
```

Checks whether two arrays are the same length, treating `null` arrays as length 0.

Parameters: `array1`—the first array, may be `null`
`array2`—the second array, may be `null`
Returns: `true` if length of arrays matches, treating `null` as an empty array

```
public static boolean isSameLength(int[] array1, int[] array2)
```

Checks whether two arrays are the same length, treating `null` arrays as length 0.

Parameters: `array1`—the first array, may be `null`
`array2`—the second array, may be `null`
Returns: `true` if length of arrays matches, treating `null` as an empty array

```
public static boolean isSameLength(short[] array1, short[] array2)
```

Checks whether two arrays are the same length, treating `null` arrays as length 0.

Parameters: `array1`—the first array, may be `null`
`array2`—the second array, may be `null`
Returns: `true` if length of arrays matches, treating `null` as an empty array

```
public static boolean isSameLength(char[] array1, char[] array2)
```

Checks whether two arrays are the same length, treating `null` arrays as length 0.

Parameters: `array1`—the first array, may be `null`
`array2`—the second array, may be `null`
Returns: `true` if length of arrays matches, treating `null` as an empty array

```
public static boolean isSameLength(byte[] array1, byte[] array2)
```

Checks whether two arrays are the same length, treating `null` arrays as length 0.

Parameters: `array1`—the first array, may be `null`
`array2`—the second array, may be `null`
Returns: `true` if length of arrays matches, treating `null` as an empty array

```
public static boolean isSameLength(double[] array1, double[] array2)
```

Checks whether two arrays are the same length, treating `null` arrays as length 0.

Parameters: `array1`—the first array, may be `null`
`array2`—the second array, may be `null`
Returns: `true` if length of arrays matches, treating `null` as an empty array

```
public static boolean isSameLength(float[] array1, float[] array2)
```

Checks whether two arrays are the same length, treating `null` arrays as length 0.

Parameters: `array1`—the first array, may be `null`
`array2`—the second array, may be `null`
Returns: `true` if length of arrays matches, treating `null` as an empty array

```
public static boolean isSameLength(boolean[] array1, boolean[] array2)
```

Checks whether two arrays are the same length, treating `null` arrays as length 0.

> **Parameters:** `array1`—the first array, may be `null`
> `array2`—the second array, may be `null`
> **Returns:** `true` if length of arrays matches, treating `null` as an empty array

```
public static boolean isSameType(java.lang.Object array1,
java.lang.Object array2)
```

Checks whether two arrays are the same type, taking into account multi-dimensional arrays.

> **Parameters:** `array1`—the first array, must not be `null`
> `array2`—the second array, must not be `null`
> **Returns:** `true` if type of arrays matches
> **Throws:** `java.lang.IllegalArgumentException`—if either array is `null`

```
public static void reverse(java.lang.Object[] array)
```

Reverses the order of the given array. There is no special handling for multi-dimensional arrays. This method does nothing if `null` array input.

> **Parameters:** `array`—the array to reverse, may be `null`

```
public static void reverse(long[] array)
```

Reverses the order of the given array. This method does nothing if `null` array input.

> **Parameters:** `array`—the array to reverse, may be `null`

```
public static void reverse(int[] array)
```

Reverses the order of the given array. This method does nothing if `null` array input.

> **Parameters:** `array`—the array to reverse, may be `null`

```
public static void reverse(short[] array)
```

Reverses the order of the given array. This method does nothing if `null` array input.

> **Parameters:** `array`—the array to reverse, may be `null`

```
public static void reverse(char[] array)
```

Reverses the order of the given array. This method does nothing if `null` array input.

Parameters: array—the array to reverse, may be null

```
public static void reverse(byte[] array)
```

Reverses the order of the given array. This method does nothing if null array input.

Parameters: array—the array to reverse, may be null

```
public static void reverse(double[] array)
```

Reverses the order of the given array. This method does nothing if null array input.

Parameters: array—the array to reverse, may be null

```
public static void reverse(float[] array)
```

Reverses the order of the given array. This method does nothing if null array input.

Parameters: array—the array to reverse, may be null

```
public static void reverse(boolean[] array)
```

Reverses the order of the given array. This method does nothing if null array input.

Parameters: array—the array to reverse, may be null

```
public static int indexOf(java.lang.Object[] array, java.lang.Object
    objectToFind)
```

Find the index of the given object in the array. This method returns -1 if null array input.

Parameters: array—the array to search through for the object, may be null

objectToFind—the object to find, may be null

Returns: the index of the object within the array, -1 if not found or null array input

```
public static int indexOf(java.lang.Object[] array, java.lang.Object
    objectToFind, int startIndex)
```

Find the index of the given object in the array starting at the given index. This method returns -1 if null array input. A negative startIndex is treated as zero. A startIndex larger than the array length will return -1.

Parameters: array—the array to search through for the object, may be null

objectToFind—the object to find, may be null

startIndex—the index to start searching at

Returns: the index of the object within the array starting at the index, -1 if not found or `null` array input

```
public static int lastIndexOf(java.lang.Object[] array,
java.lang.Object objectToFind)
```

Find the last index of the given object within the array. This method returns -1 if `null` array input.

Parameters: `array`—the array to traverse backward looking for the object, may be `null`

`objectToFind`—the object to find, may be `null`

Returns: the last index of the object within the array, -1 if not found or `null` array input

```
public static int lastIndexOf(java.lang.Object[] array,
java.lang.Object objectToFind, int startIndex)
```

Find the last index of the given object in the array starting at the given index. This method returns -1 if `null` array input. A negative `startIndex` will return -1. A `startIndex` larger than the array length will search from the end of the array.

Parameters: `array`—the array to traverse looking for the object, may be `null`

`objectToFind`—the object to find, may be `null`

`startIndex`—the start index to traverse backward from

Returns: the last index of the object within the array, -1 if not found or `null` array input

```
public static boolean contains(java.lang.Object[] array,
java.lang.Object objectToFind)
```

Checks if the object is in the given array. The method returns false if a `null` array is passed in.

Parameters: `array`—the array to search through

`objectToFind`—the object to find

Returns: `true` if the array contains the object

```
public static int indexOf(long[] array, long valueToFind)
```

Find the index of the given value in the array. This method returns -1 if `null` array input.

Parameters: `array`—the array to search through for the object, may be `null`

`valueToFind`—the value to find

Returns: the index of the value within the array, -1 if not found or `null` array input

```
public static int indexOf(long[] array, long valueToFind, int
startIndex)
```

Find the index of the given value in the array starting at the given index. This method returns -1 if `null` array input. A negative `startIndex` is treated as zero. A `startIndex` larger than the array length will return -1.

Parameters: `array`—the array to search through for the object, may be `null`
  `valueToFind`—the value to find
  `startIndex`—the index to start searching at
Returns: the index of the value within the array, `-1` if not found or `null` array input

```
public static int lastIndexOf(long[] array, long valueToFind)
```

Find the last index of the given value within the array. This method returns -1 if `null` array input.

Parameters: `array`—the array to traverse backward looking for the object, may be `null`
  `valueToFind`—the object to find
Returns: the last index of the value within the array, `-1` if not found or `null` array input

```
public static int lastIndexOf(long[] array, long valueToFind, int startIndex)
```

Find the last index of the given value in the array starting at the given index. This method returns -1 if `null` array input. A negative `startIndex` will return -1. A `startIndex` larger than the array length will search from the end of the array.

Parameters: `array`—the array to traverse looking for the object, may be `null`
  `valueToFind`—the value to find
  `startIndex`—the start index to traverse backward from
Returns: the last index of the value within the array, `-1` if not found or `null` array input

```
public static boolean contains(long[] array, long valueToFind)
```

Checks if the value is in the given array. The method returns false if a `null` array is passed in.

Parameters: `array`—the array to search through
  `valueToFind`—the value to find
Returns: `true` if the array contains the object

```
public static int indexOf(int[] array, int valueToFind)
```

Find the index of the given value in the array. This method returns -1 if `null` array input.

Parameters: `array`—the array to search through for the object, may be `null`

`valueToFind`—the value to find

Returns: the index of the value within the array, -1 if not found or `null` array input

```
public static int indexOf(int[] array, int valueToFind, int
startIndex)
```

Find the index of the given value in the array starting at the given index. This method returns -1 if `null` array input. A negative `startIndex` is treated as zero. A `startIndex` larger than the array length will return -1.

Parameters: `array`—the array to search through for the object, may be `null`

`valueToFind`—the value to find

`startIndex`—the index to start searching at

Returns: the index of the value within the array, -1 if not found or `null` array input

```
public static int lastIndexOf(int[] array, int valueToFind)
```

Find the last index of the given value within the array. This method returns -1 if `null` array input.

Parameters: `array`—the array to traverse backward looking for the object, may be `null`

`valueToFind`—the object to find

Returns: the last index of the value within the array, -1 if not found or `null` array input

```
public static int lastIndexOf(int[] array, int valueToFind, int
startIndex)
```

Find the last index of the given value in the array starting at the given index. This method returns -1 if `null` array input. A negative `startIndex` will return -1. A `startIndex` larger than the array length will search from the end of the array.

Parameters: `array`—the array to traverse looking for the object, may be `null`

`valueToFind`—the value to find

`startIndex`—the start index to traverse backward from

Returns: the last index of the value within the array, -1 if not found or `null` array input

```
public static boolean contains(int[] array, int valueToFind)
```

Checks if the value is in the given array. The method returns false if a `null` array is passed in.

Parameters: `array`—the array to search through

`valueToFind`—the value to find
Returns: `true` if the array contains the object

```
public static int indexOf(short[] array, short valueToFind)
```

Find the index of the given value in the array. This method returns -1 if `null` array input.

Parameters: `array`—the array to search through for the object, may be `null`
`valueToFind`—the value to find
Returns: the index of the value within the array, `-1` if not found or `null` array input

```
public static int indexOf(short[] array, short valueToFind, int startIndex)
```

Find the index of the given value in the array starting at the given index. This method returns -1 if `null` array input. A negative `startIndex` is treated as zero. A `startIndex` larger than the array length will return -1.

Parameters: `array`—the array to search through for the object, may be `null`
`valueToFind`—the value to find
`startIndex`—the index to start searching at
Returns: the index of the value within the array, `-1` if not found or `null` array input

```
public static int lastIndexOf(short[] array, short valueToFind)
```

Find the last index of the given value within the array. This method returns -1 if `null` array input.

Parameters: `array`—the array to traverse backward looking for the object, may be `null`
`valueToFind`—the object to find
Returns: the last index of the value within the array, `-1` if not found or `null` array input

```
public static int lastIndexOf(short[] array, short valueToFind, int startIndex)
```

Find the last index of the given value in the array starting at the given index. This method returns -1 if `null` array input. A negative `startIndex` will return -1. A `startIndex` larger than the array length will search from the end of the array.

Parameters: `array`—the array to traverse looking for the object, may be `null`
`valueToFind`—the value to find
`startIndex`—the start index to traverse backward from

Returns: the last index of the value within the array, -1 if not found or `null` array input

```
public static boolean contains(short[] array, short valueToFind)
```

Checks if the value is in the given array. The method returns false if a `null` array is passed in.

> **Parameters:** `array`—the array to search through
> `valueToFind`—the value to find
> **Returns:** `true` if the array contains the object

```
public static int indexOf(byte[] array, byte valueToFind)
```

Find the index of the given value in the array. This method returns -1 if `null` array input.

> **Parameters:** `array`—the array to search through for the object, may be `null`
> `valueToFind`—the value to find
> **Returns:** the index of the value within the array, -1 if not found or `null` array input

```
public static int indexOf(byte[] array, byte valueToFind, int
startIndex)
```

Find the index of the given value in the array starting at the given index. This method returns -1 if `null` array input. A negative `startIndex` is treated as zero. A `startIndex` larger than the array length will return -1.

> **Parameters:** `array`—the array to search through for the object, may be `null`
> `valueToFind`—the value to find
> `startIndex`—the index to start searching at
> **Returns:** the index of the value within the array, -1 if not found or `null` array input

```
public static int lastIndexOf(byte[] array, byte valueToFind)
```

Find the last index of the given value within the array. This method returns -1 if `null` array input.

> **Parameters:** `array`—the array to traverse backward looking for the object, may be `null`
> `valueToFind`—the object to find
> **Returns:** the last index of the value within the array, -1 if not found or `null` array input

```
public static int lastIndexOf(byte[] array, byte valueToFind, int
startIndex)
```

Find the last index of the given value in the array starting at the given index. This method returns -1 if `null` array input. A negative `startIndex` will return -1. A `startIndex` larger than the array length will search from the end of the array.

Parameters: `array`—the array to traverse looking for the object, may be `null`
    `valueToFind`—the value to find
    `startIndex`—the start index to traverse backward from
Returns: the last index of the value within the array, `-1` if not found or `null` array input

```
public static boolean contains(byte[] array, byte valueToFind)
```

Checks if the value is in the given array. The method returns false if a `null` array is passed in.

Parameters: `array`—the array to search through
    `valueToFind`—the value to find
Returns: `true` if the array contains the object

```
public static int indexOf(double[] array, double valueToFind)
```

Find the index of the given value in the array. This method returns -1 if `null` array input.

Parameters: `array`—the array to search through for the object, may be `null`
    `valueToFind`—the value to find
Returns: the index of the value within the array, `-1` if not found or `null` array input

```
public static int indexOf(double[] array, double valueToFind, double
    tolerance)
```

Find the index of the given value within a given tolerance in the array. This method will return the index of the first value which falls between the region defined by `valueToFind - tolerance` and `valueToFind + tolerance`. This method returns -1 if `null` array input.

Parameters: `array`—the array to search through for the object, may be `null`
    `valueToFind`—the value to find
    `tolerance`—tolerance of the search
Returns: the index of the value within the array, `-1` if not found or `null` array input

```
public static int indexOf(double[] array, double valueToFind, int
    startIndex)
```

Find the index of the given value in the array starting at the given index. This method returns -1 if `null` array input. A negative `startIndex` is treated as zero. A `startIndex` larger than the array length will return -1.

Parameters: `array`—the array to search through for the object, may be `null`
    `valueToFind`—the value to find
    `startIndex`—the index to start searching at
Returns: the index of the value within the array, -1 if not found or `null` array input

```
public static int indexOf(double[] array, double valueToFind, int
startIndex, double tolerance)
```

Find the index of the given value in the array starting at the given index. This method will return the index of the first value which falls between the region defined by `valueToFind - tolerance` and `valueToFind + tolerance`. This method returns -1 if `null` array input. A negative `startIndex` is treated as zero. A `startIndex` larger than the array length will return -1.

Parameters: `array`—the array to search through for the object, may be `null`
    `valueToFind`—the value to find
    `startIndex`—the index to start searching at
    `tolerance`—tolerance of the search
Returns: the index of the value within the array, -1 if not found or `null` array input

```
public static int lastIndexOf(double[] array, double valueToFind)
```

Find the last index of the given value within the array. This method returns -1 if `null` array input.

Parameters: `array`—the array to traverse backward looking for the object, may be `null`
    `valueToFind`—the object to find
Returns: the last index of the value within the array, -1 if not found or `null` array input

```
public static int lastIndexOf(double[] array, double valueToFind,
double tolerance)
```

Find the last index of the given value within a given tolerance in the array. This method will return the index of the last value which falls between the region defined by `valueToFind - tolerance` and `valueToFind + tolerance`. This method returns -1 if `null` array input.

Parameters: `array`—the array to search through for the object, may be `null`

valueToFind—the value to find
tolerance—tolerance of the search
Returns: the index of the value within the array, -1 if not found or `null` array input

```
public static int lastIndexOf(double[] array, double valueToFind, int startIndex)
```

Find the last index of the given value in the array starting at the given index. This method returns -1 if `null` array input. A negative `startIndex` will return -1. A `startIndex` larger than the array length will search from the end of the array.

Parameters: array—the array to traverse looking for the object, may be `null`
valueToFind—the value to find
startIndex—the start index to traverse backward from
Returns: the last index of the value within the array, -1 if not found or `null` array input

```
public static int lastIndexOf(double[] array, double valueToFind,
    int startIndex, double tolerance)
```

Find the last index of the given value in the array starting at the given index. This method will return the index of the last value which falls between the region defined by `valueToFind - tolerance` and `valueToFind + tolerance`. This method returns -1 if `null` array input. A negative `startIndex` will return -1. A `startIndex` larger than the array length will search from the end of the array.

Parameters: array—the array to traverse looking for the object, may be `null`
valueToFind—the value to find
startIndex—the start index to traverse backward from
tolerance—search for value within plus/minus this amount
Returns: the last index of the value within the array, -1 if not found or `null` array input

```
public static boolean contains(double[] array, double valueToFind)
```

Checks if the value is in the given array. The method returns false if a `null` array is passed in.

Parameters: array—the array to search through
valueToFind—the value to find
Returns: `true` if the array contains the object

```
public static boolean contains(double[] array, double valueToFind,
    double tolerance)
```

Checks if a value falling within the given tolerance is in the given array. If the array contains a value within the inclusive range defined by (`value - tolerance`) to (`value + tolerance`). The method returns false if a `null` array is passed in.

Parameters: `array`—the array to search
`valueToFind`—the value to find
`tolerance`—the array contains the tolerance of the search
Returns: true if value falling within tolerance is in array

```
public static int indexOf(float[] array, float valueToFind)
```

Find the index of the given value in the array. This method returns -1 if `null` array input.

Parameters: `array`—the array to search through for the object, may be `null`
`valueToFind`—the value to find
Returns: the index of the value within the array, -1 if not found or `null` array input

```
public static int indexOf(float[] array, float valueToFind, int startIndex)
```

Find the index of the given value in the array starting at the given index. This method returns -1 if `null` array input. A negative `startIndex` is treated as zero. A `startIndex` larger than the array length will return -1.

Parameters: `array`—the array to search through for the object, may be `null`
`valueToFind`—the value to find
`startIndex`—the index to start searching at
Returns: the index of the value within the array, -1 if not found or `null` array input

```
public static int lastIndexOf(float[] array, float valueToFind)
```

Find the last index of the given value within the array. This method returns -1 if `null` array input.

Parameters: `array`—the array to traverse backward looking for the object, may be `null`
`valueToFind`—the object to find
Returns: the last index of the value within the array, -1 if not found or `null` array input

```
public static int lastIndexOf(float[] array, float valueToFind, int startIndex)
```

Find the last index of the given value in the array starting at the given index. This method returns -1 if `null` array input. A negative `startIndex` will return -1. A `startIndex` larger than the array length will search from the end of the array.

Parameters: `array`—the array to traverse looking for the object, may be `null`

`valueToFind`—the value to find

`startIndex`—the start index to traverse backward from

Returns: the last index of the value within the array, `-1` if not found or `null` array input

```
public static boolean contains(float[] array, float valueToFind)
```

Checks if the value is in the given array. The method returns false if a `null` array is passed in.

Parameters: `array`—the array to search through

`valueToFind`—the value to find

Returns: `true` if the array contains the object

```
public static int indexOf(boolean[] array, boolean valueToFind)
```

Find the index of the given value in the array. This method returns -1 if `null` array input.

Parameters: `array`—the array to search through for the object, may be `null`

`valueToFind`—the value to find

Returns: the index of the value within the array, `-1` if not found or `null` array input

```
public static int indexOf(boolean[] array, boolean valueToFind, int
    startIndex)
```

Find the index of the given value in the array starting at the given index. This method returns -1 if `null` array input. A negative `startIndex` is treated as zero. A `startIndex` larger than the array length will return -1.

Parameters: `array`—the array to search through for the object, may be `null`

`valueToFind`—the value to find

`startIndex`—the index to start searching at

Returns: the index of the value within the array, `-1` if not found or `null` array input

```
public static int lastIndexOf(boolean[] array, boolean valueToFind)
```

Find the last index of the given value within the array. This method returns -1 if `null` array input.

Parameters: array—the array to traverse backward looking for the object, may be null

valueToFind—the object to find

Returns: the last index of the value within the array, -1 if not found or null array input

```
public static int lastIndexOf(boolean[] array, boolean valueToFind,
int startIndex)
```

Find the last index of the given value in the array starting at the given index. This method returns -1 if null array input. A negative startIndex will return -1. A startIndex larger than the array length will search from the end of the array.

Parameters: array—the array to traverse looking for the object, may be null

valueToFind—the value to find

startIndex—the start index to traverse backward from

Returns: the last index of the value within the array, -1 if not found or null array input

```
public static boolean contains(boolean[] array, boolean valueToFind)
```

Checks if the value is in the given array. The method returns false if a null array is passed in.

Parameters: array—the array to search through

valueToFind—the value to find

Returns: true if the array contains the object

```
public static long[] toPrimitive(java.lang.Long[] array)
```

Converts an array of object Longs to primitives. This method returns null if null array input.

Parameters: array—a Long array, may be null

Returns: a long array, null if null array input

Throws: java.lang.NullPointerException—if array content is null

```
public static long[] toPrimitive(java.lang.Long[] array, long
valueForNull)
```

Converts an array of object Long to primitives handling null. This method returns null if null array input.

Parameters: array—a Long array, may be null

valueForNull—the value to insert if null found

Returns: a long array, null if null array input

```
public static java.lang.Long[] toObject(long[] array)
```

Converts an array of primitive longs to objects. This method returns `null` if `null` array input.

> **Parameters:** array—a `long` array
> **Returns:** a `Long` array, `null` if `null` array input

```
public static int[] toPrimitive(java.lang.Integer[] array)
```

Converts an array of object Integers to primitives. This method returns `null` if `null` array input.

> **Parameters:** array—an `Integer` array, may be `null`
> **Returns:** an `int` array, `null` if `null` array input
> **Throws:** `java.lang.NullPointerException`—if array content is `null`

```
public static int[] toPrimitive(java.lang.Integer[] array,
     int valueForNull)
```

Converts an array of object Integer to primitives handling `null`. This method returns `null` if `null` array input.

> **Parameters:** array—an `Integer` array, may be `null`
> valueForNull—the value to insert if `null` found
> **Returns:** an `int` array, `null` if `null` array input

```
public static java.lang.Integer[] toObject(int[] array)
```

Converts an array of primitive ints to objects. This method returns `null` if `null` array input.

> **Parameters:** array—an `int` array
> **Returns:** an `Integer` array, `null` if `null` array input

```
public static short[] toPrimitive(java.lang.Short[] array)
```

Converts an array of object Shorts to primitives. This method returns `null` if `null` array input.

> **Parameters:** array—a `Short` array, may be `null`
> **Returns:** a `byte` array, `null` if `null` array input
> **Throws:** `java.lang.NullPointerException`—if array content is `null`

```
public static short[] toPrimitive(java.lang.Short[] array,
     short valueForNull)
```

Converts an array of object Short to primitives handling `null`. This method returns `null` if `null` array input.

> **Parameters:** array—a `Short` array, may be `null`
> valueForNull—the value to insert if `null` found
> **Returns:** a `byte` array, `null` if `null` array input

```
public static java.lang.Short[] toObject(short[] array)
```

Converts an array of primitive shorts to objects. This method returns `null` if `null` array input.

> **Parameters:** `array`—a `short` array
> **Returns:** a `Short` array, `null` if `null` array input

```
public static byte[] toPrimitive(java.lang.Byte[] array)
```

Converts an array of object Bytes to primitives. This method returns `null` if `null` array input.

> **Parameters:** `array`—a `Byte` array, may be `null`
> **Returns:** a `byte` array, `null` if `null` array input
> **Throws:** `java.lang.NullPointerException`—if array content is `null`

```
public static byte[] toPrimitive(java.lang.Byte[] array, byte
valueForNull)
```

Converts an array of object Bytes to primitives handling `null`. This method returns `null` if `null` array input.

> **Parameters:** `array`—a `Byte` array, may be `null`
> `valueForNull`—the value to insert if `null` found
> **Returns:** a `byte` array, `null` if `null` array input

```
public static java.lang.Byte[] toObject(byte[] array)
```

Converts an array of primitive bytes to objects. This method returns `null` if `null` array input.

> **Parameters:** `array`—a `byte` array
> **Returns:** a `Byte` array, `null` if `null` array input

```
public static double[] toPrimitive(java.lang.Double[] array)
```

Converts an array of object Doubles to primitives. This method returns `null` if `null` array input.

> **Parameters:** `array`—a `Double` array, may be `null`
> **Returns:** a `double` array, `null` if `null` array input
> **Throws:** `java.lang.NullPointerException`—if array content is `null`

```
public static double[] toPrimitive(java.lang.Double[] array, double
valueForNull)
```

Converts an array of object Doubles to primitives handling `null`. This method returns `null` if `null` array input.

> **Parameters:** `array`—a `Double` array, may be `null`
> `valueForNull`—the value to insert if `null` found

Returns: a `double` array, `null` if `null` array input

```
public static java.lang.Double[] toObject(double[] array)
```

Converts an array of primitive doubles to objects. This method returns `null` if `null` array input.

Parameters: `array`—a `double` array
Returns: a `Double` array, `null` if `null` array input

```
public static float[] toPrimitive(java.lang.Float[] array)
```

Converts an array of object Floats to primitives. This method returns `null` if `null` array input.

Parameters: `array`—a `Float` array, may be `null`
Returns: a `float` array, `null` if `null` array input
Throws: `java.lang.NullPointerException`—if array content is `null`

```
public static float[] toPrimitive(java.lang.Float[] array,
float valueForNull)
```

Converts an array of object Floats to primitives handling `null`. This method returns `null` if `null` array input.

Parameters: `array`—a `Float` array, may be `null`
`valueForNull`—the value to insert if `null` found
Returns: a `float` array, `null` if `null` array input

```
public static java.lang.Float[] toObject(float[] array)
```

Converts an array of primitive floats to objects. This method returns `null` if `null` array input.

Parameters: `array`—a `float` array
Returns: a `Float` array, `null` if `null` array input

```
public static boolean[] toPrimitive(java.lang.Boolean[] array)
```

Converts an array of object `Boolean`s to primitives. This method returns `null` if `null` array input.

Parameters: `array`—a `Boolean` array, may be `null`
Returns: a `boolean` array, `null` if `null` array input
Throws: `java.lang.NullPointerException`—if array content is `null`

```
public static boolean[] toPrimitive(java.lang.Boolean[] array, boolean
valueForNull)
```

Converts an array of object `Boolean`s to primitives handling `null`. This method returns `null` if `null` array input.

Parameters: array—a `Boolean` array, may be `null`
valueForNull—the value to insert if `null` found
Returns: a `boolean` array, `null` if `null` array input

```
public static java.lang.Boolean[] toObject(boolean[] array)
```

Converts an array of primitive `boolean`s to objects. This method returns `null` if `null` array input.

Parameters: array—a `boolean` array
Returns: a `Boolean` array, `null` if `null` array input

ORG.APACHE.COMMONS.LANG.BITFIELD

Operations on bit-mapped fields.

Constructor Detail

```
public BitField(int mask)
```

Creates a BitField instance.

Parameters: mask—the mask specifying which bits apply to this `BitField`. Bits that are set in this mask are the bits that this `BitField` operates on

Method Detail

```
public int getValue(int holder)
```

Obtains the value for the specified `BitField`, appropriately shifted right.

Many users of a `BitField` will want to treat the specified bits as an int value, and will not want to be aware that the value is stored as a `BitField` (and so shifted left so many bits).

Parameters: holder—the int data containing the bits we're interested in
Returns: the selected bits, shifted right appropriately
See Also: `setValue(int, int)`

```
public short getShortValue(short holder)
```

Obtains the value for the specified `BitField`, appropriately shifted right, as a short.

Many users of a `BitField` will want to treat the specified bits as an int value, and will not want to be aware that the value is stored as a `BitField` (and so shifted left so many bits).

Parameters: holder—the short data containing the bits we're interested in

Returns: the selected bits, shifted right appropriately
See Also: setShortValue(short, short)

```
public int getRawValue(int holder)
```

Obtains the value for the specified BitField, unshifted.

Parameters: holder—the int data containing the bits we're interested in
Returns: the selected bits

```
public short getShortRawValue(short holder)
```

Obtains the value for the specified BitField, unshifted.

Parameters: holder—the short data containing the bits we're interested in
Returns: the selected bits

```
public boolean isSet(int holder)
```

Returns whether the field is set or not.

This is most commonly used for a single-bit field, which is often used to represent a boolean value; the result of using it for a multi-bit field is to determine whether *any* of its bits are set.

Parameters: holder—the int data containing the bits we're interested in
Returns: true if any of the bits are set, else false

```
public boolean isAllSet(int holder)
```

Returns whether all of the bits are set or not.

This is a stricter test than isSet(int), in that all of the bits in a multi-bit set must be set for this method to return true.

Parameters: holder—the int data containing the bits we're interested in
Returns: true if all of the bits are set, else false

```
public int setValue(int holder, int value)
```

Replaces the bits with new values.

Parameters: holder—the int data containing the bits we're interested in
value—the new value for the specified bits
Returns: the value of holder with the bits from the value parameter replacing the old bits
See Also: getValue(int)

```
public short setShortValue(short holder, short value)
```

Replaces the bits with new values.

Parameters: `holder`—the short data containing the bits we're interested in

`value`—the new value for the specified bits

Returns: the value of holder with the bits from the value parameter replacing the old bits

See Also: `getShortValue(short)`

```
public int clear(int holder)
```

Clears the bits.

Parameters: `holder`—the int data containing the bits we're interested in
Returns: the value of holder with the specified bits cleared (set to 0)

```
public short clearShort(short holder)
```

Clears the bits.

Parameters: `holder`—the short data containing the bits we're interested in

Returns: the value of holder with the specified bits cleared (set to 0)

```
public byte clearByte(byte holder)
```

Clears the bits.

Parameters: `holder`—the byte data containing the bits we're interested in
Returns: the value of holder with the specified bits cleared (set to 0)

```
public int set(int holder)
```

Sets the bits.

Parameters: `holder`—the int data containing the bits we're interested in
Returns: the value of holder with the specified bits set to 1

```
public short setShort(short holder)
```

Sets the bits.

Parameters: `holder`—the short data containing the bits we're interested in

Returns: the value of holder with the specified bits set to 1

```
public byte setByte(byte holder)
```

Sets the bits.

Parameters: `holder`—the byte data containing the bits we're interested in
Returns: the value of holder with the specified bits set to 1

```
public int setBoolean(int holder, boolean flag)
```

Sets a `boolean` BitField.

> **Parameters:** `holder`—the int data containing the bits we're interested in
> `flag`—indicating whether to set or clear the bits
> **Returns:** the value of holder with the specified bits set or cleared

```
public short setShortBoolean(short holder, boolean flag)
```

Sets a `boolean` BitField.

> **Parameters:** `holder`—the short data containing the bits we're interested in
> `flag`—indicating whether to set or clear the bits
> **Returns:** the value of holder with the specified bits set or cleared

```
public byte setByteBoolean(byte holder, boolean flag)
```

Sets a `boolean` BitField.

> **Parameters:** `holder`—the byte data containing the bits we're interested in
> `flag`—indicating whether to set or clear the bits
> **Returns:** the value of holder with the specified bits set or cleared

ORG.APACHE.COMMONS.LANG.BOOLEANUTILS

> java.lang.Object
> **org.apache.commons.lang.BooleanUtils**

Operations on `boolean` primitives and `Boolean` objects.

This class tries to handle `null` input gracefully. An exception will not be thrown for a `null` input. Each method documents its behavior in more detail.

Constructor Detail

```
public BooleanUtils()
```

BooleanUtils instances should NOT be constructed in standard programming. Instead, the class should be used as `BooleanUtils.toBooleanObject(true);`.

This constructor is public to permit tools that require a JavaBean instance to operate.

Method Detail

```
public static java.lang.Boolean negate(java.lang.Boolean bool)
```

Negates the specified `boolean`. If `null` is passed in, `null` will be returned.

> **Parameters:** `bool`—the `Boolean` to negate, may be `null`

Returns: the negated `Boolean`, or `null` if `null` input

```
public static java.lang.Boolean toBooleanObject(boolean bool)
```

`Boolean` factory that avoids creating new `Boolean` objecs all the time. This method was added to JDK1.4 but is available here for earlier JDKs.

Parameters: `bool`—the `boolean` to convert
Returns: Boolean.TRUE or Boolean.FALSE as appropriate

```
public static boolean toBoolean(java.lang.Boolean bool)
```

Converts a `Boolean` to a `boolean` handling `null` by returning false.

Parameters: `bool`—the `boolean` to convert
Returns: `true` or `false`, `null` returns `false`

```
public static boolean toBooleanDefaultIfNull(java.lang.Boolean bool,
boolean valueIfNull)
```

Converts a `Boolean` to a `boolean` handling `null`.

Parameters: `bool`—the `boolean` to convert
`valueIfNull`—the `boolean` value to return if `null`
Returns: `true` or `false`

```
public static boolean toBoolean(int value)
```

Converts an int to a `boolean` using the convention that zero is false.

Parameters: `value`—the int to convert
Returns: `true` if non-zero, `false` if zero

```
public static java.lang.Boolean toBooleanObject(int value)
```

Converts an int to a `Boolean` using the convention that zero is false.

Parameters: `value`—the int to convert
Returns: Boolean.TRUE if non-zero, Boolean.FALSE if zero, `null` if `null`

```
public static java.lang.Boolean toBooleanObject(java.lang.Integer
value)
```

Converts an Integer to a `Boolean` using the convention that zero is false. `null` will be converted to `null`.

Parameters: `value`—the Integer to convert
Returns: Boolean.TRUE if non-zero, Boolean.FALSE if zero, `null` if `null` input

```
public static boolean toBoolean(int value, int trueValue, int
falseValue)
```

Converts an int to a `boolean` specifying the conversion values.

> **Parameters:** `value`—the Integer to convert
> `trueValue`—the value to match for `true`
> `falseValue`—the value to match for `false`
> **Returns:** `true` or `false`
> **Throws:** `java.lang.IllegalArgumentException`—if no match

```
public static boolean toBoolean(java.lang.Integer value,
java.lang.Integer trueValue, java.lang.Integer falseValue)
```

Converts an Integer to a `boolean` specifying the conversion values.

> **Parameters:** `value`—the Integer to convert
> `trueValue`—the value to match for `true`, may be `null`
> `falseValue`—the value to match for `false`, may be `null`
> **Returns:** `true` or `false`
> **Throws:** `java.lang.IllegalArgumentException`—if no match

```
public static java.lang.Boolean toBooleanObject(int value,
int trueValue, int falseValue, int nullValue)
```

Converts an int to a `Boolean` specifying the conversion values.

> **Parameters:** `value`—the Integer to convert
> `trueValue`—the value to match for `true`
> `falseValue`—the value to match for `false`
> `nullValue`—the value to match for `null`
> **Returns:** Boolean.TRUE, Boolean.FALSE, or `null`
> **Throws:** `java.lang.IllegalArgumentException`—if no match

```
public static java.lang.Boolean toBooleanObject(java.lang.Integer
value, java.lang.Integer trueValue, java.lang.Integer falseValue,
java.lang.Integer nullValue)
```

Converts an Integer to a `Boolean` specifying the conversion values.

> **Parameters:** `value`—the Integer to convert
> `trueValue`—the value to match for `true`, may be `null`
> `falseValue`—the value to match for `false`, may be `null`
> `nullValue`—the value to match for `null`, may be `null`
> **Returns:** Boolean.TRUE, Boolean.FALSE, or `null`
> **Throws:** `java.lang.IllegalArgumentException`—if no match

```
public static int toInteger(boolean bool)
```

Converts a `boolean` to an int using the convention that zero is false.

> **Parameters:** `bool`—the `boolean` to convert
> **Returns:** one if `true`, zero if `false`

```
public static java.lang.Integer toIntegerObject(boolean bool)
```

Converts a `boolean` to an Integer using the convention that zero is false.

> **Parameters:** `bool`—the `Boolean` to convert
> **Returns:** one if `true`, zero if `false`

```
public static java.lang.Integer toIntegerObject(java.lang.Boolean
bool)
```

Converts a `Boolean` to a Integer using the convention that zero is false. `null` will be converted to `null`.

> **Parameters:** `bool`—the `Boolean` to convert
> **Returns:** one if Boolean.TRUE, zero if Boolean.FALSE, `null` if `null`

```
public static int toInteger(boolean bool, int trueValue,
int falseValue)
```

Converts a `boolean` to an int specifying the conversion values.

> **Parameters:** `bool`—the `Boolean` to convert
> `trueValue`—the value to return if `true`
> `falseValue`—the value to return if `false`
> **Returns:** the appropriate value

```
public static int toInteger(java.lang.Boolean bool, int trueValue,
int falseValue, int nullValue)
```

Converts a `Boolean` to an int specifying the conversion values.

> **Parameters:** `bool`—the `Boolean` to convert
> `trueValue`—the value to return if `true`
> `falseValue`—the value to return if `false`
> `nullValue`—the value to return if `null`
> **Returns:** the appropriate value

```
public static java.lang.Integer toIntegerObject(boolean bool,
java.lang.Integer trueValue, java.lang.Integer falseValue)
```

Converts a `boolean` to an Integer specifying the conversion values.

> **Parameters:** `bool`—the `Boolean` to convert
> `trueValue`—the value to return if `true`, may be `null`
> `falseValue`—the value to return if `false`, may be `null`
> **Returns:** the appropriate value

```
public static java.lang.Integer toIntegerObject(java.lang.Boolean
bool, java.lang.Integer trueValue, java.lang.Integer falseValue,
java.lang.Integer nullValue)
```

Converts a `Boolean` to an Integer specifying the conversion values.

> **Parameters:** `bool`—the `Boolean` to convert
> `trueValue`—the value to return if `true`, may be `null`

falseValue—the value to return if `false`, may be `null`
nullValue—the value to return if `null`, may be `null`
Returns: the appropriate value

```
public static java.lang.Boolean toBooleanObject(java.lang.String str)
```

Converts a `String` to a `Boolean`. 'true', 'on' or 'yes' (case insensitive) will return true. 'false', 'off' or 'no' (case insensitive) will return false. Otherwise, `null` is returned.

Parameters: str—the `String` to check
Returns: the `Boolean` value of the string, `null` if no match or `null` input

```
public static java.lang.Boolean toBooleanObject(java.lang.String str,
java.lang.String trueString, java.lang.String falseString,
java.lang.String nullString)
```

Converts a `String` to a `Boolean` throwing an exception if no match.

Parameters: str—the `String` to check
trueString—the `String` to match for `true` (case sensitive), may be `null`
falseString—the `String` to match for `false` (case sensitive), may be `null`
nullString—the `String` to match for `null` (case sensitive), may be `null`
Returns: the `Boolean` value of the string, `null` if no match or `null` input

```
public static boolean toBoolean(java.lang.String str)
```

Converts a `String` to a `boolean`. 'true', 'on' or 'yes' (case insensitive) will return true. Otherwise, false is returned.

Parameters: str—the `String` to check
Returns: the `boolean` value of the string, `false` if no match

```
public static boolean toBoolean(java.lang.String str, java.lang.String
trueString, java.lang.String falseString)
```

Converts a `String` to a `Boolean` throwing an exception if no match found. `null` is returned if there is no match.

Parameters: str—the `String` to check
trueString—the `String` to match for `true` (case sensitive), may be `null`
falseString—the `String` to match for `false` (case sensitive), may be `null`
Returns: the `boolean` value of the string
Throws: `java.lang.IllegalArgumentException`—if the `String` doesn't match

```
public static java.lang.String toStringTrueFalse(java.lang.Boolean
bool)
```

Converts a `Boolean` to a `String` returning 'true', 'false', or `null`.

> **Parameters:** `bool`—the `Boolean` to check
> **Returns:** `'true'`, `'false'`, or `null`

```
public static java.lang.String toStringOnOff(java.lang.Boolean bool)
```

Converts a `Boolean` to a `String` returning 'on', 'off', or `null`.

> **Parameters:** `bool`—the `Boolean` to check
> **Returns:** `'on'`, `'off'`, or `null`

```
public static java.lang.String toStringYesNo(java.lang.Boolean bool)
```

Converts a `Boolean` to a `String` returning 'yes', 'no', or `null`.

> **Parameters:** `bool`—the `Boolean` to check
> **Returns:** `'yes'`, `'no'`, or `null`

```
public static java.lang.String toString(java.lang.Boolean bool,
    java.lang.String trueString, java.lang.String falseString,
    java.lang.String nullString)
```

Converts a `Boolean` to a `String` returning one of the input `String`s.

> **Parameters:** `bool`—the `Boolean` to check
> `trueString`—the `String` to return if `true`, may be `null`
> `falseString`—the `String` to return if `false`, may be `null`
> `nullString`—the `String` to return if `null`, may be `null`
> **Returns:** one of the three input `String`s

```
public static java.lang.String toStringTrueFalse(boolean bool)
```

Converts a `boolean` to a `String` returning 'true' or 'false'.

> **Parameters:** `bool`—the `Boolean` to check
> **Returns:** `'true'`, `'false'`, or `null`

```
public static java.lang.String toStringOnOff(boolean bool)
```

Converts a `boolean` to a `String` returning 'on' or 'off'.

> **Parameters:** `bool`—the `Boolean` to check
> **Returns:** `'on'`, `'off'`, or `null`

```
public static java.lang.String toStringYesNo(boolean bool)
```

Converts a `boolean` to a `String` returning 'yes' or 'no'.

> **Parameters:** `bool`—the `Boolean` to check
> **Returns:** `'yes'`, `'no'`, or `null`

```
public static java.lang.String toString(boolean bool, java.lang.String
trueString, java.lang.String falseString)
```

Converts a `boolean` to a `String` returning one of the input `String`s.

> **Parameters:** `bool`—the `Boolean` to check
> `trueString`—the `String` to return if `true`, may be `null`
> `falseString`—the `String` to return if `false`, may be `null`
> **Returns:** one of the two input `String`s

```
public static boolean xor(boolean[] array)
```

Performs an xor on a set of `boolean`s.

> **Parameters:** `array`—an array of `boolean`s
> **Returns:** `true` if the xor is successful.
> **Throws:** `java.lang.IllegalArgumentException`–if array is `null`
> `java.lang.IllegalArgumentException`–if array is empty.

```
public static java.lang.Boolean xor(java.lang.Boolean[] array)
```

Performs an xor on an array of `Boolean`s.

> **Parameters:** `array`–an array of Booleans
> **Returns:** `true` if the xor is successful
> **Throws:** `java.lang.IllegalArgumentException`–if array is `null`
> `java.lang.IllegalArgumentException`–if array is empty.
> `java.lang.IllegalArgumentException`—if array contains a `null`

org.apache.commons.lang.CharRange

```
public final class CharRange implements java.io.Serializable
```

A contiguous range of characters, optionally negated. Instances are immutable.

Constructor Detail

```
public CharRange(char ch)
```

Constructs a CharRange over a single character.

> **Parameters:** `ch`—only character in this range

```
public CharRange(char ch, boolean negated)
```

Constructs a CharRange over a single character, optionally negating the range. A negated range includes everything except the specified char.

> **Parameters:** `ch`—only character in this range

negated—true to express everything except the range

```
public CharRange(char start, char end)
```

Constructs a CharRange over a set of characters.

Parameters: start—first character, inclusive, in this range
end—last character, inclusive, in this range

```
public CharRange(char start, char end, boolean negated)
```

Constructs a CharRange over a set of characters, optionally negating the range. A negated range includes everything except that defined by the start and end characters. If start and end are in the wrong order, they are reversed. Thus a-e is the same as e-a.

Parameters: start—first character, inclusive, in this range
end—last character, inclusive, in this range
negated—true to express everything except the range

Method Detail

```
public char getStart()
```

Gets the start character for this character range.

Returns: the start char (inclusive)

```
public char getEnd()
```

Gets the end character for this character range.

Returns: the end char (inclusive)

```
public boolean isNegated()
```

Is this CharRange negated. A negated range includes everything except that defined by the start and end characters.

Returns: true is negated

```
public boolean contains(char ch)
```

Is the character specified contained in this range.

Parameters: ch—the character to check
Returns: true if this range contains the input character

```
public boolean contains(CharRange range)
```

Are all the characters of the passed in range contained in this range.

Parameters: range—the range to check against

Returns: true if this range entirely contains the input range
Throws: java.lang.IllegalArgumentException—if null input

```
public boolean equals(java.lang.Object obj)
```

Compares two CharRange objects, returning true if they represent exactly the same range of characters defined in the same way.

Parameters: obj—the object to compare to
Returns: true if equal

```
public int hashCode()
```

Gets a hashCode compatable with the equals method.

Returns: a suitable hashCode

```
public java.lang.String toString()
```

Gets a string representation of the character range.

Returns: string representation of this range

org.apache.commons.lang.CharSet

```
public class CharSet implements java.io.Serializable
```

A set of characters. Instances are immutable, but instances of subclasses may not be.

Field Summary

```
public static final CharSet EMPTY
```

A CharSet defining no characters.

```
public static final CharSet ASCII_ALPHA
```

A CharSet defining ASCII alphabetic characters "a-zA-Z".

```
public static final CharSet ASCII_ALPHA_LOWER
```

A CharSet defining ASCII alphabetic characters "a-z".

```
public static final CharSet ASCII_ALPHA_UPPER
```

A CharSet defining ASCII alphabetic characters "A-Z".

```
public static final CharSet ASCII_NUMERIC
```

A CharSet defining ASCII alphabetic characters "0-9".

Method Detail

```
public static CharSet getInstance(java.lang.String setStr)
```

Factory method to create a new CharSet using a special syntax.

- `null` or empty string ("")—set containing no characters
- Single character, such as "a"—set containing just that character
- Multi character, such as "a-e"—set containing characters from one character to the other
- Negated, such as "^a" or "^a-e"—set containing all characters except those defined
- Combinations, such as "abe-g"—set containing all the characters from the individual sets

The matching order is:

1. Negated multi character range, such as "^a-e"
2. Ordinary multi character range, such as "a-e"
3. Negated single character, such as "^a"
4. Ordinary single character, such as "a"

Matching works left to right. Once a match is found the search starts again from the next character. If the same range is defined twice using the same syntax, only one range will be kept. Thus, "a-ca-c" creates only one range of "a-c". If the start and end of a range are in the wrong order, they are reversed. Thus "a-e" is the same as "e-a". As a result, "a-ee-a" would create only one range, as the "a-e" and "e-a" are the same.

The set of characters represented is the union of the specified ranges. All CharSet objects returned by this method will be immutable.

Parameters: setStr—the String describing the set, may be null
Returns: a CharSet instance

```
public CharRange[] getCharRanges()
```

Gets the internal set as an array of CharRange objects.

Returns: an array of immutable CharRange objects

```
public boolean contains(char ch)
```

Does the CharSet contain the specified character ch.

Parameters: ch—the character to check for
Returns: true if the set contains the characters

```
public boolean equals(java.lang.Object obj)
```

Compares two CharSet objects, returning true if they represent exactly the same set of characters defined in the same way.

The two sets abc and a-c are not equal according to this method.

Parameters: `obj`—the object to compare to
Returns: true if equal

```
public int hashCode()
```

Gets a hashCode compatible with the equals method.

Returns: a suitable hashCode

```
public java.lang.String toString()
```

Gets a string representation of the set.

Returns: string representation of the set

org.apache.commons.lang.CharSetUtils

This class handles `null` input gracefully. An exception will not be thrown for a `null` input. Each method documents its behavior in more detail.

Constructor Detail

```
public CharSetUtils()
```

CharSetUtils instances should NOT be constructed in standard programming. Instead, the class should be used as CharSetUtils.evaluateSet(null);. This constructor is public to permit tools that require a JavaBean instance to operate.

Method Detail

```
public static java.lang.String squeeze(java.lang.String str,
java.lang.String set)
```

Squeezes any repetitions of a character that is mentioned in the supplied set.

```
CharSetUtils.squeeze(null, *)       = null
CharSetUtils.squeeze("", *)         = ""
CharSetUtils.squeeze(*, null)       = *
CharSetUtils.squeeze(*, "")         = *
CharSetUtils.squeeze("hello", "k-p") = "helo"
CharSetUtils.squeeze("hello", "a-e") = "hello"
```

Parameters: `str`—the string to squeeze, may be `null`
`set`—the character set to use for manipulation, may be `null`
Returns: modified `string`, `null` if `null` string input
See Also: for set-syntax.

```
public static java.lang.String squeeze(java.lang.String str,
java.lang.String[] set)
```

Squeezes any repetitions of a character that is mentioned in the supplied set. An example is:

```
squeeze("hello", {"el"}) => "helo"
```

Parameters: str—the string to squeeze, may be null
set—the character set to use for manipulation, may be null
Returns: modified string, null if null string input
See Also: for set-syntax.

```
public static int count(java.lang.String str,  java.lang.String set)
```

Takes an argument in set-syntax, see evaluateSet, and returns the number of characters present in the specified string.

```
CharSetUtils.count(null, *) = 0
CharSetUtils.count("", *) = 0
CharSetUtils.count(*, null) = 0
CharSetUtils.count(*, "") = 0
CharSetUtils.count("hello", "k-p") = 3
CharSetUtils.count("hello", "a-e") = 1
```

Parameters: str—String to count characters in, may be null
set—String set of characters to count, may be null
Returns: character count, zero if null string input
See Also: for set-syntax.

```
public static int count(java.lang.String str, java.lang.String[] set)
```

Takes an argument in set-syntax, see evaluateSet, and returns the number of characters present in the specified string.
    An example would be:

```
count("hello", {"c-f", "o"}) returns 2.
```

Parameters: str—String to count characters in, may be null
set—String[] set of characters to count, may be null
Returns: character count, zero if null string input
See Also: for set-syntax.

```
public static java.lang.String keep(java.lang.String str,
java.lang.String set)
```

Takes an argument in set-syntax, see evaluateSet, and keeps any of the characters present in the specified string.

```
CharSetUtils.keep(null, *) = null
CharSetUtils.keep("", *) = ""
CharSetUtils.keep(*, null) = ""
```

```
CharSetUtils.keep(*, "") = ""
CharSetUtils.keep("hello", "hl") = "hll"
CharSetUtils.keep("hello", "le") = "ell"
```

Parameters: str—String to keep characters from, may be null
set—String set of characters to keep, may be null
Returns: modified String, null if null string input
See Also: for set-syntax.

```
public static java.lang.String keep(java.lang.String str,
java.lang.String[] set)
```

Takes an argument in set-syntax, see evaluateSet, and keeps any of the characters present in the specified string.
An example would be:

```
keep("hello", {"c-f", "o"}) returns "hll"
```

Parameters: str—String to keep characters from, may be null
set—String[] set of characters to keep, may be null
Returns: modified String, null if null string input
See Also: for set-syntax.

```
public static java.lang.String delete(java.lang.String str,
java.lang.String set)
```

Takes an argument in set-syntax, see evaluateSet, and deletes any of the characters present in the specified string.

```
CharSetUtils.delete(null, *) = null
CharSetUtils.delete("", *) = ""
CharSetUtils.delete(*, null) = *
CharSetUtils.delete(*, "") = *
CharSetUtils.delete("hello", "hl") = "hll"
CharSetUtils.delete("hello", "le") = "ell"
```

Parameters: str—String to delete characters from, may be null
set—String set of characters to delete, may be null
Returns: modified String, null if null string input
See Also: for set-syntax.

```
public static java.lang.String delete(java.lang.String str,
java.lang.String[] set)
```

Takes an argument in set-syntax, see evaluateSet, and deletes any of the characters present in the specified string.
An example would be:

```
delete("hello", {"c-f", "o"}) returns "hll"
```

Parameters: str—String to delete characters from, may be null
set—String[] set of characters to delete, may be null
Returns: modified String, null if null string input
See Also: for set-syntax.

org.apache.commons.lang.ClassUtils

Operates on classes without using reflection.

This class handles invalid null inputs as best it can. Each method documents its behavior in more detail.

Field Detail

    public static final char PACKAGE_SEPARATOR_CHAR

The package separator character: ..

> **See Also:** Constant Field Values

    public static final java.lang.String PACKAGE_SEPARATOR

The package separator String: . .

    public static final char INNER_CLASS_SEPARATOR_CHAR

The inner class separator character: $.

> **See Also:** Constant Field Values

    public static final java.lang.String INNER_CLASS_SEPARATOR

The inner class separator String: $.

Constructor Detail

    public ClassUtils()

ClassUtils instances should NOT be constructed in standard programming. Instead, the class should be used as ClassUtils.getShortClassName(cls).

This constructor is public to permit tools that require a JavaBean instance to operate.

Method Detail

    public static java.lang.String getShortClassName(java.lang.Object
    object, java.lang.String valueIfNull)

Gets the class name minus the package name for an Object.

> **Parameters:** object—the class to get the short name for, may be null
> valueIfNull—the value to return if null

Returns: the class name of the object without the package name, or the `null` value

```
public static java.lang.String getShortClassName(java.lang.Class cls)
```

Gets the class name minus the package name from a Class.

Parameters: `cls`—the class to get the short name for, must not be `null`
Returns: the class name without the package name
Throws: `java.lang.IllegalArgumentException`—if the class is `null`

```
public static java.lang.String getShortClassName(java.lang.String
className)
```

Gets the class name minus the package name from a `string`. The string passed in is assumed to be a class name—it is not checked.

Parameters: `className`—the className to get the short name for, must not be empty or `null`
Returns: the class name of the class without the package name
Throws: `java.lang.IllegalArgumentException`—if the className is empty

```
public static java.lang.String getPackageName(java.lang.Object object,
java.lang.String valueIfNull)
```

Gets the package name of an Object.

Parameters: `object`—the class to get the package name for, may be `null`
`valueIfNull`—the value to return if `null`
Returns: the package name of the object, or the `null` value

```
public static java.lang.String getPackageName(java.lang.Class cls)
```

Gets the package name of a Class.

Parameters: `cls`—the class to get the package name for, must not be `null`
Returns: the package name
Throws: `java.lang.IllegalArgumentException`—if the class is `null`

```
public static java.lang.String getPackageName(java.lang.String
className)
```

Gets the package name from a `string`. The string passed in is assumed to be a class name—it is not checked.

Parameters: `className`—the className to get the package name for, must not be empty or `null`
Returns: the package name
Throws: `java.lang.IllegalArgumentException`—if the className is empty

```
public static java.util.List getAllSuperclasses(java.lang.Class cls)
```

Gets a List of superclasses for the given class.

Parameters: `cls`—the class to look up, must not be `null`
Returns: the `List` of superclasses in order going up from this one, `null` if `null` input

```
public static java.util.List getAllInterfaces(java.lang.Class cls)
```

Gets a List of all interfaces implemented by the given class and its superclasses. The order is determined by looking through each interface in turn as declared in the source file and following its hieracrchy up. Then each superclass is considered in the same way. Later duplicates are ignored, so the order is maintained.

Parameters: `cls`—the class to look up, must not be `null`
Returns: the `List` of interfaces in order, `null` if `null` input

```
public static java.util.List convertClassNamesToClasses(java.util.List
    classNames)
```

Given a List of class names, this method converts them into classes. A new List is returned. If the class name cannot be found, `null` is stored in the List. If the class name in the List is `null`, `null` is stored in the output List.

Parameters: `classNames`—the classNames to change
Returns: a `List` of Class objects corresponding to the class names, `null` if `null` input
Throws: `java.lang.ClassCastException`—if classNames contains a non `String` entry

```
public static java.util.List convertClassesToClassNames(java.util.List
    classes)
```

Given a List of Class objects, this method converts them into class names. A new List is returned. `null` objects will be copied into the returned list as `null`.

Parameters: `classes`—the classes to change
Returns: a `List` of Class objects corresponding to the class names, `null` if `null` input
Throws: `java.lang.ClassCastException`—if classNames contains a non Class or `null` entry

```
public static boolean isAssignable(java.lang.Class[] classArray,
    java.lang.Class[] toClassArray)
```

Checks if an array of Classes can be assigned to another array of Classes.

This method calls `isAssignable` for each Class pair in the input arrays. It can be used to check if a set of arguments (the first parameter) are suitably compatible with a set of method parameter types (the second parameter).

Unlike the Class.isAssignableFrom(java.lang.Class) method, this method takes into account widenings of primitive classes and `null`s.

Primitive widenings allow an int to be assigned to a long, float or double. This method returns the correct result for these cases.

Null may be assigned to any reference type. This method will return true if `null` is passed in and the toClass is non-primitive.

Specifically, this method tests whether the type represented by the specified Class parameter can be converted to the type represented by this Class object via an identity conversion widening primitive or widening reference conversion. See The Java Language Specification, sections 5.1.1, 5.1.2 and 5.1.4 for details.

Parameters: classArray—the array of Classes to check, may be `null`
toClassArray—the array of Classes to try to assign into, may be `null`
Returns: `true` if assignment possible

```
public static boolean isAssignable(java.lang.Class cls,
java.lang.Class toClass)
```

Checks if one Class can be assigned to a variable of another Class.

Unlike the Class.isAssignableFrom(java.lang.Class) method, this method takes into account widenings of primitive classes and `null`s.

Primitive widenings allow an int to be assigned to a long, float or double. This method returns the correct result for these cases.

Null may be assigned to any reference type. This method will return true if `null` is passed in and the toClass is non-primitive.

Specifically, this method tests whether the type represented by the specified Class parameter can be converted to the type represented by this Class object via an identity conversion widening primitive or widening reference conversion. See The Java Language Specification, sections 5.1.1, 5.1.2 and 5.1.4 for details.

Parameters: cls—the Class to check, may be `null`
toClass—the Class to try to assign into, returns `false` if `null`
Returns: `true` if assignment possible

```
public static boolean isInnerClass(java.lang.Class cls)
```

Is the specified class an inner class or static nested class.

Parameters: cls—the class to check
Returns: `true` if the class is an inner or static nested class, `false` if not or null

org.apache.commons.lang.ObjectUtils

This class tries to handle `null` input gracefully. An exception will generally not be thrown for a `null` input. Each method documents its behavior in more detail.

Nested Class Summary
`static class ObjectUtils.Null`

Field Detail

`public static final ObjectUtils.Null NULL`

Singleton used as a `null` placeholder where `null` has another meaning.

For example, in a HashMap the HashMap.get(java.lang.Object) method returns `null` if the Map contains `null` or if there is no matching key. The Null placeholder can be used to distinguish between these two cases.

Another example is Hashtable, where `null` cannot be stored.

This instance is Serializable.

Constructor Detail

`public ObjectUtils()`

ObjectUtils instances should NOT be constructed in standard programming. Instead, the class should be used as `ObjectUtils.defaultIfNull("a","b");`. This constructor is public to permit tools that require a JavaBean instance to operate.

Method Detail

`public static java.lang.Object defaultIfNull(java.lang.Object object, java.lang.Object defaultValue)`

Returns a default value if the object passed is `null`.

```
ObjectUtils.defaultIfNull(null, null)  = null
ObjectUtils.defaultIfNull(null, "")    = ""
ObjectUtils.defaultIfNull(null, "zz")  = "zz"
ObjectUtils.defaultIfNull("abc", *)    = "abc"
ObjectUtils.defaultIfNull(Boolean.TRUE, *) = Boolean.TRUE
```

Parameters: `object`—the `Object` to test, may be `null`
`defaultValue`—the default value to return, may be `null`
Returns: `object` if it is not `null`, defaultValue otherwise

`public static boolean equals(java.lang.Object object1, java.lang.Object object2)`

Compares two objects for equality, where either one or both objects may be `null`.

```
ObjectUtils.equals(null, null) = true
ObjectUtils.equals(null, "") = false
ObjectUtils.equals("", null) = false
ObjectUtils.equals("", "") = true
ObjectUtils.equals(Boolean.TRUE, null) = false
ObjectUtils.equals(Boolean.TRUE, "true") = false
ObjectUtils.equals(Boolean.TRUE, Boolean.TRUE) = true
ObjectUtils.equals(Boolean.TRUE, Boolean.FALSE) = false
```

Parameters: `object1`—the first object, may be `null`
`object2`—the second object, may be `null`
Returns: `true` if the values of both objects are the same

```
public static java.lang.String identityToString(java.lang.Object
object)
```

Gets the `toString` that would be produced by Object if a class did not override `toString` itself. `null` will return `null`.

```
ObjectUtils.identityToString(null) = null
ObjectUtils.identityToString("") = "java.lang.String@1e23"
ObjectUtils.identityToString(Boolean.TRUE) = "java.lang.Boolean@7fa"
```

Parameters: `object`—the object to create a `toString` for, may be `null`
Returns: the default `toString` text, or `null` if `null` passed in

```
public static java.lang.StringBuffer
appendIdentityToString(java.lang.StringBuffer buffer, java.lang.Object
object)
```

Appends the `toString` that would be produced by Object if a class did not override `toString` itself. `null` will return `null`.

```
ObjectUtils.appendIdentityToString(*, null) = null
ObjectUtils.appendIdentityToString(null, "") = "java.lang.String@1e23"
ObjectUtils.appendIdentityToString(null, Boolean.TRUE) =
"java.lang.Boolean@7fa"
ObjectUtils.appendIdentityToString(buf, Boolean.TRUE) =
buf.append("java.lang.Boolean@7fa")
```

Parameters: `buffer`—the buffer to append to, may be `null`
`object`—the object to create a `toString` for, may be `null`
Returns: the default `toString` text, or `null` if `null` passed in

```
public static java.lang.String toString(java.lang.Object obj)
```

Gets the `toString` of an Object returning an empty string (`""`) if `null` input.

```
ObjectUtils.toString(null)         = ""
ObjectUtils.toString("")           = ""
ObjectUtils.toString("bat")        = "bat"
ObjectUtils.toString(Boolean.TRUE) = "true"
```

Parameters: `obj`—the Object to `toString`, may be `null`
Returns: the passed in Object's `toString`, or nullStr if `null` input
See Also: `StringUtils.defaultString(String)`, `String.valueOf(Object)`

```
public static java.lang.String toString(java.lang.Object obj,
java.lang.String nullStr)
```

Gets the `toString` of an Object returning a specified text if `null` input.

```
ObjectUtils.toString(null, null)           = null
ObjectUtils.toString(null, "null")         = "null"
ObjectUtils.toString("", "null")           = ""
ObjectUtils.toString("bat", "null")        = "bat"
ObjectUtils.toString(Boolean.TRUE, "null") = "true"
```

Parameters: `obj`—the Object to `toString`, may be `null`
`nullStr`—the `String` to return if `null` input, may be `null`
Returns: the passed in Object's `toString`, or nullStr if `null` input
See Also: `StringUtils.defaultString(String,String)`, `String.valueOf(Object)`

org.apache.commons.lang.ObjectUtils.Null

```
public static class ObjectUtils.Null implements java.io.Serializable
```

Class used as a `null` placeholder where `null` has another meaning.

For example, in a HashMap the HashMap.get(java.lang.Object) method returns `null` if the Map contains `null` or if there is no matching key. The Null placeholder can be used to distinguish between these two cases.

Another example is Hashtable, where `null` cannot be stored.
See Also: Serialized Form

org.apache.commons.lang.RandomStringUtils

Operations for random `strings`.

Constructor Detail

```
public RandomStringUtils()
```

RandomStringUtils instances should NOT be constructed in standard programming. Instead, the class should be used as `RandomStringUtils.random(5);`.

This constructor is public to permit tools that require a JavaBean instance to operate.

Method Detail

```
public static java.lang.String random(int count)
```

Creates a random string whose length is the number of characters specified. Characters will be chosen from the set of all characters.

Parameters: count—the length of random string to create
Returns: the random string

```
public static java.lang.String randomAscii(int count)
```

Creates a random string whose length is the number of characters specified. Characters will be chosen from the set of characters whose ASCII value is between 32 and 126 (inclusive).

Parameters: count—the length of random string to create
Returns: the random string

```
public static java.lang.String randomAlphabetic(int count)
```

Creates a random string whose length is the number of characters specified. Characters will be chosen from the set of alphabetic characters.

Parameters: count—the length of random string to create
Returns: the random string

```
public static java.lang.String randomAlphanumeric(int count)
```

Creates a random string whose length is the number of characters specified. Characters will be chosen from the set of alpha-numeric characters.

Parameters: count—the length of random string to create
Returns: the random string

```
public static java.lang.String randomNumeric(int count)
```

Creates a random string whose length is the number of characters specified. Characters will be chosen from the set of numeric characters.

Parameters: count—the length of random string to create
Returns: the random string

```
public static java.lang.String random(int count, boolean letters,
boolean numbers)
```

Creates a random string whose length is the number of characters specified. Characters will be chosen from the set of alpha-numeric characters as indicated by the arguments.

Parameters: `count`—the length of random string to create
`letters`—if `true`, generated string will include alphabetic characters
`numbers`—if `true`, generatd string will include numeric characters
Returns: the random string

```
public static java.lang.String random(int count, int start, int end,
boolean letters, boolean numbers)
```

Creates a random string whose length is the number of characters specified. Characters will be chosen from the set of alpha-numeric characters as indicated by the arguments.

Parameters: `count`—the length of random string to create
`start`—the position in set of chars to start at
`end`—the position in set of chars to end before
`letters`—if `true`, generated string will include alphabetic characters
`numbers`—if `true`, generated string will include numeric characters
Returns: the random string

```
public static java.lang.String random(int count, int start, int end,
boolean letters, boolean numbers, char[] chars)
```

Creates a random string based on a variety of options, using default source of randomness. This method has exactly the same semantics as `random(int,int,int,boolean,boolean,char[],Random)`, but instead of using an externally supplied source of randomness, it uses the internal static Random instance.

Parameters: `count`—the length of random string to create
`start`—the position in set of chars to start at
`end`—the position in set of chars to end before
`letters`—only allow letters?
`numbers`—only allow numbers?
`chars`—the set of chars to choose randoms from. If `null`, then it will use the set of all chars.
Returns: the random string
Throws: `java.lang.ArrayIndexOutOfBoundsException`—if there are not (end−start) + 1 characters in the set array.

```
public static java.lang.String random(int count, int start, int end,
boolean letters, boolean numbers, char[] chars, java.util.Random
random)
```

Creates a random string based on a variety of options, using supplied source of randomness.

If start and end are both 0, start and end are set to ' ' and 'z', the ASCII printable characters will be used, unless letters and numbers are both false, in which case, start and end are set to 0 and Integer.MAX_VALUE. If set is not `null`, characters between start and end are chosen.

This method accepts a user-supplied Random instance to use as a source of randomness. By seeding a single Random instance with a fixed seed and using it for each call, the same random sequence of strings can be generated repeatedly and predictably.

Parameters: `count`—the length of random string to create
`start`—the position in set of chars to start at
`end`—the position in set of chars to end before
`letters`—only allow letters?
`numbers`—only allow numbers?
`chars`—the set of chars to choose randoms from. If `null`, then it will use the set of all chars.
`random`—a source of randomness
Returns: the random string
Throws: `java.lang.ArrayIndexOutOfBoundsException`—if there are not `(end-start) + 1` characters in the set array.
`java.lang.IllegalArgumentException`—if count < 0.

```
public static java.lang.String random(int count, java.lang.String chars)
```

Creates a random string whose length is the number of characters specified. Characters will be chosen from the set of characters specified.

Parameters: `count`—the length of random string to create
`chars`—the `String` containing the set of characters to use, may be `null`
Returns: the random string
Throws: `java.lang.IllegalArgumentException`—if count < 0.

```
public static java.lang.String random(int count, char[] chars)
```

Creates a random string whose length is the number of characters specified. Characters will be chosen from the set of characters specified.

Parameters: `count`—the length of random string to create
`chars`—the character array containing the set of characters to use, may be `null`
Returns: the random string
Throws: `java.lang.IllegalArgumentException`—if count < 0.

org.apache.commons.lang.SerializationUtils

Assists with the serialization process and performs additional functionality based on serialization.

- ☞ Deep clone using serialization
- ☞ Serialize managing finally and IOException
- ☞ Deserialize managing finally and IOException

This class throws exceptions for invalid `null` inputs. Each method documents its behavior in more detail.

Constructor Detail

```
public SerializationUtils()
```

SerializationUtils instances should NOT be constructed in standard programming. Instead, the class should be used as `SerializationUtils.clone(object)`. This constructor is public to permit tools that require a JavaBean instance to operate.

Method Detail

```
public static java.lang.Object clone(java.io.Serializable object)
```

Deep clone an Object using serialization. This is many times slower than writing clone methods by hand on all objects in your object graph. However, for complex object graphs, or for those that don't support deep cloning, this can be a simple alternative implementation. Of course all the objects must be Serializable.

> **Parameters:** `object`—the `Serializable` object to clone
> **Returns:** the cloned object
> **Throws:** `SerializationException`—(runtime) if the serialization fails

```
public static void serialize(java.io.Serializable obj,
java.io.OutputStream outputStream)
```

Serializes an Object to the specified stream.

The stream will be closed once the object is written. This avoids the need for a finally clause, and maybe also exception handling, in the application code.

The stream passed in is not buffered internally within this method. This is the responsibility of your application if desired.

> **Parameters:** `obj`—the object to serialize to bytes, may be `null`
> `outputStream`—the stream to write to, must not be `null`
> **Throws:** `java.lang.IllegalArgumentException`—if `outputStream` is `null`
> `SerializationException`—(runtime) if the serialization fails

```
public static byte[] serialize(java.io.Serializable obj)
```

Serializes an Object to a byte array for storage/serialization.

> **Parameters:** `obj`—the object to serialize to bytes
> **Returns:** a byte[] with the converted Serializable
> **Throws:** `SerializationException`—(runtime) if the serialization fails

```
public static java.lang.Object deserialize(java.io.InputStream
inputStream)
```

Deserializes an Object from the specified stream. The stream will be closed once the object is written. This avoids the need for a finally clause, and maybe also exception handling, in the application code.

The stream passed in is not buffered internally within this method. This is the responsibility of your application if desired.

> **Parameters:** `inputStream`—the serialized object input stream, must not be `null`
>
> **Returns:** the deserialized object
>
> **Throws:** `java.lang.IllegalArgumentException`—if `inputStream` is `null`
> `SerializationException`—(runtime) if the serialization fails

```
public static java.lang.Object deserialize(byte[] objectData)
```

Deserializes a single Object from an array of bytes.

> **Parameters:** `objectData`—the serialized object, must not be `null`
>
> **Returns:** the deserialized object
>
> **Throws:** `java.lang.IllegalArgumentException`—if `objectData` is `null`
> `SerializationException`—(runtime) if the serialization fails

org.apache.commons.lang.StringEscapeUtils

Escapes and unescapes `Strings` for Java, Java Script, HTML, XML, and SQL.

Constructor Detail

```
public StringEscapeUtils()
```

StringEscapeUtils instances should NOT be constructed in standard programming. Instead, the class should be used as:

```
StringEscapeUtils.escapeJava("foo");
```

This constructor is public to permit tools that require a JavaBean instance to operate.

Method Detail

```
public static java.lang.String escapeJava(java.lang.String str)
```

Escapes the characters in a `String` using Java `String` rules. Deals correctly with quotes and control-chars (tab, backslash, cr, ff, etc.). So a tab becomes the characters '\\' and 't'. The only difference between Java strings and JavaScript strings is that in JavaScript, a single quote must be escaped.

Example:

```
input string:  He didn't say, "Stop!"
output string: He didn't say, \"Stop!\"
```

Parameters: str—String to escape values in, may be null
Returns: String with escaped values, null if null string input

```
public static void escapeJava(java.io.Writer out, java.lang.String str)
    throws java.io.IOException
```

Escapes the characters in a String using Java String rules to a Writer. A null string input has no effect.

Parameters: out—Writer to write escaped string into
str—String to escape values in, may be null
Throws: java.lang.IllegalArgumentException—if the Writer is null
java.io.IOException—if error occurs on underlying Writer
See Also: escapeJava(java.lang.String)

```
public static java.lang.String escapeJavaScript(java.lang.String str)
```

Escapes the characters in a String using JavaScript String rules. Escapes any values it finds into their JavaScript String form. Deals correctly with quotes and control-chars (tab, backslash, cr, ff, etc.). So a tab becomes the characters '\\' and 't'.

The only difference between Java strings and JavaScript strings is that in JavaScript, a single quote must be escaped.

Example:

```
input string: He didn't say, "Stop!"
output string: He didn\'t say, \"Stop!\"
```

Parameters: str—String to escape values in, may be null
Returns: String with escaped values, null if null string input

```
public static void escapeJavaScript(java.io.Writer out,
    java.lang.String str) throws java.io.IOException
```

Escapes the characters in a String using JavaScript String rules to a Writer. A null string input has no effect.

Parameters: out—Writer to write escaped string into
str—String to escape values in, may be null
Throws: java.lang.IllegalArgumentException—if the Writer is null
java.io.IOException—if error occurs on underlying Writer
See Also: escapeJavaScript(java.lang.String)

```
public static java.lang.String unescapeJava(java.lang.String str)
```

Unescapes any Java literals found in the String. For example, it will turn a sequence of '\' and 'n' into a newline character, unless the '\' is preceded by another '\'.

Parameters: `str`—the `String` to unescape, may be `null`
Returns: a new unescaped `String`, `null` if `null` string input

```
public static void unescapeJava(java.io.Writer out,
java.lang.String str)
    throws java.io.IOException
```

Unescapes any Java literals found in the `String` to a Writer. For example, it will turn a sequence of '\' and 'n' into a newline character, unless the '\' is preceded by another '\'. A `null` string input has no effect.

Parameters: `out`—the `Writer` used to output unescaped characters
`str`—the `String` to unescape, may be `null`
Throws: `java.lang.IllegalArgumentException`—if the Writer is `null`
`java.io.IOException`—if error occurs on underlying Writer

```
public static java.lang.String unescapeJavaScript(java.lang.String
str)
```

Unescapes any JavaScript literals found in the `String`. For example, it will turn a sequence of '\' and 'n' into a newline character, unless the '\' is preceded by another '\'.

Parameters: `str`—the `String` to unescape, may be `null`
Returns: A new unescaped `String`, `null` if `null` string input
See Also: `unescapeJava(String)`

```
public static void unescapeJavaScript(java.io.Writer out,
java.lang.String str) throws java.io.IOException
```

Unescapes any JavaScript literals found in the `String` to a Writer.

For example, it will turn a sequence of '\' and 'n' into a newline character, unless the '\' is preceded by another '\'.

A `null` string input has no effect.

Parameters: `out`—the `Writer` used to output unescaped characters
`str`—the `String` to unescape, may be `null`
Throws: `java.lang.IllegalArgumentException`—if the Writer is `null`
`java.io.IOException`—if error occurs on underlying Writer
See Also: `unescapeJava(Writer,String)`

```
public static java.lang.String escapeHtml(java.lang.String str)
```

Escapes the characters in a `String` using HTML entities.

For example: "bread" & "butter" => "bread" & "butter".

Supports all known HTML 4.0 entities, including funky accents.

Parameters: `str`—the `String` to escape, may be `null`
Returns: a new escaped `String`, `null` if `null` string input

See Also: unescapeHtml(String), ISO Entities, HTML 3.2 Character Entities for ISO Latin-1, HTML 4.0 Character entity references, HTML 4.01 Character References, HTML 4.01 Code positions

```
public static java.lang.String unescapeHtml(java.lang.String str)
```

Unescapes a string containing entity escapes to a string containing the actual Unicode characters corresponding to the escapes. Supports HTML 4.0 entities.

For example, the string "<Français>" will become "<Français>"

If an entity is unrecognized, it is left alone, and inserted verbatim into the result string. e.g. ">&zzzz;x" will become ">&zzzz;x".

Parameters: str—the String to unescape, may be null
Returns: a new unescaped String, null if null string input
See Also: escapeHtml(String)

```
public static java.lang.String escapeXml(java.lang.String str)
```

Escapes the characters in a string using XML entities.

For example: "bread" & "butter" => "bread" & "butter".

Supports only the four basic XML entities (gt, lt, quot, amp). Does not support DTDs or external entities.

Parameters: str—the String to escape, may be null
Returns: a new escaped String, null if null string input
See Also: unescapeXml(java.lang.String)

```
public static java.lang.String unescapeXml(java.lang.String str)
```

Unescapes a string containing XML entity escapes to a string containing the actual Unicode characters corresponding to the escapes.

Supports only the four basic XML entities (gt, lt, quot, amp). Does not support DTDs or external entities.

Parameters: str—the String to unescape, may be null
Returns: a new unescaped String, null if null string input
See Also: escapeXml(String)

```
public static java.lang.String escapeSql(java.lang.String str)
```

Escapes the characters in a string to be suitable to pass to an SQL query. For example,

```
statement.executeQuery("SELECT * FROM MOVIES WHERE TITLE='" +
StringEscapeUtils.escapeSql("McHale's Navy") +
"'");
```

At present, this method only turns single-quotes into doubled single-quotes ("McHale's Navy" => "McHale's Navy"). It does not handle the cases of percent (%) or underscore (_) for use in LIKE clauses.

> see `http://www.jguru.com/faq/view.jsp?EID=8881`

Parameters: `str`—the string to escape, may be `null`
Returns: a new `String`, escaped for SQL, `null` if `null` string input

org.apache.commons.lang.StringUtils

Operations on `String` that are `null` safe.

- `IsEmpty/IsBlank`—checks if a `String` contains text
- `Trim/Strip`—removes leading and trailing whitespace
- `Equals`—compares two strings `null`-safe
- `IndexOf/LastIndexOf/Contains`—`null`-safe index-of checks
- `IndexOfAny/LastIndexOfAny/IndexOfAnyBut/LastIndexOfAnyBut`—index-of any of a set of `strings`
- `ContainsOnly/ContainsNone`—does `String` contains only/none of these characters
- `Substring/Left/Right/Mid`—`null`-safe substring extractions
- `SubstringBefore/SubstringAfter/SubstringBetween`—substring extraction relative to other strings
- `Split/Join`—splits a `String` into an array of substrings and vice versa
- `Replace/Delete/Overlay`—Searches a `String` and replaces one `String` with another
- `Chomp/Chop`—removes the last part of a `String`
- `LeftPad/RightPad/Center/Repeat`—pads a `String`
- `UpperCase/LowerCase/SwapCase/Capitalize/Uncapitalize`—changes the case of a `String`
- `CountMatches`—counts the number of occurrences of one `string` in another
- `IsAlpha/IsNumeric/IsWhitespace`—checks the characters in a `String`
- `DefaultString`—protects against a `null` input `string`
- `Reverse/ReverseDelimited`—reverses a `String`
- `Abbreviate`—abbreviates a `string` using ellipsis
- `Difference`—compares two `strings` and reports on their differences
- `LevensteinDistance`—the number of changes needed to change one `String` into another

The StringUtils class defines certain words related to `string` handling.

- `null`—`null`
- empty—a zero-length string (`""`)

- ☞ space—the space character (' ', char 32)
- ☞ whitespace—the characters defined by `Character.isWhitespace(char)`
- ☞ trim—the characters <= 32 as in `String.trim()`

StringUtils handles `null` input `String`s quietly. That is to say that a `null` input will return `null`. Where a `boolean` or int is being returned, details vary by method.

A side effect of the `null` handling is that a NullPointerException should be considered a bug in StringUtils (except for deprecated methods).

Methods in this class give sample code to explain their operation. The symbol * is used to indicate any input including `null`.

Field Detail

    public static final java.lang.String EMPTY

The empty `String` `""`.
See Also: Constant Field Values

Constructor Detail

    public StringUtils()

StringUtils instances should NOT be constructed in standard programming. Instead, the class should be used as `StringUtils.trim("foo");`.

This constructor is public to permit tools that require a JavaBean instance to operate.

Method Detail

    public static boolean isEmpty(java.lang.String str)

Checks if a `String` is empty ("") or `null`.

```
StringUtils.isEmpty(null)      = true
StringUtils.isEmpty("")        = true
StringUtils.isEmpty(" ")       = false
StringUtils.isEmpty("bob")     = false
StringUtils.isEmpty(" bob ")   = false
```

NOTE: This method changed in Lang version 2.0. It no longer trims the `String`. That functionality is available in isBlank().

Parameters: str—the `String` to check, may be `null`
Returns: `true` if the `String` is empty or `null`

    public static boolean isNotEmpty(java.lang.String str)

Checks if a `String` is not empty ("") and not `null`.

```
StringUtils.isNotEmpty(null)  = false
StringUtils.isNotEmpty("")    = false
StringUtils.isNotEmpty(" ")   = true
StringUtils.isNotEmpty("bob") = true
StringUtils.isNotEmpty(" bob ") = true
```

Parameters: `str`—the `String` to check, may be `null`
Returns: `true` if the `String` is not empty and not `null`

```
public static boolean isBlank(java.lang.String str)
```

Checks if a `String` is whitespace, empty ("") or `null`.

```
StringUtils.isBlank(null)  = true
StringUtils.isBlank("")    = true
StringUtils.isBlank(" ")   = true
StringUtils.isBlank("bob") = false
StringUtils.isBlank(" bob ") = false
```

Parameters: `str`—the `String` to check, may be `null`
Returns: `true` if the `String` is `null`, empty or whitespace

```
public static boolean isNotBlank(java.lang.String str)
```

Checks if a `String` is not empty (""), not `null` and not whitespace only.

```
StringUtils.isNotBlank(null)  = false
StringUtils.isNotBlank("")    = false
StringUtils.isNotBlank(" ")   = false
StringUtils.isNotBlank("bob") = true
StringUtils.isNotBlank(" bob ") = true
```

Parameters: `str`—the `String` to check, may be `null`
Returns: `true` if the `String` is not empty and not `null` and not whitespace

```
public static java.lang.String trim(java.lang.String str)
```

Removes control characters (char <= 32) from both ends of this `String`, handling `null` by returning `null`.

The `String` is trimmed using `String.trim()`. Trim removes start and end characters <= 32. To strip whitespace use `strip(String)`. To trim your choice of characters, use the `strip(String, String)` methods.

```
StringUtils.trim(null)    = null
StringUtils.trim("")      = ""
StringUtils.trim("   ")   = ""
StringUtils.trim("abc")   = "abc"
StringUtils.trim("  abc ") = "abc"
```

Parameters: `str`—the `String` to be trimmed, may be `null`
Returns: the trimmed string, `null` if `null` String input

```
public static java.lang.String trimToNull(java.lang.String str)
```

Removes control characters (char <= 32) from both ends of this `String` returning `null` if the `String` is empty ("") after the trim or if it is `null`. The `String` is trimmed using `String.trim()`. Trim removes start and end characters <= 32. To strip whitespace use `stripToNull(String)`.

```
StringUtils.trimToNull(null)  = null
StringUtils.trimToNull("")    = null
StringUtils.trimToNull("   ") = null
StringUtils.trimToNull("abc") = "abc"
StringUtils.trimToNull("  abc  ") = "abc"
```

Parameters: `str`—the `String` to be trimmed, may be `null`
Returns: the trimmed `String`, `null` if only chars <= 32, empty or `null` String input

```
public static java.lang.String trimToEmpty(java.lang.String str)
```

Removes control characters (char <= 32) from both ends of this `String` returning an empty `String` ("") if the `String` is empty ("") after the trim or if it is `null`.

The `String` is trimmed using `String.trim()`. Trim removes start and end characters <= 32. To strip whitespace use `stripToEmpty(String)`.

```
StringUtils.trimToEmpty(null)  = ""
StringUtils.trimToEmpty("")    = ""
StringUtils.trimToEmpty("   ") = ""
StringUtils.trimToEmpty("abc") = "abc"
StringUtils.trimToEmpty("  abc  ") = "abc"
```

Parameters: `str`—the `String` to be trimmed, may be `null`
Returns: the trimmed `String`, or an empty `String` if `null` input

```
public static java.lang.String strip(java.lang.String str)
```

Strips whitespace from the start and end of a `String`.

This is similar to `trim(String)` but removes whitespace. Whitespace is defined by `Character.isWhitespace(char)`.

A `null` input `String` returns `null`.

```
StringUtils.strip(null)  = null
StringUtils.strip("")    = ""
StringUtils.strip("   ") = ""
StringUtils.strip("abc") = "abc"
```

```
StringUtils.strip(" abc") = "abc"
StringUtils.strip("abc ") = "abc"
StringUtils.strip(" abc ") = "abc"
StringUtils.strip(" ab c ") = "ab c"
```

Parameters: `str`—the `String` to remove whitespace from, may be `null`
Returns: the stripped `String`, `null` if `null` `String` input

```
public static java.lang.String stripToNull(java.lang.String str)
```

Strips whitespace from the start and end of a `String` returning `null` if the `String` is empty (`""`) after the strip.

This is similar to `trimToNull(String)` but removes whitespace. Whitespace is defined by `Character.isWhitespace(char)`.

```
StringUtils.strip(null) = null
StringUtils.strip("") = null
StringUtils.strip(" ") = null
StringUtils.strip("abc") = "abc"
StringUtils.strip(" abc") = "abc"
StringUtils.strip("abc ") = "abc"
StringUtils.strip(" abc ") = "abc"
StringUtils.strip(" ab c ") = "ab c"
```

Parameters: `str`—the `String` to be stripped, may be `null`
Returns: the stripped `String`, `null` if whitespace, empty or `null` `String` input

```
public static java.lang.String stripToEmpty(java.lang.String str)
```

Strips whitespace from the start and end of a `String` returning an empty `String` if `null` input.

This is similar to `trimToEmpty(String)` but removes whitespace. Whitespace is defined by `Character.isWhitespace(char)`.

```
StringUtils.strip(null) = ""
StringUtils.strip("") = ""
StringUtils.strip(" ") = ""
StringUtils.strip("abc") = "abc"
StringUtils.strip(" abc") = "abc"
StringUtils.strip("abc ") = "abc"
StringUtils.strip(" abc ") = "abc"
StringUtils.strip(" ab c ") = "ab c"
```

Parameters: `str`—the `String` to be stripped, may be `null`
Returns: the trimmed `String`, or an empty `String` if `null` input

```
public static java.lang.String strip(java.lang.String str,
       java.lang.String stripChars)
```

Strips any of a set of characters from the start and end of a `string`. This is similar to `string.trim()` but allows the characters to be stripped to be controlled.

A `null` input `string` returns `null`. An empty string ("") input returns the empty string. If the stripChars `string` is `null`, whitespace is stripped as defined by `Character.isWhitespace(char)`. Alternatively use `strip(String)`.

```
StringUtils.strip(null, *)        = null
StringUtils.strip("", *)          = ""
StringUtils.strip("abc", null)    = "abc"
StringUtils.strip(" abc", null)   = "abc"
StringUtils.strip("abc ", null)   = "abc"
StringUtils.strip(" abc ", null)  = "abc"
StringUtils.strip(" abcyx", "xyz") = " abc"
```

Parameters: str—the `String` to remove characters from, may be `null`
stripChars—the characters to remove, `null` treated as whitespace
Returns: the stripped `String`, `null` if `null` String input

```
public static java.lang.String stripStart(java.lang.String str,
java.lang.String stripChars)
```

Strips any of a set of characters from the start of a `string`. A `null` input `string` returns `null`. An empty string ("") input returns the empty string. If the stripChars `string` is `null`, whitespace is stripped as defined by `Character.isWhitespace(char)`.

```
StringUtils.stripStart(null, *)       = null
StringUtils.stripStart("", *)         = ""
StringUtils.stripStart("abc", "")     = "abc"
StringUtils.stripStart("abc", null)   = "abc"
StringUtils.stripStart(" abc", null)  = "abc"
StringUtils.stripStart("abc ", null)  = "abc "
StringUtils.stripStart(" abc ", null) = "abc "
StringUtils.stripStart("yxabc ", "xyz") = "abc "
```

Parameters: str—the `String` to remove characters from, may be `null`
stripChars—the characters to remove, `null` treated as whitespace
Returns: the stripped `String`, `null` if `null` String input

```
public static java.lang.String stripEnd(java.lang.String str,
java.lang.String stripChars)
```

Strips any of a set of characters from the end of a `string`. A `null` input `string` returns `null`. An empty string ("") input returns the empty string. If the `stripChars String` is `null`, whitespace is stripped as defined by `Character.isWhitespace(char)`.

```
StringUtils.stripEnd(null, *)     = null
StringUtils.stripEnd("", *)       = ""
StringUtils.stripEnd("abc", "")   = "abc"
```

```
StringUtils.stripEnd("abc", null)    = "abc"
StringUtils.stripEnd("  abc", null)  = "  abc"
StringUtils.stripEnd("abc  ", null)  = "abc"
StringUtils.stripEnd(" abc ", null)  = " abc"
StringUtils.stripEnd("  abcyx", "xyz") = "  abc"
```

Parameters: str—the String to remove characters from, may be null
stripChars—the characters to remove, null treated as whitespace
Returns: the stripped String, null if null String input

```
public static java.lang.String[] stripAll(java.lang.String[] strs)
```

Strips whitespace from the start and end of every String in an array. Whitespace is defined by Character.isWhitespace(char).

A new array is returned each time, except for length zero. A null array will return null. An empty array will return itself. A null array entry will be ignored.

```
StringUtils.stripAll(null)             = null
StringUtils.stripAll([])               = []
StringUtils.stripAll(["abc", "  abc"]) = ["abc", "abc"]
StringUtils.stripAll(["abc ", null])   = ["abc", null]
```

Parameters: strs—the array to remove whitespace from, may be null
Returns: the stripped Strings, null if null array input

```
public static java.lang.String[] stripAll(java.lang.String[] strs,
    java.lang.String stripChars)
```

Strips any of a set of characters from the start and end of every String in an array. Whitespace is defined by Character.isWhitespace(char).

A new array is returned each time, except for length zero. A null array will return null. An empty array will return itself. A null array entry will be ignored. A null stripChars will strip whitespace as defined by Character.isWhitespace(char).

```
StringUtils.stripAll(null, *)                = null
StringUtils.stripAll([], *)                  = []
StringUtils.stripAll(["abc", "  abc"], null) = ["abc", "abc"]
StringUtils.stripAll(["abc ", null], null)   = ["abc", null]
StringUtils.stripAll(["abc ", null], "yz")   = ["abc ", null]
StringUtils.stripAll(["yabcz", null], "yz")  = ["abc", null]
```

Parameters: strs—the array to remove characters from, may be null
stripChars—the characters to remove, null treated as whitespace
Returns: the stripped Strings, null if null array input

```
public static boolean equals(java.lang.String str1, java.lang.String
    str2)
```

Compares two strings, returning true if they are equal. nulls are handled without exceptions. Two null references are considered to be equal. The comparison is case sensitive.

```
StringUtils.equals(null, null) = true
StringUtils.equals(null, "abc") = false
StringUtils.equals("abc", null) = false
StringUtils.equals("abc", "abc") = true
StringUtils.equals("abc", "ABC") = false
```

Parameters: str1—the first String, may be null
str2—the second String, may be null
Returns: true if the strings are equal, case sensitive, or both null
See Also: String.equals(Object)

```
public static boolean equalsIgnoreCase(java.lang.String str1,
    java.lang.String str2)
```

Compares two strings, returning true if they are equal ignoring the case. nulls are handled without exceptions. Two null references are considered equal. Comparison is case insensitive.

```
StringUtils.equalsIgnoreCase(null, null) = true
StringUtils.equalsIgnoreCase(null, "abc") = false
StringUtils.equalsIgnoreCase("abc", null) = false
StringUtils.equalsIgnoreCase("abc", "abc") = true
StringUtils.equalsIgnoreCase("abc", "ABC") = true
```

Parameters: str1—the first String, may be null
str2—the second String, may be null
Returns: true if the strings are equal, case insensitive, or both null
See Also: String.equalsIgnoreCase(String)

```
public static int indexOf(java.lang.String str, char searchChar)
```

Finds the first index within a string, handling null. This method uses String.indexOf(int). A null or empty ("") String will return -1.

```
StringUtils.indexOf(null, *) = -1
StringUtils.indexOf("", *) = -1
StringUtils.indexOf("aabaabaa", 'a') = 0
StringUtils.indexOf("aabaabaa", 'b') = 2
```

Parameters: str—the String to check, may be null
searchChar—the character to find
Returns: the first index of the search character, -1 if no match or null string input

```
public static int indexOf(java.lang.String str, char searchChar, int
    startPos)
```

Finds the first index within a String from a start position, handling null. This method uses String.indexOf(int, int).

A null or empty ("") String will return -1. A negative start position is treated as zero. A start position greater than the string length returns -1.

```
StringUtils.indexOf(null, *, *)          = -1
StringUtils.indexOf("", *, *)            = -1
StringUtils.indexOf("aabaabaa", 'b', 0)  = 2
StringUtils.indexOf("aabaabaa", 'b', 3)  = 5
StringUtils.indexOf("aabaabaa", 'b', 9)  = -1
StringUtils.indexOf("aabaabaa", 'b', -1) = 2
```

Parameters: str—the String to check, may be null
searchChar—the character to find
startPos—the start position, negative treated as zero
Returns: the first index of the search character, -1 if no match or null string input

```
public static int indexOf(java.lang.String str, java.lang.String
    searchStr)
```

Finds the first index within a String, handling null. This method uses String.indexOf(String). A null String will return -1.

```
StringUtils.indexOf(null, *)             = -1
StringUtils.indexOf(*, null)             = -1
StringUtils.indexOf("", "")              = 0
StringUtils.indexOf("aabaabaa", "a")     = 0
StringUtils.indexOf("aabaabaa", "b")     = 2
StringUtils.indexOf("aabaabaa", "ab")    = 1
StringUtils.indexOf("aabaabaa", "")      = 0
```

Parameters: str—the String to check, may be null
searchStr—the String to find, may be null
Returns: the first index of the search String, -1 if no match or null String input

```
public static int indexOf(java.lang.String str, java.lang.String
    searchStr, int startPos)
```

Finds the first index within a String, handling null. This method uses String.indexOf(String, int).

A null String will return -1. A negative start position is treated as zero. An empty ("") search String always matches. A start position greater than the string length only matches an empty search String.

```
StringUtils.indexOf(null, *, *)          = -1
StringUtils.indexOf(*, null, *)          = -1
StringUtils.indexOf("", "", 0)           = 0
StringUtils.indexOf("aabaabaa", "a", 0)  = 0
```

```
StringUtils.indexOf("aabaabaa", "b", 0) = 2
StringUtils.indexOf("aabaabaa", "ab", 0) = 1
StringUtils.indexOf("aabaabaa", "b", 3) = 5
StringUtils.indexOf("aabaabaa", "b", 9) = -1
StringUtils.indexOf("aabaabaa", "b", -1) = 2
StringUtils.indexOf("aabaabaa", "", 2) = 2
StringUtils.indexOf("abc", "", 9) = 3
```

Parameters: str—the String to check, may be null
searchStr—the String to find, may be null
startPos—the start position, negative treated as zero

Returns: the first index of the search string, -1 if no match or null string input

```
public static int lastIndexOf(java.lang.String str, char searchChar)
```

Finds the last index within a String, handling null. This method uses String.lastIndexOf(int).

A null or empty ("") String will return -1.

```
StringUtils.lastIndexOf(null, *) = -1
StringUtils.lastIndexOf("", *) = -1
StringUtils.lastIndexOf("aabaabaa", 'a') = 7
StringUtils.lastIndexOf("aabaabaa", 'b') = 5
```

Parameters: str—the String to check, may be null
searchChar—the character to find

Returns: the last index of the search character, -1 if no match or null string input

```
public static int lastIndexOf(java.lang.String str, char searchChar,
    int startPos)
```

Finds the last index within a String from a start position, handling null. This method uses String.lastIndexOf(int, int).

A null or empty ("") String will return -1. A negative start position returns -1. A start position greater than the string length searches the whole string.

```
StringUtils.lastIndexOf(null, *, *) = -1
StringUtils.lastIndexOf("", *, *) = -1
StringUtils.lastIndexOf("aabaabaa", 'b', 8) = 5
StringUtils.lastIndexOf("aabaabaa", 'b', 4) = 2
StringUtils.lastIndexOf("aabaabaa", 'b', 0) = -1
StringUtils.lastIndexOf("aabaabaa", 'b', 9) = 5
StringUtils.lastIndexOf("aabaabaa", 'b', -1) = -1
StringUtils.lastIndexOf("aabaabaa", 'a', 0) = 0
```

Parameters: str—the String to check, may be null
searchChar—the character to find
startPos—the start position

Returns: the last index of the search character, -1 if no match or `null` string input

```
public static int lastIndexOf(java.lang.String str, java.lang.String searchStr)
```

Finds the last index within a `String`, handling `null`. This method uses `String.lastIndexOf(String)`.

A `null` `String` will return -1.

```
StringUtils.lastIndexOf(null, *)         = -1
StringUtils.lastIndexOf(*, null)         = -1
StringUtils.lastIndexOf("", "")          = 0
StringUtils.lastIndexOf("aabaabaa", "a") = 0
StringUtils.lastIndexOf("aabaabaa", "b") = 2
StringUtils.lastIndexOf("aabaabaa", "ab") = 1
StringUtils.lastIndexOf("aabaabaa", "")  = 8
```

Parameters: `str`—the `String` to check, may be `null`
`searchStr`—the `String` to find, may be `null`
Returns: the last index of the search `string`, -1 if no match or `null` string input

```
public static int lastIndexOf(java.lang.String str, java.lang.String searchStr, int startPos)
```

Finds the first index within a `String`, handling `null`. This method uses `String.lastIndexOf(String, int)`.

A `null` `String` will return -1. A negative start position returns -1. An empty (`""`) search `String` always matches unless the start position is negative. A start position greater than the string length searches the whole string.

```
StringUtils.lastIndexOf(null, *, *)            = -1
StringUtils.lastIndexOf(*, null, *)            = -1
StringUtils.lastIndexOf("aabaabaa", "a", 8)    = 7
StringUtils.lastIndexOf("aabaabaa", "b", 8)    = 5
StringUtils.lastIndexOf("aabaabaa", "ab", 8)   = 4
StringUtils.lastIndexOf("aabaabaa", "b", 9)    = 5
StringUtils.lastIndexOf("aabaabaa", "b", -1)   = -1
StringUtils.lastIndexOf("aabaabaa", "a", 0)    = 0
StringUtils.lastIndexOf("aabaabaa", "b", 0)    = -1
```

Parameters: `str`—the `String` to check, may be `null`
`searchStr`—the `String` to find, may be `null`
`startPos`—the start position, negative treated as zero
Returns: the first index of the search `string`, -1 if no match or `null` string input

```
public static boolean contains(java.lang.String str, char searchChar)
```

Checks if `string` contains a search character, handling `null`. This method uses `String.indexOf(int)`. A `null` or empty ("") `string` will return false.

```
StringUtils.contains(null, *)    = false
StringUtils.contains("", *)      = false
StringUtils.contains("abc", 'a') = true
StringUtils.contains("abc", 'z') = false
```

Parameters: str—the `string` to check, may be `null`
searchChar—the character to find
Returns: true if the `string` contains the search character, false if not or `null` string input

```
public static boolean contains(java.lang.String str, java.lang.String
searchStr)
```

Find the first index within a `string`, handling `null`. This method uses `String.indexOf(int)`. A `null` `string` will return false.

```
StringUtils.contains(null, *)    = false
StringUtils.contains(*, null)    = false
StringUtils.contains("", "")     = true
StringUtils.contains("abc", "")  = true
StringUtils.contains("abc", "a") = true
StringUtils.contains("abc", "z") = false
```

Parameters: str—the `string` to check, may be `null`
searchStr—the `string` to find, may be `null`
Returns: true if the `string` contains the search character, false if not or `null` string input

```
public static int indexOfAny(java.lang.String str, char[] searchChars)
```

Search a `string` to find the first index of any character in the given set of characters.

A `null` `string` will return -1. A `null` or zero length search array will return -1.

```
StringUtils.indexOfAny(null, *)                = -1
StringUtils.indexOfAny("", *)                  = -1
StringUtils.indexOfAny(*, null)                = -1
StringUtils.indexOfAny(*, [])                  = -1
StringUtils.indexOfAny("zzabyycdxx",['z','a']) = 0
StringUtils.indexOfAny("zzabyycdxx",['b','y']) = 3
StringUtils.indexOfAny("aba", ['z'])           = -1
```

Parameters: str—the `string` to check, may be `null`
searchChars—the chars to search for, may be `null`

Returns: the index of any of the chars, -1 if no match or `null` input

```
public static int indexOfAny(java.lang.String str, java.lang.String
searchChars)
```

Search a `String` to find the first index of any character in the given set of characters.

A `null` `String` will return -1. A `null` search string will return -1.

```
StringUtils.indexOfAny(null, *) = -1
StringUtils.indexOfAny("", *) = -1
StringUtils.indexOfAny(*, null) = -1
StringUtils.indexOfAny(*, "") = -1
StringUtils.indexOfAny("zzabyycdxx", "za") = 0
StringUtils.indexOfAny("zzabyycdxx", "by") = 3
StringUtils.indexOfAny("aba","z") = -1
```

Parameters: str—the `String` to check, may be `null`
searchChars—the chars to search for, may be `null`
Returns: the index of any of the chars, -1 if no match or `null` input

```
public static int indexOfAnyBut(java.lang.String str, char[]
searchChars)
```

Search a `String` to find the first index of any character not in the given set of characters.

A `null` `String` will return -1. A `null` or zero length search array will return -1.

```
StringUtils.indexOfAnyBut(null, *) = -1
StringUtils.indexOfAnyBut("", *) = -1
StringUtils.indexOfAnyBut(*, null) = -1
StringUtils.indexOfAnyBut(*, []) = -1
StringUtils.indexOfAnyBut("zzabyycdxx",'za') = 3
StringUtils.indexOfAnyBut("zzabyycdxx", '') = 0
StringUtils.indexOfAnyBut("aba", 'ab') = -1
```

Parameters: str—the `String` to check, may be `null`
searchChars—the chars to search for, may be `null`
Returns: the index of any of the chars, -1 if no match or `null` input

```
public static int indexOfAnyBut(java.lang.String str, java.lang.String
searchChars)
```

Search a `String` to find the first index of any character not in the given set of characters.

A `null` `String` will return -1. A `null` search string will return -1.

```
StringUtils.indexOfAnyBut(null, *) = -1
StringUtils.indexOfAnyBut("", *) = -1
StringUtils.indexOfAnyBut(*, null) = -1
```

```
StringUtils.indexOfAnyBut(*, "") = -1
StringUtils.indexOfAnyBut("zzabyycdxx", "za") = 3
StringUtils.indexOfAnyBut("zzabyycdxx", "") = 0
StringUtils.indexOfAnyBut("aba","ab") = -1
```

Parameters: `str`—the `String` to check, may be `null`
searchChars—the chars to search for, may be `null`
Returns: the index of any of the chars, -1 if no match or `null` input

```
public static boolean containsOnly(java.lang.String str, char[] valid)
```

Checks if the `string` contains only certain characters.

A `null` `String` will return false. A `null` valid character array will return false. An empty `string` (`""`) always returns true.

```
StringUtils.containsOnly(null, *) = false
StringUtils.containsOnly(*, null) = false
StringUtils.containsOnly("", *) = true
StringUtils.containsOnly("ab", '') = false
StringUtils.containsOnly("abab", 'abc') = true
StringUtils.containsOnly("ab1", 'abc') = false
StringUtils.containsOnly("abz", 'abc') = false
```

Parameters: `str`—the `String` to check, may be `null`
valid—an array of valid chars, may be `null`
Returns: `true` if it only contains valid chars and is non-`null`

```
public static boolean containsOnly(java.lang.String str,
java.lang.String validChars)
```

Checks if the `string` contains only certain characters.

A `null` `String` will return false. A `null` valid character `string` will return false. An empty `string` (`""`) always returns true.

```
StringUtils.containsOnly(null, *) = false
StringUtils.containsOnly(*, null) = false
StringUtils.containsOnly("", *) = true
StringUtils.containsOnly("ab", "") = false
StringUtils.containsOnly("abab", "abc") = true
StringUtils.containsOnly("ab1", "abc") = false
StringUtils.containsOnly("abz", "abc") = false
```

Parameters: `str`—the `String` to check, may be `null`
validChars—a `String` of valid chars, may be `null`
Returns: `true` if it only contains valid chars and is non-`null`

```
public static boolean containsNone(java.lang.String str, char[]
invalidChars)
```

Checks that the `string` does not contain certain characters.

A `null` `String` will return true. A `null` invalid character array will return true. An empty `String` (" ") always returns true.

```
StringUtils.containsNone(null, *) = true
StringUtils.containsNone(*, null) = true
StringUtils.containsNone("", *) = true
StringUtils.containsNone("ab", '') = true
StringUtils.containsNone("abab", 'xyz') = true
StringUtils.containsNone("ab1", 'xyz') = true
StringUtils.containsNone("abz", 'xyz') = false
```

Parameters: str—the `String` to check, may be `null`
invalidChars—an array of invalid chars, may be `null`
Returns: `true` if it contains none of the invalid chars, or is `null`

```
public static boolean containsNone(java.lang.String str,
    java.lang.String invalidChars)
```

Checks that the `String` does not contain certain characters.

A `null` `String` will return true. A `null` invalid character array will return true. An empty `String` (" ") always returns true.

```
StringUtils.containsNone(null, *) = true
StringUtils.containsNone(*, null) = true
StringUtils.containsNone("", *) = true
StringUtils.containsNone("ab", "") = true
StringUtils.containsNone("abab", "xyz") = true
StringUtils.containsNone("ab1", "xyz") = true
StringUtils.containsNone("abz", "xyz") = false
```

Parameters: str—the `String` to check, may be `null`
invalidChars—a `String` of invalid chars, may be `null`
Returns: `true` if it contains none of the invalid chars, or is `null`

```
public static int indexOfAny(java.lang.String str, java.lang.String[]
    searchStrs)
```

Find the first index of any of a set of potential substrings.

A `null` `String` will return -1. A `null` or zero length search array will return -1. A `null` search array entry will be ignored, but a search array containing "" will return 0 if str is not `null`. This method uses `String.indexOf(String)`.

```
StringUtils.indexOfAny(null, *) = -1
StringUtils.indexOfAny(*, null) = -1
StringUtils.indexOfAny(*, []) = -1
StringUtils.indexOfAny("zzabyycdxx", ["ab","cd"]) = 2
StringUtils.indexOfAny("zzabyycdxx", ["cd","ab"]) = 2
StringUtils.indexOfAny("zzabyycdxx", ["mn","op"]) = -1
StringUtils.indexOfAny("zzabyycdxx", ["zab","aby"]) = 1
StringUtils.indexOfAny("zzabyycdxx", [""]) = 0
StringUtils.indexOfAny("", [""]) = 0
StringUtils.indexOfAny("", ["a"]) = -1
```

Parameters: str—the String to check, may be null
searchStrs—the Strings to search for, may be null
Returns: the first index of any of the searchStrs in str, -1 if no match

```
public static int lastIndexOfAny(java.lang.String str,
java.lang.String[] searchStrs)
```

Find the latest index of any of a set of potential substrings.

A null String will return -1. A null search array will return -1. A null or zero length search array entry will be ignored, but a search array containing "" will return the length of str if str is not null. This method uses String.indexOf(String).

```
StringUtils.lastIndexOfAny(null, *) = -1
StringUtils.lastIndexOfAny(*, null) = -1
StringUtils.lastIndexOfAny(*, []) = -1
StringUtils.lastIndexOfAny(*, [null]) = -1
StringUtils.lastIndexOfAny("zzabyycdxx", ["ab","cd"]) = 6
StringUtils.lastIndexOfAny("zzabyycdxx", ["cd","ab"]) = 6
StringUtils.lastIndexOfAny("zzabyycdxx", ["mn","op"]) = -1
StringUtils.lastIndexOfAny("zzabyycdxx", ["mn","op"]) = -1
StringUtils.lastIndexOfAny("zzabyycdxx", ["mn",""]) = 10
```

Parameters: str—the String to check, may be null
searchStrs—the Strings to search for, may be null
Returns: the last index of any of the Strings, -1 if no match

```
public static java.lang.String substring(java.lang.String str, int start)
```

Gets a substring from the specified String avoiding exceptions.

A negative start position can be used to start n characters from the end of the String.

A null String will return null. An empty ("") String will return "".

```
StringUtils.substring(null, *) = null
StringUtils.substring("", *) = ""
StringUtils.substring("abc", 0) = "abc"
StringUtils.substring("abc", 2) = "c"
StringUtils.substring("abc", 4) = ""
StringUtils.substring("abc", -2) = "bc"
StringUtils.substring("abc", -4) = "abc"
```

Parameters: str—the String to get the substring from, may be null
start—the position to start from, negative means count back from the end of the String by this many characters
Returns: substring from start position, null if null String input

```
public static java.lang.String substring(java.lang.String str, int start, int end)
```

Gets a substring from the specified `string` avoiding exceptions.

A negative start position can be used to start/end n characters from the end of the `string`.

The returned substring starts with the character in the start position and ends before the end position. All postion counting is zero-based—i.e., to start at the beginning of the string, use `start = 0`. Negative start and end positions can be used to specify offsets relative to the end of the `string`.

If `start` is not strictly to the left of `end`, `""` is returned.

```
StringUtils.substring(null, *, *)    = null
StringUtils.substring("", * , *)     = "";
StringUtils.substring("abc", 0, 2)   = "ab"
StringUtils.substring("abc", 2, 0)   = ""
StringUtils.substring("abc", 2, 4)   = "c"
StringUtils.substring("abc", 4, 6)   = ""
StringUtils.substring("abc", 2, 2)   = ""
StringUtils.substring("abc", -2, -1) = "b"
StringUtils.substring("abc", -4, 2)  = "ab"
```

Parameters: str—the `string` to get the substring from, may be `null`

start—the position to start from, negative means count back from the end of the `string` by this many characters

end—the position to end at (exclusive), negative means count back from the end of the `string` by this many characters

Returns: substring from start position to end positon, `null` if `null` String input

```
public static java.lang.String left(java.lang.String str, int len)
```

Gets the leftmost len characters of a `string`.

If len characters are not available, or the `string` is `null`, the `string` will be returned without an exception. An exception is thrown if len is negative.

```
StringUtils.left(null, *)    = null
StringUtils.left(*, -ve)     = ""
StringUtils.left("", *)      = ""
StringUtils.left("abc", 0)   = ""
StringUtils.left("abc", 2)   = "ab"
StringUtils.left("abc", 4)   = "abc"
```

Parameters: str—the `string` to get the leftmost characters from, may be `null`

len—the length of the required `string`, must be zero or positive

Returns: the leftmost characters, `null` if `null` String input

```
public static java.lang.String right(java.lang.String str, int len)
```

Gets the rightmost len characters of a `string`.

If len characters are not available, or the `string` is `null`, the `string` will be returned without an an exception. An exception is thrown if len is negative.

```
StringUtils.right(null, *)     = null
StringUtils.right(*, -ve)      = ""
StringUtils.right("", *)       = ""
StringUtils.right("abc", 0)    = ""
StringUtils.right("abc", 2)    = "bc"
StringUtils.right("abc", 4)    = "abc"
```

Parameters: `str`—the `string` to get the rightmost characters from, may be `null`
    `len`—the length of the required `string`, must be zero or positive
Returns: the rightmost characters, `null` if `null` `String` input

```
public static java.lang.String mid(java.lang.String str, int pos,
    int len)
```

Gets len characters from the middle of a `string`.

If len characters are not available, the remainder of the `string` will be returned without an exception. If the `string` is `null`, `null` will be returned. An exception is thrown if len is negative.

```
StringUtils.mid(null, *, *)    = null
StringUtils.mid(*, *, -ve)     = ""
StringUtils.mid("", 0, *)      = ""
StringUtils.mid("abc", 0, 2)   = "ab"
StringUtils.mid("abc", 0, 4)   = "abc"
StringUtils.mid("abc", 2, 4)   = "c"
StringUtils.mid("abc", 4, 2)   = ""
StringUtils.mid("abc", -2, 2)  = "ab"
```

Parameters: `str`—the `string` to get the characters from, may be `null`
    `pos`—the position to start from, negative treated as zero
    `len`—the length of the required `string`, must be zero or positive
Returns: the middle characters, `null` if `null` `String` input

```
public static java.lang.String substringBefore(java.lang.String str,
    java.lang.String separator)
```

Gets the substring before the first occurence of a separator. The separator is not returned. A `null` string input will return `null`. An empty ("") string input will return the empty string. A `null` separator will return the input string.

```
StringUtils.substringBefore(null, *)       = null
StringUtils.substringBefore("", *)         = ""
StringUtils.substringBefore("abc", "a")    = ""
StringUtils.substringBefore("abcba", "b")  = "a"
StringUtils.substringBefore("abc", "c")    = "ab"
```

```
StringUtils.substringBefore("abc", "d") = "abc"
StringUtils.substringBefore("abc", "") = ""
StringUtils.substringBefore("abc", null) = "abc"
```

Parameters: `str`—the `String` to get a substring from, may be `null`
`separator`—the `String` to search for, may be `null`
Returns: the substring before the first occurence of the separator, `null` if `null` `String` input

```
public static java.lang.String substringAfter(java.lang.String str,
java.lang.String separator)
```

Gets the substring after the first occurence of a separator. The separator is not returned.

A `null` string input will return `null`. An empty (`""`) string input will return the empty string. A `null` separator will return the empty string if the input string is not `null`.

```
StringUtils.substringAfter(null, *) = null
StringUtils.substringAfter("", *) = ""
StringUtils.substringAfter(*, null) = ""
StringUtils.substringAfter("abc", "a") = "bc"
StringUtils.substringAfter("abcba", "b") = "cba"
StringUtils.substringAfter("abc", "c") = ""
StringUtils.substringAfter("abc", "d") = ""
StringUtils.substringAfter("abc", "") = "abc"
```

Parameters: `str`—the `String` to get a substring from, may be `null`
`separator`—the `String` to search for, may be `null`
Returns: the substring after the first occurence of the separator, `null` if `null` `String` input

```
public static java.lang.String substringBeforeLast(java.lang.String
str, java.lang.String separator)
```

Gets the substring before the last occurence of a separator. The separator is not returned.

A `null` string input will return `null`. An empty (`""`) string input will return the empty string. An empty or `null` separator will return the input string.

```
StringUtils.substringBeforeLast(null, *) = null
StringUtils.substringBeforeLast("", *) = ""
StringUtils.substringBeforeLast("abcba", "b") = "abc"
StringUtils.substringBeforeLast("abc", "c") = "ab"
StringUtils.substringBeforeLast("a", "a") = ""
StringUtils.substringBeforeLast("a", "z") = "a"
StringUtils.substringBeforeLast("a", null) = "a"
StringUtils.substringBeforeLast("a", "") = "a"
```

Parameters: `str`—the `String` to get a substring from, may be `null`
separator—the `String` to search for, may be `null`
Returns: the substring before the last occurence of the separator, `null` if `null` String input

```
public static java.lang.String substringAfterLast(java.lang.String
str, java.lang.String separator)
```

Gets the substring after the last occurence of a separator. The separator is not returned.

A `null` string input will return `null`. An empty ("") string input will return the empty string. An empty or `null` separator will return the empty string if the input string is not `null`.

```
StringUtils.substringAfterLast(null, *)       = null
StringUtils.substringAfterLast("", *)         = ""
StringUtils.substringAfterLast(*, "")         = ""
StringUtils.substringAfterLast(*, null)       = ""
StringUtils.substringAfterLast("abc", "a")    = "bc"
StringUtils.substringAfterLast("abcba", "b")  = "a"
StringUtils.substringAfterLast("abc", "c")    = ""
StringUtils.substringAfterLast("a", "a")      = ""
StringUtils.substringAfterLast("a", "z")      = ""
```

Parameters: `str`—the `String` to get a substring from, may be `null`
separator—the `String` to search for, may be `null`
Returns: the substring after the last occurence of the separator, `null` if `null` String input

```
public static java.lang.String substringBetween(java.lang.String str,
java.lang.String tag)
```

Gets the `String` that is nested in between two instances of the same `String`.

A `null` input `String` returns `null`. A `null` tag returns `null`.

```
StringUtils.substringBetween(null, *)            = null
StringUtils.substringBetween("", "")             = ""
StringUtils.substringBetween("", "tag")          = null
StringUtils.substringBetween("tagabctag", null)  = null
StringUtils.substringBetween("tagabctag", "")    = ""
StringUtils.substringBetween("tagabctag", "tag") = "abc"
```

Parameters: `str`—the `String` containing the substring, may be `null`
tag—the `String` before and after the substring, may be `null`
Returns: the substring, `null` if no match

```
public static java.lang.String substringBetween(java.lang.String str,
java.lang.String open, java.lang.String close)
```

Gets the `String` that is nested in between two `Strings`. Only the first match is returned.

A `null` input `String` returns `null`. A `null` open/close returns `null` (no match). An empty ("") open/close returns an empty string.

```
StringUtils.substringBetween(null, *, *) = null
StringUtils.substringBetween("", "", "") = ""
StringUtils.substringBetween("", "", "tag") = null
StringUtils.substringBetween("", "tag", "tag") = null
StringUtils.substringBetween("yabcz", null, null) = null
StringUtils.substringBetween("yabcz", "", "") = ""
StringUtils.substringBetween("yabcz", "y", "z") = "abc"
StringUtils.substringBetween("yabczyabcz", "y", "z") = "abc"
```

Parameters: str—the `String` containing the substring, may be `null`
open—the `String` before the substring, may be `null`
close—the `String` after the substring, may be `null`
Returns: the substring, `null` if no match

```
public static java.lang.String[] split(java.lang.String str)
```

Splits the provided text into an array, using whitespace as the separator. Whitespace is defined by `Character.isWhitespace(char)`.

The separator is not included in the returned `String` array. Adjacent separators are treated as one separator.

A `null` input `String` returns `null`.

```
StringUtils.split(null) = null
StringUtils.split("") = []
StringUtils.split("abc def") = ["abc", "def"]
StringUtils.split("abc  def") = ["abc", "def"]
StringUtils.split(" abc ") = ["abc"]
```

Parameters: str—the `String` to parse, may be `null`
Returns: an array of parsed `strings`, `null` if `null` String input

```
public static java.lang.String[] split(java.lang.String str, char
separatorChar)
```

Splits the provided text into an array, separator specified. This is an alternative to using `StringTokenizer`. The separator is not included in the returned `String` array. Adjacent separators are treated as one separator. A `null` input `String` returns `null`.

```
StringUtils.split(null, *) = null
StringUtils.split("", *) = []
StringUtils.split("a.b.c", '.') = ["a", "b", "c"]
StringUtils.split("a..b.c", '.') = ["a", "b", "c"]
StringUtils.split("a:b:c", '.') = ["a:b:c"]
StringUtils.split("a\tb\nc", null) = ["a", "b", "c"]
StringUtils.split("a b c", ' ') = ["a", "b", "c"]
```

Parameters: str—the String to parse, may be null
separatorChar—the character used as the delimiter, null splits on whitespace
Returns: an array of parsed Strings, null if null String input

```
public static java.lang.String[] split(java.lang.String str,
java.lang.String separatorChars)
```

Splits the provided text into an array, separators specified. This is an alternative to using StringTokenizer.

The separator is not included in the returned string array. Adjacent separators are treated as one separator.

A null input String returns null. A null separatorChars splits on whitespace.

```
StringUtils.split(null, *) = null
StringUtils.split("", *) = []
StringUtils.split("abc def", null) = ["abc", "def"]
StringUtils.split("abc def", " ") = ["abc", "def"]
StringUtils.split("abc def", " ") = ["abc", "def"]
StringUtils.split("ab:cd:ef", ":") = ["ab", "cd", "ef"]
```

Parameters: str—the String to parse, may be null
separatorChars—the characters used as the delimiters, null splits on whitespace
Returns: an array of parsed Strings, null if null String input

```
public static java.lang.String[] split(java.lang.String str,
java.lang.String separatorChars, int max)
```

Splits the provided text into an array, separators specified. This is an alternative to using StringTokenizer.

The separator is not included in the returned string array. Adjacent separators are treated as one separator.

A null input String returns null. A null separatorChars splits on whitespace.

```
StringUtils.split(null, *, *) = null
StringUtils.split("", *, *) = []
StringUtils.split("ab de fg", null, 0) = ["ab", "cd", "ef"]
StringUtils.split("ab de fg", null, 0) = ["ab", "cd", "ef"]
StringUtils.split("ab:cd:ef", ":", 0) = ["ab", "cd", "ef"]
StringUtils.split("ab:cd:ef", ":", 2) = ["ab", "cdef"]
```

Parameters: str—the String to parse, may be null
separatorChars—the characters used as the delimiters, null splits on whitespace
max—the maximum number of elements to include in the array. A zero or negative value implies no limit

Returns: an array of parsed strings, null if null String input

```
public static java.lang.String join(java.lang.Object[] array)
```

Joins the elements of the provided array into a single string containing the provided list of elements.

No separator is added to the joined string. Null objects or empty strings within the array are represented by empty strings.

```
StringUtils.join(null) = null
StringUtils.join([]) = ""
StringUtils.join([null]) = ""
StringUtils.join(["a", "b", "c"]) = "abc"
StringUtils.join([null, "", "a"]) = "a"
```

Parameters: array—the array of values to join together, may be null
Returns: the joined string, null if null array input

```
public static java.lang.String join(java.lang.Object[] array, char
    separator)
```

Joins the elements of the provided array into a single string containing the provided list of elements.

No delimiter is added before or after the list. Null objects or empty strings within the array are represented by empty strings.

```
StringUtils.join(null, *) = null
StringUtils.join([], *) = ""
StringUtils.join([null], *) = ""
StringUtils.join(["a", "b", "c"], ';') = "a;b;c"
StringUtils.join(["a", "b", "c"], null) = "abc"
StringUtils.join([null, "", "a"], ';') = ";;a"
```

Parameters: array—the array of values to join together, may be null
separator—the separator character to use
Returns: the joined string, null if null array input

```
public static java.lang.String join(java.lang.Object[] array,
    java.lang.String separator)
```

Joins the elements of the provided array into a single string containing the provided list of elements.

No delimiter is added before or after the list. A null separator is the same as an empty string (""). Null objects or empty strings within the array are represented by empty strings.

```
StringUtils.join(null, *) = null
StringUtils.join([], *) = ""
StringUtils.join([null], *) = ""
```

```
StringUtils.join(["a", "b", "c"], "--") = "a--b--c"
StringUtils.join(["a", "b", "c"], null) = "abc"
StringUtils.join(["a", "b", "c"], "") = "abc"
StringUtils.join([null, "", "a"], ',') = ",,a"
```

Parameters: array—the array of values to join together, may be `null`
separator—the separator character to use, `null` treated as " "
Returns: the joined `String`, `null` if `null` array input

```
public static java.lang.String join(java.util.Iterator iterator, char
separator)
```

Joins the elements of the provided Iterator into a single `String` containing the provided elements.

No delimiter is added before or after the list. Null objects or empty strings within the iteration are represented by empty strings.

See the examples here: `join(Object[],char)`.

Parameters: iterator—the `Iterator` of values to join together, may be `null`
separator—the separator character to use
Returns: the joined String, `null` if `null` iterator input

```
public static java.lang.String join(java.util.Iterator iterator,
java.lang.String separator)
```

Joins the elements of the provided Iterator into a single `String` containing the provided elements.

No delimiter is added before or after the list. A `null` separator is the same as an empty `String` (" ").

See the examples here: `join(Object[],String)`.

Parameters: iterator—the `Iterator` of values to join together, may be `null`
separator—the separator character to use, `null` treated as " "
Returns: the joined `String`, `null` if `null` iterator input

```
public static java.lang.String deleteWhitespace(java.lang.String str)
```

Deletes all whitespaces from a `String` as defined by `Character.isWhitespace(char)`.

```
StringUtils.deleteWhitespace(null) = null
StringUtils.deleteWhitespace("") = ""
StringUtils.deleteWhitespace("abc") = "abc"
StringUtils.deleteWhitespace(" ab c ") = "abc"
```

Parameters: str—the `String` to delete whitespace from, may be `null`
Returns: the `String` without whitespaces, `null` if `null` `String` input

```
public static java.lang.String replaceOnce(java.lang.String text,
java.lang.String repl, java.lang.String with)
```

Replaces a string with another string inside a larger string, once.
A null reference passed to this method is a no-op.

```
StringUtils.replaceOnce(null, *, *) = null
StringUtils.replaceOnce("", *, *) = ""
StringUtils.replaceOnce("aba", null, null) = "aba"
StringUtils.replaceOnce("aba", null, null) = "aba"
StringUtils.replaceOnce("aba", "a", null) = "aba"
StringUtils.replaceOnce("aba", "a", "") = "aba"
StringUtils.replaceOnce("aba", "a", "z") = "zba"
```

Parameters: text—text to search and replace in, may be null
repl—the String to search for, may be null
with—the String to replace with, may be null
Returns: the text with any replacements processed, null if null String input
See Also: replace(String text, String repl, String with, int max)

```
public static java.lang.String replace(java.lang.String text,
java.lang.String repl, java.lang.String with)
```

Replaces all occurances of a string within another string. A null reference passed to this method is a no-op.

```
StringUtils.replace(null, *, *) = null
StringUtils.replace("", *, *) = ""
StringUtils.replace("aba", null, null) = "aba"
StringUtils.replace("aba", null, null) = "aba"
StringUtils.replace("aba", "a", null) = "aba"
StringUtils.replace("aba", "a", "") = "aba"
StringUtils.replace("aba", "a", "z") = "zbz"
```

Parameters: text—text to search and replace in, may be null
repl—the String to search for, may be null
with—the String to replace with, may be null
Returns: the text with any replacements processed, null if null String input
See Also: replace(String text, String repl, String with, int max)

```
public static java.lang.String replace(java.lang.String text,
java.lang.String repl, java.lang.String with, int max)
```

Replaces a string with another string inside a larger string, for the first max values of the search string.

A null reference passed to this method is a no-op.

```
StringUtils.replace(null, *, *, *) = null
StringUtils.replace("", *, *, *) = ""
StringUtils.replace("abaa", null, null, 1) = "abaa"
```

```
StringUtils.replace("abaa", null, null, 1) = "abaa"
StringUtils.replace("abaa", "a", null, 1) = "abaa"
StringUtils.replace("abaa", "a", "", 1) = "abaa"
StringUtils.replace("abaa", "a", "z", 0) = "abaa"
StringUtils.replace("abaa", "a", "z", 1) = "zbaa"
StringUtils.replace("abaa", "a", "z", 2) = "zbza"
StringUtils.replace("abaa", "a", "z", -1) = "zbzz"
```

Parameters: text—text to search and replace in, may be null
repl—the String to search for, may be null
with—the String to replace with, may be null
max—maximum number of values to replace, or -1 if no maximum
Returns: the text with any replacements processed, null if null String input

```
public static java.lang.String replaceChars(java.lang.String str, char
searchChar, char replaceChar)
```

Replaces all occurrences of a character in a String with another. This is a null-safe version of String.replace(char, char).

A null string input returns null. An empty ("") string input returns an empty string.

```
StringUtils.replaceChars(null, *, *) = null
StringUtils.replaceChars("", *, *) = ""
StringUtils.replaceChars("abcba", 'b', 'y') = "aycya"
StringUtils.replaceChars("abcba", 'z', 'y') = "abcba"
```

Parameters: str—String to replace characters in, may be null
searchChar—the character to search for, may be null
replaceChar—the character to replace, may be null
Returns: modified String, null if null String input

```
public static java.lang.String replaceChars(java.lang.String str,
java.lang.String searchChars, java.lang.String replaceChars)
```

Replaces multiple characters in a String in one go. This method can also be used to delete characters.

For example:

```
replaceChars("hello", "ho", "jy") = jelly.
```

A null string input returns null. An empty ("") string input returns an empty string. A null or empty set of search characters returns the input string.

The length of the search characters should normally equal the length of the replace characters. If the search characters are longer, then the extra search characters are deleted. If the search characters are shorter, then the extra replace characters are ignored.

```
StringUtils.replaceChars(null, *, *)         = null
StringUtils.replaceChars("", *, *)           = ""
StringUtils.replaceChars("abc", null, *)     = "abc"
StringUtils.replaceChars("abc", "", *)       = "abc"
StringUtils.replaceChars("abc", "b", null)   = "ac"
StringUtils.replaceChars("abc", "b", "")     = "ac"
StringUtils.replaceChars("abcba", "bc", "yz") = "ayzya"
StringUtils.replaceChars("abcba", "bc", "y")  = "ayya"
StringUtils.replaceChars("abcba", "bc", "yzx") = "ayzya"
```

Parameters: str—String to replace characters in, may be null
searchChars—a set of characters to search for, may be null
replaceChars—a set of characters to replace, may be null
Returns: modified String, null if null string input

```
public static java.lang.String overlay(java.lang.String str,
java.lang.String overlay, int start, int end)
```

Overlays part of a String with another String.

A null string input returns null. A negative index is treated as zero. An index greater than the string length is treated as the string length. The start index is always the smaller of the two indices.

```
StringUtils.overlay(null, *, *, *)            = null
StringUtils.overlay("", "abc", 0, 0)          = "abc"
StringUtils.overlay("abcdef", null, 2, 4)     = "abef"
StringUtils.overlay("abcdef", "", 2, 4)       = "abef"
StringUtils.overlay("abcdef", "", 4, 2)       = "abef"
StringUtils.overlay("abcdef", "zzzz", 2, 4)   = "abzzzzef"
StringUtils.overlay("abcdef", "zzzz", 4, 2)   = "abzzzzef"
StringUtils.overlay("abcdef", "zzzz", -1, 4)  = "zzzzef"
StringUtils.overlay("abcdef", "zzzz", 2, 8)   = "abzzzz"
StringUtils.overlay("abcdef", "zzzz", -2, -3) = "zzzzabcdef"
StringUtils.overlay("abcdef", "zzzz", 8, 10)  = "abcdefzzzz"
```

Parameters: str—the String to do overlaying in, may be null
overlay—the String to overlay, may be null
start—the position to start overlaying at
end—the position to stop overlaying before
Returns: overlayed String, null if null String input

```
public static java.lang.String chomp(java.lang.String str)
```

Removes one newline from end of a String if it's there, otherwise leave it alone. A newline is "\n", "\r", or "\r\n".

NOTE: This method changed in 2.0. It now more closely matches Perl chomp.

```
StringUtils.chomp(null) = null
StringUtils.chomp("")   = ""
```

```
StringUtils.chomp("abc \r") = "abc "
StringUtils.chomp("abc\n") = "abc"
StringUtils.chomp("abc\r\n") = "abc"
StringUtils.chomp("abc\r\n\r\n") = "abc\r\n"
StringUtils.chomp("abc\n\r") = "abc\n"
StringUtils.chomp("abc\n\rabc") = "abc\n\rabc"
StringUtils.chomp("\r") = ""
StringUtils.chomp("\n") = ""
StringUtils.chomp("\r\n") = ""
```

Parameters: str—the String to chomp a newline from, may be null
Returns: String without newline, null if null String input

```
public static java.lang.String chomp(java.lang.String str,
java.lang.String separator)
```

Removes separator from the end of str if it's there, otherwise leave it alone.

NOTE: This method changed in version 2.0. It now more closely matches Perl chomp. For the previous behavior, use substringBeforeLast(String, String). This method uses String.endsWith(String).

```
StringUtils.chomp(null, *) = null
StringUtils.chomp("", *) = ""
StringUtils.chomp("foobar", "bar") = "foo"
StringUtils.chomp("foobar", "baz") = "foobar"
StringUtils.chomp("foo", "foo") = ""
StringUtils.chomp("foo ", "foo") = "foo "
StringUtils.chomp(" foo", "foo") = " "
StringUtils.chomp("foo", "foooo") = "foo"
StringUtils.chomp("foo", "") = "foo"
StringUtils.chomp("foo", null) = "foo"
```

Parameters: str—the String to chomp from, may be null
separator—separator String, may be null
Returns: String without trailing separator, null if null String input

```
public static java.lang.String chop(java.lang.String str)
```

Remove the last character from a String. If the String ends in \r\n, then remove both of them.

```
StringUtils.chop(null) = null
StringUtils.chop("") = ""
StringUtils.chop("abc \r") = "abc "
StringUtils.chop("abc\n") = "abc"
StringUtils.chop("abc\r\n") = "abc"
StringUtils.chop("abc") = "ab"
StringUtils.chop("abc\nabc") = "abc\nab"
StringUtils.chop("a") = ""
StringUtils.chop("\r") = ""
StringUtils.chop("\n") = ""
StringUtils.chop("\r\n") = ""
```

Parameters: `str`—the `String` to chop last character from, may be `null`
Returns: `String` without last character, `null` if `null` `String` input

```
public static java.lang.String repeat(java.lang.String str, int repeat)
```

Repeat a `String` `repeat` times to form a new `String`.

```
StringUtils.repeat(null, 2)  = null
StringUtils.repeat("", 0)    = ""
StringUtils.repeat("", 2)    = ""
StringUtils.repeat("a", 3)   = "aaa"
StringUtils.repeat("ab", 2)  = "abab"
StringUtils.repeat("a", -2)  = ""
```

Parameters: `str`—the `String` to repeat, may be `null`
`repeat`—number of times to repeat str, negative treated as zero
Returns: a new `String` consisting of the original `String` repeated, `null` if `null` `String` input

```
public static java.lang.String rightPad(java.lang.String str, int size)
```

Right pad a `String` with spaces (' ').
The `String` is padded to the size of size.

```
StringUtils.rightPad(null, *)   = null
StringUtils.rightPad("", 3)     = "   "
StringUtils.rightPad("bat", 3)  = "bat"
StringUtils.rightPad("bat", 5)  = "bat  "
StringUtils.rightPad("bat", 1)  = "bat"
StringUtils.rightPad("bat", -1) = "bat"
```

Parameters: `str`—the `String` to pad out, may be `null`
`size`—the size to pad to
Returns: right padded `String` or original `String` if no padding is necessary, `null` if `null` `String` input

```
public static java.lang.String rightPad(java.lang.String str, int size, char padChar)
```

Right pad a `String` with a specified character. The `String` is padded to the size of size.

```
StringUtils.rightPad(null, *, *)      = null
StringUtils.rightPad("", 3, 'z')      = "zzz"
StringUtils.rightPad("bat", 3, 'z')   = "bat"
StringUtils.rightPad("bat", 5, 'z')   = "batzz"
StringUtils.rightPad("bat", 1, 'z')   = "bat"
StringUtils.rightPad("bat", -1, 'z')  = "bat"
```

Parameters: `str`—the `String` to pad out, may be `null`
`size`—the size to pad to
`padChar`—the character to pad with
Returns: right padded `string` or original `string` if no padding is necessary, `null` if `null` String input

```
public static java.lang.String rightPad(java.lang.String str, int
size, java.lang.String padStr)
```

Right pad a `string` with a specified `string`.
The `string` is padded to the size of size.

```
StringUtils.rightPad(null, *, *) = null
StringUtils.rightPad("", 3, "z") = "zzz"
StringUtils.rightPad("bat", 3, "yz") = "bat"
StringUtils.rightPad("bat", 5, "yz") = "batyz"
StringUtils.rightPad("bat", 8, "yz") = "batyzyzy"
StringUtils.rightPad("bat", 1, "yz") = "bat"
StringUtils.rightPad("bat", -1, "yz") = "bat"
StringUtils.rightPad("bat", 5, null) = "bat  "
StringUtils.rightPad("bat", 5, "") = "bat  "
```

Parameters: `str`—the `String` to pad out, may be `null`
`size`—the size to pad to
`padStr`—the `string` to pad with, `null` or empty treated as single space
Returns: right padded `string` or original `string` if no padding is necessary, `null` if `null` String input

```
public static java.lang.String leftPad(java.lang.String str, int size)
```

Left pad a `string` with spaces (' '). The `string` is padded to the size of size.

```
StringUtils.leftPad(null, *) = null
StringUtils.leftPad("", 3) = "   "
StringUtils.leftPad("bat", 3) = "bat"
StringUtils.leftPad("bat", 5) = "  bat"
StringUtils.leftPad("bat", 1) = "bat"
StringUtils.leftPad("bat", -1) = "bat"
```

Parameters: `str`—the `String` to pad out, may be `null`
`size`—the size to pad to
Returns: left padded `string` or original `string` if no padding is necessary, `null` if `null` String input

```
public static java.lang.String leftPad(java.lang.String str, int size,
char padChar)
```

Left pad a `string` with a specified character.
Pad to a size of size.

```
StringUtils.leftPad(null, *, *)     = null
StringUtils.leftPad("", 3, 'z')     = "zzz"
StringUtils.leftPad("bat", 3, 'z')  = "bat"
StringUtils.leftPad("bat", 5, 'z')  = "zzbat"
StringUtils.leftPad("bat", 1, 'z')  = "bat"
StringUtils.leftPad("bat", -1, 'z') = "bat"
```

Parameters: str—the String to pad out, may be null
size—the size to pad to
padChar—the character to pad with
Returns: left padded String or original String if no padding is necessary, null if null String input

```
public static java.lang.String leftPad(java.lang.String str, int size,
java.lang.String padStr)
```

Left pad a String with a specified String.
Pad to a size of size.

```
StringUtils.leftPad(null, *, *)      = null
StringUtils.leftPad("", 3, "z")      = "zzz"
StringUtils.leftPad("bat", 3, "yz")  = "bat"
StringUtils.leftPad("bat", 5, "yz")  = "yzbat"
StringUtils.leftPad("bat", 8, "yz")  = "yzyzybat"
StringUtils.leftPad("bat", 1, "yz")  = "bat"
StringUtils.leftPad("bat", -1, "yz") = "bat"
StringUtils.leftPad("bat", 5, null)  = "  bat"
StringUtils.leftPad("bat", 5, "")    = "  bat"
```

Parameters: str—the String to pad out, may be null
size—the size to pad to
padStr—the String to pad with, null or empty treated as single space
Returns: left padded String or original String if no padding is necessary, null if null String input

```
public static java.lang.String center(java.lang.String str, int size)
```

Centers a String in a larger String of size size using the space character (' '). If the size is less than the String length, the String is returned. A null String returns null. A negative size is treated as zero. Equivalent to center(str, size, "").

```
StringUtils.center(null, *)       = null
StringUtils.center("", 4)         = "    "
StringUtils.center("ab", -1)      = "ab"
StringUtils.center("ab", 4)       = " ab "
StringUtils.center("abcd", 2)     = "abcd"
StringUtils.center("a", 4)        = " a  "
```

Parameters: str—the String to center, may be null
size—the int size of new String, negative treated as zero

Returns: centered String, null if null String input

```
public static java.lang.String center(java.lang.String str, int size,
    char padChar)
```

Centers a String in a larger String of size size. Uses a supplied character as the value to pad the String with.

If the size is less than the String length, the String is returned. A null String returns null. A negative size is treated as zero.

```
StringUtils.center(null, *, *)    = null
StringUtils.center("", 4, ' ')    = "    "
StringUtils.center("ab", -1, ' ') = "ab"
StringUtils.center("ab", 4, ' ')  = " ab "
StringUtils.center("abcd", 2, ' ') = "abcd"
StringUtils.center("a", 4, ' ')   = "  a  "
StringUtils.center("a", 4, 'y')   = "yayy"
```

Parameters: str—the String to center, may be null
size—the int size of new String, negative treated as zero
padChar—the character to pad the new String with
Returns: centered String, null if null String input

```
public static java.lang.String center(java.lang.String str, int size,
    java.lang.String padStr)
```

Centers a String in a larger String of size size. Uses a supplied String as the value to pad the String with.

If the size is less than the String length, the String is returned. A null String returns null. A negative size is treated as zero.

```
StringUtils.center(null, *, *)      = null
StringUtils.center("", 4, " ")      = "    "
StringUtils.center("ab", -1, " ")   = "ab"
StringUtils.center("ab", 4, " ")    = " ab "
StringUtils.center("abcd", 2, " ")  = "abcd"
StringUtils.center("a", 4, " ")     = "  a  "
StringUtils.center("a", 4, "yz")    = "yayz"
StringUtils.center("abc", 7, null)  = "  abc  "
StringUtils.center("abc", 7, "")    = "  abc  "
```

Parameters: str—the String to center, may be null
size—the int size of new String, negative treated as zero
padStr—the String to pad the new String with, must not be null or empty
Returns: centered String, null if null String input
Throws: java.lang.IllegalArgumentException—if padStr is null or empty

```
public static java.lang.String upperCase(java.lang.String str)
```

Converts a String to upper case as per String.toUpperCase().

A null input String returns null.

```
StringUtils.upperCase(null) = null
StringUtils.upperCase("") = ""
StringUtils.upperCase("aBc") = "ABC"
```

Parameters: str—the String to upper case, may be null
Returns: the upper cased String, null if null String input

```
public static java.lang.String lowerCase(java.lang.String str)
```

Converts a String to lower case as per String.toLowerCase().
A null input String returns null.

```
StringUtils.lowerCase(null) = null
StringUtils.lowerCase("") = ""
StringUtils.lowerCase("aBc") = "abc"
```

Parameters: str—the String to lower case, may be null
Returns: the lower cased String, null if null String input

```
public static java.lang.String capitalize(java.lang.String str)
```

Capitalizes a String changing the first letter to title case as per Character.toTitleCase(char). No other letters are changed.

For a word based algorithm, see WordUtils.capitalize(String). A null input String returns null.

```
StringUtils.capitalize(null) = null
StringUtils.capitalize("") = ""
StringUtils.capitalize("cat") = "Cat"
StringUtils.capitalize("cAt") = "CAt"
```

Parameters: str—the String to capitalize, may be null
Returns: the capitalized String, null if null String input
See Also: WordUtils.capitalize(String), uncapitalize(String)

```
public static java.lang.String uncapitalize(java.lang.String str)
```

Uncapitalizes a String changing the first letter to title case as per Character.toLowerCase(char). No other letters are changed.

For a word based algorithm, see WordUtils.uncapitalize(String). A null input String returns null.

```
StringUtils.uncapitalize(null) = null
StringUtils.uncapitalize("") = ""
StringUtils.uncapitalize("Cat") = "cat"
StringUtils.uncapitalize("CAT") = "cAT"
```

Parameters: `str`—the `String` to uncapitalize, may be `null`
Returns: the uncapitalized `String`, `null` if `null` `String` input
See Also: `WordUtils.uncapitalize(String)`, `capitalize(String)`

```
public static java.lang.String swapCase(java.lang.String str)
```

Swaps the case of a `String` changing upper and title case to lower case, and lower case to upper case.

- ☞ Upper case character converts to Lower case
- ☞ Title case character converts to Lower case
- ☞ Lower case character converts to Upper case

For a word based algorithm, see `WordUtils.swapCase(String)`. A `null` input `String` returns `null`.

```
StringUtils.swapCase(null) = null
StringUtils.swapCase("")   = ""
StringUtils.swapCase("The dog has a BONE") = "tHE DOG HAS A bone"
```

NOTE: This method changed in Lang version 2.0. It no longer performs a word based algorithm. If you only use ASCII, you will notice no change. That functionality is available in WordUtils.

Parameters: `str`—the `String` to swap case, may be `null`
Returns: the changed `String`, `null` if `null` `String` input

```
public static int countMatches(java.lang.String str, java.lang.String sub)
```

Counts how many times the substring appears in the larger `String`.

A `null` or empty (`""`) `String` input returns 0.

```
StringUtils.countMatches(null, *)       = 0
StringUtils.countMatches("", *)         = 0
StringUtils.countMatches("abba", null)  = 0
StringUtils.countMatches("abba", "")    = 0
StringUtils.countMatches("abba", "a")   = 2
StringUtils.countMatches("abba", "ab")  = 1
StringUtils.countMatches("abba", "xxx") = 0
```

Parameters: `str`—the `String` to check, may be `null`
`sub`—the substring to count, may be `null`
Returns: the number of occurences, 0 if either `string` is `null`

```
public static boolean isAlpha(java.lang.String str)
```

Checks if the `string` contains only unicode letters.

`null` will return false. An empty `string` (`""`) will return true.

```
StringUtils.isAlpha(null) = false
StringUtils.isAlpha("") = true
StringUtils.isAlpha(" ") = false
StringUtils.isAlpha("abc") = true
StringUtils.isAlpha("ab2c") = false
StringUtils.isAlpha("ab-c") = false
```

Parameters: str—the String to check, may be null
Returns: true if only contains letters, and is non-null

```
public static boolean isAlphaSpace(java.lang.String str)
```

Checks if the String contains only unicode letters and space (' '). null will return false An empty String ("") will return true.

```
StringUtils.isAlphaSpace(null) = false
StringUtils.isAlphaSpace("") = true
StringUtils.isAlphaSpace(" ") = true
StringUtils.isAlphaSpace("abc") = true
StringUtils.isAlphaSpace("ab c") = true
StringUtils.isAlphaSpace("ab2c") = false
StringUtils.isAlphaSpace("ab-c") = false
```

Parameters: str—the String to check, may be null
Returns: true if only contains letters and space, and is non-null

```
public static boolean isAlphanumeric(java.lang.String str)
```

Checks if the String contains only unicode letters or digits. null will return false. An empty String ("") will return true.

```
StringUtils.isAlphanumeric(null) = false
StringUtils.isAlphanumeric("") = true
StringUtils.isAlphanumeric(" ") = false
StringUtils.isAlphanumeric("abc") = true
StringUtils.isAlphanumeric("ab c") = false
StringUtils.isAlphanumeric("ab2c") = true
StringUtils.isAlphanumeric("ab-c") = false
```

Parameters: str—the String to check, may be null
Returns: true if only contains letters or digits, and is non-null

```
public static boolean isAlphanumericSpace(java.lang.String str)
```

Checks if the String contains only unicode letters, digits or space (' '). null will return false. An empty String ("") will return true.

```
StringUtils.isAlphanumeric(null) = false
StringUtils.isAlphanumeric("") = true
```

```
StringUtils.isAlphanumeric(" ")    = true
StringUtils.isAlphanumeric("abc")  = true
StringUtils.isAlphanumeric("ab c") = true
StringUtils.isAlphanumeric("ab2c") = true
StringUtils.isAlphanumeric("ab-c") = false
```

Parameters: str—the String to check, may be null
Returns: true if only contains letters, digits or space, and is non-null

```
public static boolean isNumeric(java.lang.String str)
```

Checks if the String contains only unicode digits. A decimal point is not a unicode digit and returns false.

null will return false. An empty String ("") will return true.

```
StringUtils.isNumeric(null)   = false
StringUtils.isNumeric("")     = true
StringUtils.isNumeric(" ")    = false
StringUtils.isNumeric("123")  = true
StringUtils.isNumeric("12 3") = false
StringUtils.isNumeric("ab2c") = false
StringUtils.isNumeric("12-3") = false
StringUtils.isNumeric("12.3") = false
```

Parameters: str—the String to check, may be null
Returns: true if only contains digits, and is non-null

```
public static boolean isNumericSpace(java.lang.String str)
```

Checks if the String contains only unicode digits or space (' '). A decimal point is not a unicode digit and returns false.

null will return false. An empty String ("") will return true.

```
StringUtils.isNumeric(null)   = false
StringUtils.isNumeric("")     = true
StringUtils.isNumeric(" ")    = true
StringUtils.isNumeric("123")  = true
StringUtils.isNumeric("12 3") = true
StringUtils.isNumeric("ab2c") = false
StringUtils.isNumeric("12-3") = false
StringUtils.isNumeric("12.3") = false
```

Parameters: str—the String to check, may be null
Returns: true if only contains digits or space, and is non-null

```
public static boolean isWhitespace(java.lang.String str)
```

Checks if the String contains only whitespace.

null will return false. An empty String ("") will return true.

```
StringUtils.isWhitespace(null)  = false
StringUtils.isWhitespace("")    = true
StringUtils.isWhitespace("  ")  = true
StringUtils.isWhitespace("abc") = false
StringUtils.isWhitespace("ab2c")= false
StringUtils.isWhitespace("ab-c")= false
```

Parameters: str—the String to check, may be null
Returns: true if only contains whitespace, and is non-null

```
public static java.lang.String defaultString(java.lang.String str)
```

Returns either the passed in String, or if the String is null, an empty String ("").

```
StringUtils.defaultString(null)  = ""
StringUtils.defaultString("")    = ""
StringUtils.defaultString("bat") = "bat"
```

Parameters: str—the String to check, may be null
Returns: the passed in String, or the empty String if it was null
See Also: ObjectUtils.toString(Object), String.valueOf(Object)

```
public static java.lang.String defaultString(java.lang.String str,
java.lang.String defaultStr)
```

Returns either the passed in String, or if the String is null, an empty String ("").

```
StringUtils.defaultString(null, "null")  = "null"
StringUtils.defaultString("", "null")    = ""
StringUtils.defaultString("bat", "null") = "bat"
```

Parameters: str—the String to check, may be null
defaultStr—the default String to return if the input is null, may be null
Returns: the passed in String, or the default if it was null
See Also: ObjectUtils.toString(Object,String), String.valueOf(Object)

```
public static java.lang.String reverse(java.lang.String str)
```

Reverses a String as per StringBuffer.reverse().
null String returns null.

```
StringUtils.reverse(null)  = null
StringUtils.reverse("")    = ""
StringUtils.reverse("bat") = "tab"
```

Parameters: str—the String to reverse, may be null
Returns: the reversed String, null if null String input

```
public static java.lang.String reverseDelimited(java.lang.String str,
char separatorChar)
```

Reverses a `String` that is delimited by a specific character.

The `String`s between the delimiters are not reversed. Thus `java.lang.String` becomes `String.lang.java` (if the delimiter is '.').

```
StringUtils.reverseDelimited(null, *)      = null
StringUtils.reverseDelimited("", *)        = ""
StringUtils.reverseDelimited("a.b.c", 'x') = "a.b.c"
StringUtils.reverseDelimited("a.b.c", ".") = "c.b.a"
```

Parameters: str—the `String` to reverse, may be `null`
separatorChar—the separator character to use
Returns: the reversed `String`, `null` if `null` `String` input

```
public static java.lang.String abbreviate(java.lang.String str,
int maxWidth)
```

Abbreviates a `String` using ellipses. This will turn "Now is the time for all good men" into "Now is the time for..."

Specifically:

☞ If str is less than maxWidth characters long, return it.
☞ Else abbreviate it to (`substring(str, 0, max-3) + "..."`).
☞ If maxWidth is less than 4, throw an `IllegalArgumentException`.
☞ In no case will it return a `String` of length greater than maxWidth.

```
StringUtils.abbreviate(null, *)         = null
StringUtils.abbreviate("", 4)           = ""
StringUtils.abbreviate("abcdefg", 6)    = "abc..."
StringUtils.abbreviate("abcdefg", 7)    = "abcdefg"
StringUtils.abbreviate("abcdefg", 8)    = "abcdefg"
StringUtils.abbreviate("abcdefg", 4)    = "a..."
StringUtils.abbreviate("abcdefg", 3)    = IllegalArgumentException
```

Parameters: str—the `String` to check, may be `null`
maxWidth—maximum length of result `String`, must be at least 4
Returns: abbreviated `String`, `null` if `null` `String` input
Throws: `java.lang.IllegalArgumentException`—if the width is too small

```
public static java.lang.String abbreviate(java.lang.String str, int
offset, int maxWidth)
```

Abbreviates a `String` using ellipses. This will turn "Now is the time for all good men" into "...is the time for..."

Works like `abbreviate(String, int)`, but allows you to specify a "left edge" offset. Note that this left edge is not necessarily going to be the leftmost character in the result, or the first character following the ellipses, but it will appear somewhere in the result.

In no case will it return a string of length greater than maxWidth.

```
StringUtils.abbreviate(null, *, *) = null
StringUtils.abbreviate("", 0, 4) = ""
StringUtils.abbreviate("abcdefghijklmno", -1, 10) = "abcdefg..."
StringUtils.abbreviate("abcdefghijklmno", 0, 10) = "abcdefg..."
StringUtils.abbreviate("abcdefghijklmno", 1, 10) = "abcdefg..."
StringUtils.abbreviate("abcdefghijklmno", 4, 10) = "abcdefg..."
StringUtils.abbreviate("abcdefghijklmno", 5, 10) = "...fghi..."
StringUtils.abbreviate("abcdefghijklmno", 6, 10) = "...ghij..."
StringUtils.abbreviate("abcdefghijklmno", 8, 10) = "...ijklmno"
StringUtils.abbreviate("abcdefghijklmno", 10, 10) = "...ijklmno"
StringUtils.abbreviate("abcdefghijklmno", 12, 10) = "...ijklmno"
StringUtils.abbreviate("abcdefghij", 0, 3) = IllegalArgumentException
StringUtils.abbreviate("abcdefghij", 5, 6) = IllegalArgumentException
```

Parameters: str—the String to check, may be null
offset—left edge of source string
maxWidth—maximum length of result string, must be at least 4
Returns: abbreviated string, null if null String input
Throws: java.lang.IllegalArgumentException—if the width is too small

```
public static java.lang.String difference(java.lang.String str1,
java.lang.String str2)
```

Compares two strings, and returns the portion where they differ. (More precisely, return the remainder of the second string, starting from where it's different from the first.)

For example, difference("i am a machine", "i am a robot") -> "robot".

```
StringUtils.difference(null, null) = null
StringUtils.difference("", "") = ""
StringUtils.difference("", "abc") = "abc"
StringUtils.difference("abc", "") = ""
StringUtils.difference("abc", "abc") = ""
StringUtils.difference("ab", "abxyz") = "xyz"
StringUtils.difference("abcde", "abxyz") = "xyz"
StringUtils.difference("abcde", "xyz") = "xyz"
```

Parameters: str1—the first string, may be null
str2—the second string, may be null
Returns: the portion of str2 where it differs from str1; returns the empty string if they are equal

```
public static int indexOfDifference(java.lang.String str1,
java.lang.String str2)
```

Compares two strings, and returns the index at which the strings begin to differ.

For example, indexOfDifference("i am a machine", "i am a robot") -> 7

```
StringUtils.indexOfDifference(null, null) = -1
StringUtils.indexOfDifference("", "") = -1
StringUtils.indexOfDifference("", "abc") = 0
StringUtils.indexOfDifference("abc", "") = 0
StringUtils.indexOfDifference("abc", "abc") = -1
StringUtils.indexOfDifference("ab", "abxyz") = 2
StringUtils.indexOfDifference("abcde", "abxyz") = 2
StringUtils.indexOfDifference("abcde", "xyz") = 0
```

Parameters: str1—the first String, may be null
str2—the second String, may be null
Returns: the index where str2 and str1 begin to differ; -1 if they are equal

```
public static int getLevenshteinDistance(java.lang.String s,
java.lang.String t)
```

Find the Levenshtein distance between two Strings.

This is the number of changes needed to change one String into another, where each change is a single character modification (deletion, insertion or substitution).

This implementation of the Levenshtein distance algorithm is from http://www.merriampark.com/ld.htm

```
StringUtils.getLevenshteinDistance(null, *) = IllegalArgumentException
StringUtils.getLevenshteinDistance(*, null) = IllegalArgumentException
StringUtils.getLevenshteinDistance("","") = 0
StringUtils.getLevenshteinDistance("","a") = 1
StringUtils.getLevenshteinDistance("aaapppp", "") = 7
StringUtils.getLevenshteinDistance("frog", "fog") = 1
StringUtils.getLevenshteinDistance("fly", "ant") = 3
StringUtils.getLevenshteinDistance("elephant", "hippo") = 7
StringUtils.getLevenshteinDistance("hippo", "elephant") = 7
StringUtils.getLevenshteinDistance("hippo", "zzzzzzzz") = 8
StringUtils.getLevenshteinDistance("hello", "hallo") = 1
```

Parameters: s—the first String, must not be null
t—the second String, must not be null
Returns: result distance
Throws: java.lang.IllegalArgumentException—if either String input null

org.apache.commons.lang.SystemUtils

Helpers for java.lang.System.

If a system property cannot be read due to security restrictions, the corresponding field in this class will be set to null and a message will be written to System.err.

Field Detail

```
public static final java.lang.String FILE_ENCODING
```

The `file.encoding` System Property. File encoding, such as Cp1252. Defaults to `null` if the runtime does not have security access to read this property or the property does not exist.
> **Since:** Java 1.2.

```
public static final java.lang.String FILE_SEPARATOR
```

The `file.separator` System Property. File separator ("/" on UNIX). Defaults to `null` if the runtime does not have security access to read this property or the property does not exist.
> **Since:** Java 1.1.

```
public static final java.lang.String JAVA_CLASS_PATH
```

The `java.class.path` System Property. Java class path. Defaults to `null` if the runtime does not have security access to read this property or the property does not exist.
> **Since:** Java 1.1.

```
public static final java.lang.String JAVA_CLASS_VERSION
```

The `java.class.version` System Property. Java class format version number. Defaults to `null` if the runtime does not have security access to read this property or the property does not exist.
> **Since:** Java 1.1.

```
public static final java.lang.String JAVA_COMPILER
```

The `java.compiler` System Property. Name of JIT compiler to use. First in JDK version 1.2. Not used in Sun JDKs after 1.2. Defaults to `null` if the runtime does not have security access to read this property or the property does not exist.
> **Since:** Java 1.2. Not used in Sun versions after 1.2.

```
public static final java.lang.String JAVA_EXT_DIRS
```

The `java.ext.dirs` System Property. Path of extension directory or directories. Defaults to `null` if the runtime does not have security access to read this property or the property does not exist.
> **Since:** Java 1.3

```
public static final java.lang.String JAVA_HOME
```

The `java.home` System Property. Java installation directory. Defaults to `null` if the runtime does not have security access to read this property or the property does not exist.
> **Since:** Java 1.1

```
public static final java.lang.String JAVA_IO_TMPDIR
```

The `java.io.tmpdir` System Property. Default temp file path. Defaults to `null` if the runtime does not have security access to read this property or the property does not exist.
Since: Java 1.2

```
public static final java.lang.String JAVA_LIBRARY_PATH
```

The `java.library.path` System Property. List of paths to search when loading libraries. Defaults to `null` if the runtime does not have security access to read this property or the property does not exist.
Since: Java 1.2

```
public static final java.lang.String JAVA_RUNTIME_NAME
```

The `java.runtime.name` System Property. Java Runtime Environment name. Defaults to `null` if the runtime does not have security access to read this property or the property does not exist.
Since: Java 1.3

```
public static final java.lang.String JAVA_RUNTIME_VERSION
```

The `java.runtime.version` System Property. Java Runtime Environment version. Defaults to `null` if the runtime does not have security access to read this property or the property does not exist.
Since: Java 1.3

```
public static final java.lang.String JAVA_SPECIFICATION_NAME
```

The `java.specification.name` System Property. Java Runtime Environment specification name. Defaults to `null` if the runtime does not have security access to read this property or the property does not exist.
Since: Java 1.2

```
public static final java.lang.String JAVA_SPECIFICATION_VENDOR
```

The `java.specification.vendor` System Property. Java Runtime Environment specification vendor. Defaults to `null` if the runtime does not have security access to read this property or the property does not exist.
Since: Java 1.2

```
public static final java.lang.String JAVA_SPECIFICATION_VERSION
```

The `java.specification.version` System Property. Java Runtime Environment specification version. Defaults to `null` if the runtime does not have security access to read this property or the property does not exist.
Since: Java 1.3

```
public static final java.lang.String JAVA_VENDOR
```

The `java.vendor` System Property. Java vendor-specific string. Defaults to `null` if the runtime does not have security access to read this property or the property does not exist.
Since: Java 1.1

```
public static final java.lang.String JAVA_VENDOR_URL
```

The `java.vendor.url` System Property. Java vendor URL. Defaults to `null` if the runtime does not have security access to read this property or the property does not exist.
Since: Java 1.1

```
public static final java.lang.String JAVA_VERSION
```

The `java.version` System Property. Java version number. Defaults to `null` if the runtime does not have security access to read this property or the property does not exist.
Since: Java 1.1

```
public static final java.lang.String JAVA_VM_INFO
```

The `java.vm.info` System Property. Java Virtual Machine implementation info. Defaults to `null` if the runtime does not have security access to read this property or the property does not exist.
Since: Java 1.2

```
public static final java.lang.String JAVA_VM_NAME
```

The `java.vm.name` System Property. Java Virtual Machine implementation name. Defaults to `null` if the runtime does not have security access to read this property or the property does not exist.
Since: Java 1.2

```
public static final java.lang.String JAVA_VM_SPECIFICATION_NAME
```

The `java.vm.specification.name` System Property. Java Virtual Machine specification name. Defaults to `null` if the runtime does not have security access to read this property or the property does not exist.
Since: Java 1.2

```
public static final java.lang.String JAVA_VM_SPECIFICATION_VENDOR
```

The `java.vm.specification.vendor` System Property. Java Virtual Machine specification vendor. Defaults to `null` if the runtime does not have security access to read this property or the property does not exist.
Since: Java 1.2

```
public static final java.lang.String JAVA_VM_SPECIFICATION_VERSION
```

The `java.vm.specification.version` System Property. Java Virtual Machine specification version. Defaults to `null` if the runtime does not have security access to read this property or the property does not exist.
Since: Java 1.2

```
public static final java.lang.String JAVA_VM_VENDOR
```

The `java.vm.vendor` System Property. Java Virtual Machine implementation vendor. Defaults to `null` if the runtime does not have security access to read this property or the property does not exist.
Since: Java 1.2

```
public static final java.lang.String JAVA_VM_VERSION
```

The `java.vm.version` System Property. Java Virtual Machine implementation version. Defaults to `null` if the runtime does not have security access to read this property or the property does not exist.
Since: Java 1.2

```
public static final java.lang.String LINE_SEPARATOR
```

The `line.separator` System Property. Line separator ("\n<" on UNIX). Defaults to `null` if the runtime does not have security access to read this property or the property does not exist.
Since: Java 1.1

```
public static final java.lang.String OS_ARCH
```

The `os.arch` System Property. Operating system architecture. Defaults to `null` if the runtime does not have security access to read this property or the property does not exist.
Since: Java 1.1

```
public static final java.lang.String OS_NAME
```

The `os.name` System Property. Operating system name. Defaults to `null` if the runtime does not have security access to read this property or the property does not exist.
Since: Java 1.1

```
public static final java.lang.String OS_VERSION
```

The `os.version` System Property. Operating system version. Defaults to `null` if the runtime does not have security access to read this property or the property does not exist.
Since: Java 1.1

```
public static final java.lang.String PATH_SEPARATOR
```

The `path.separator` System Property. Path separator (":" on UNIX). Defaults to `null` if the runtime does not have security access to read this property or the property does not exist.
Since: Java 1.1

```
public static final java.lang.String USER_COUNTRY
```

The `user.country` or user.region System Property. User's country code, such as GB. First in JDK version 1.2 as user.region. Renamed to user.country in 1.4. Defaults to `null` if the runtime does not have security access to read this property or the property does not exist.
Since: Java 1.2

```
public static final java.lang.String USER_DIR
```

The `user.dir` System Property. User's current working directory. Defaults to `null` if the runtime does not have security access to read this property or the property does not exist.
Since: Java 1.1

```
public static final java.lang.String USER_HOME
```

The `user.home` System Property. User's home directory. Defaults to `null` if the runtime does not have security access to read this property or the property does not exist.
Since: Java 1.1

```
public static final java.lang.String USER_LANGUAGE
```

The `user.language` System Property. User's language code, such as 'en'. Defaults to `null` if the runtime does not have security access to read this property or the property does not exist.
Since: Java 1.2

```
public static final java.lang.String USER_NAME
```

The `user.name` System Property. User's account name. Defaults to `null` if the runtime does not have security access to read this property or the property does not exist.
Since: Java 1.1

```
public static final float JAVA_VERSION_FLOAT
```

Gets the Java version as a float. Example return values:

- `1.2f` for JDK 1.2
- `1.31f` for JDK 1.3.1

The field will return zero if JAVA_VERSION is null.

```
public static final int JAVA_VERSION_INT
```

Gets the Java version as an int. Example return values:

- ☞ 120 for JDK 1.2
- ☞ 131 for JDK 1.3.1

The field will return zero if JAVA_VERSION is null.

```
public static final boolean IS_JAVA_1_1
```

Is true if this is Java version 1.1 (also 1.1.x versions). The field will return false if JAVA_VERSION is null.

```
public static final boolean IS_JAVA_1_2
```

Is true if this is Java version 1.2 (also 1.2.x versions). The field will return false if JAVA_VERSION is null.

```
public static final boolean IS_JAVA_1_3
```

Is true if this is Java version 1.3 (also 1.3.x versions). The field will return false if JAVA_VERSION is null.

```
public static final boolean IS_JAVA_1_4
```

Is true if this is Java version 1.4 (also 1.4.x versions). The field will return false if JAVA_VERSION is null.

```
public static final boolean IS_JAVA_1_5
```

Is true if this is Java version 1.5 (also 1.5.x versions). The field will return false if JAVA_VERSION is null.

```
public static final boolean IS_OS_AIX
```

Is true if this is AIX. The field will return false if OS_NAME is null.

```
public static final boolean IS_OS_HP_UX
```

Is true if this is HP-UX. The field will return false if OS_NAME is null.

```
public static final boolean IS_OS_IRIX
```

Is true if this is Irix. The field will return false if OS_NAME is null.

```
public static final boolean IS_OS_LINUX
```

Is true if this is Linux. The field will return false if `OS_NAME` is `null`.

```
public static final boolean IS_OS_MAC
```

Is true if this is Mac. The field will return false if `OS_NAME` is `null`.

```
public static final boolean IS_OS_MAC_OSX
```

Is true if this is MacOSX. The field will return false if `OS_NAME` is `null`.

```
public static final boolean IS_OS_OS2
```

Is true if this is OS/2. The field will return false if `OS_NAME` is `null`.

```
public static final boolean IS_OS_SOLARIS
```

Is true if this is Solaris. The field will return false if `OS_NAME` is `null`.

```
public static final boolean IS_OS_SUN_OS
```

Is true if this is SunOS. The field will return false if `OS_NAME` is `null`.

```
public static final boolean IS_OS_WINDOWS
```

Is true if this is Windows. The field will return false if `OS_NAME` is `null`.

```
public static final boolean IS_OS_WINDOWS_2000
```

Is true if this is Windows 2000. The field will return false if `OS_NAME` is `null`.

```
public static final boolean IS_OS_WINDOWS_95
```

Is true if this is Windows 95. The field will return false if `OS_NAME` is `null`.

```
public static final boolean IS_OS_WINDOWS_98
```

Is true if this is Windows 98. The field will return false if `OS_NAME` is `null`.

```
public static final boolean IS_OS_WINDOWS_ME
```

Is true if this is Windows ME. The field will return false if `OS_NAME` is `null`.

```
public static final boolean IS_OS_WINDOWS_NT
```

Is true if this is Windows NT. The field will return false if `OS_NAME` is `null`.

```
public static final boolean IS_OS_WINDOWS_XP
```

Is true if this is Windows XP. The field will return false if `OS_NAME` is `null`.

Constructor Detail

```
public SystemUtils()
```

SystemUtils instances should NOT be constructed in standard programming. Instead, the class should be used as `SystemUtils.FILE_SEPARATOR`.

This constructor is public to permit tools that require a JavaBean instance to operate.

Method Detail

```
public static boolean isJavaVersionAtLeast(float requiredVersion)
```

Is the Java version at least the requested version.
Example input:

- ☞ `1.2f` to test for JDK 1.2
- ☞ `1.31f` to test for JDK 1.3.1

Parameters: `requiredVersion`—the required version, for example 1.31f
Returns: `true` if the actual version is equal or greater than the required version

```
public static boolean isJavaVersionAtLeast(int requiredVersion)
```

Is the Java version at least the requested version.
Example input:

- ☞ `120` to test for JDK 1.2 or greater
- ☞ `131` to test for JDK 1.3.1 or greater

Parameters: `requiredVersion`—the required version, for example 131
Returns: `true` if the actual version is equal or greater than the required version

org.apache.commons.lang.Validate

Assists in validating arguments. The class is based along the lines of JUnit. If an argument value is deemed invalid, an `IllegalArgumentException` is thrown. For example:

```
Validate.isTrue( i>0, "The value must be greater than zero: ", i);
Validate.notNull( surname, "The surname must not be null");
```

Constructor Detail

```
public Validate()
```

Constructor. This class should not normally be instantiated.

Method Detail

```
public static void isTrue(boolean expression, java.lang.String
message, java.lang.Object value)
```

Validate an argument, throwing IllegalArgumentException if the test result is false. This is used when validating according to an arbitrary boolean expression, such as validating a primitive number or using your own custom validation expression.

```
Validate.isTrue( myObject.isOk(), "The object is not OK: ", myObject);
```

For performance reasons, the object is passed as a separate parameter and appended to the message string only in the case of an error.

Parameters: expression—a boolean expression
message—the exception message you would like to see if the expression is false
value—the value to append to the message in case of error
Throws: java.lang.IllegalArgumentException—if expression is false

```
public static void isTrue(boolean expression, java.lang.String
message, long value)
```

Validate an argument, throwing IllegalArgumentException if the test result is false.

This is used when validating according to an arbitrary boolean expression, such as validating a primitive number or using your own custom validation expression.

```
Validate.isTrue( i<0, "The value must be greater than zero: ", i);
```

For performance reasons, the object is passed as a separate parameter and appended to the message string only in the case of an error.

Parameters: expression—a boolean expression
message—the exception message you would like to see if the expression is false
value—the value to append to the message in case of error
Throws: java.lang.IllegalArgumentException—if expression is false

```
public static void isTrue(boolean expression, java.lang.String
message, double value)
```

Validate an argument, throwing IllegalArgumentException if the test result is false.

This is used when validating according to an arbitrary boolean expression, such as validating a primitive number or using your own custom validation expression.

```
Validate.isTrue( d>0.0, "The value must be greater than zero: ", d);
```

For performance reasons, the object is passed as a separate parameter and appended to the message string only in the case of an error.

Parameters: `expression`—a `boolean` expression

`message`—the exception message you would like to see if the expression is `false`

`value`—the value to append to the message in case of error

Throws: `java.lang.IllegalArgumentException`—if expression is `false`

```
public static void isTrue(boolean expression, java.lang.String
message)
```

Validate an argument, throwing `IllegalArgumentException` if the test result is false.

This is used when validating according to an arbitrary `boolean` expression, such as validating a primitive number or using your own custom validation expression.

```
Validate.isTrue( (i>0), "The value must be greater than zero");
Validate.isTrue( myObject.isOk(), "The object is not OK");
```

For performance reasons, the message string should not involve a string append, instead use the `isTrue(boolean, String, Object)` method.

Parameters: `expression`—a `boolean` expression

`message`—the exception message you would like to see if the expression is `false`

Throws: `java.lang.IllegalArgumentException`—if expression is `false`

```
public static void isTrue(boolean expression)
```

Validate an argument, throwing `IllegalArgumentException` if the test result is false.

This is used when validating according to an arbitrary `boolean` expression, such as validating a primitive number or using your own custom validation expression.

```
Validate.isTrue( i>0 );
Validate.isTrue( myObject.isOk() );
```

The message in the exception is 'The validated expression is false'.

Parameters: `expression`—a `boolean` expression

Throws: `java.lang.IllegalArgumentException`—if expression is `false`

```
public static void notNull(java.lang.Object object, java.lang.String
message)
```

Validate an argument, throwing `IllegalArgumentException` if the argument is `null`.

```
Validate.notNull(myObject, "The object must not be null");
```

Parameters: `object`—the object to check is not `null`
`message`—the exception message you would like to see if the object is `null`
Throws: `java.lang.IllegalArgumentException`—if the object is `null`

```
public static void notNull(java.lang.Object object)
```

Validate an argument, throwing `IllegalArgumentException` if the argument is `null`.

```
Validate.notNull(myObject);
```

The message in the exception is 'The validated object is `null`'.
Parameters: `object`—the object to check is not `null`
Throws: `java.lang.IllegalArgumentException`—if the object is `null`

```
public static void notEmpty(java.lang.Object[] array, java.lang.String message)
```

Validate an argument, throwing `IllegalArgumentException` if the argument array is empty (`null` or no elements).

```
Validate.notEmpty(myArray, "The array must not be empty");
```

Parameters: `array`—the array to check is not empty
`message`—the exception message you would like to see if the array is empty
Throws: `java.lang.IllegalArgumentException`—if the array is empty

```
public static void notEmpty(java.lang.Object[] array)
```

Validate an argument, throwing `IllegalArgumentException` if the argument array is empty (`null` or no elements).

```
Validate.notEmpty(myArray);
```

The message in the exception is 'The validated array is empty'.
Parameters: `array`—the array to check is not empty
Throws: `java.lang.IllegalArgumentException`—if the array is empty

```
public static void notEmpty(java.util.Collection collection,
java.lang.String message)
```

Validate an argument, throwing `IllegalArgumentException` if the argument Collection is empty (`null` or no elements).

```
Validate.notEmpty(myCollection, "The collection must not be empty");
```

Parameters: `collection`—the collection to check is not empty

message—the exception message you would like to see if the collection is empty
Throws: `java.lang.IllegalArgumentException`—if the collection is empty

```
public static void notEmpty(java.util.Collection collection)
```

Validate an argument, throwing `IllegalArgumentException` if the argument Collection is empty (`null` or no elements).

```
Validate.notEmpty(myCollection);
```

The message in the exception is 'The validated collection is empty'.
Parameters: collection—the collection to check is not empty
Throws: `java.lang.IllegalArgumentException`—if the collection is empty

```
public static void notEmpty(java.util.Map map, java.lang.String message)
```

Validate an argument, throwing `IllegalArgumentException` if the argument Map is empty (`null` or no elements).

```
Validate.notEmpty(myMap, "The collection must not be empty");
```

Parameters: map—the map to check is not empty
message—the exception message you would like to see if the map is empty
Throws: `java.lang.IllegalArgumentException`—if the map is empty

```
public static void notEmpty(java.util.Map map)
```

Validate an argument, throwing `IllegalArgumentException` if the argument Map is empty (`null` or no elements).

```
Validate.notEmpty(myMap);
```

The message in the exception is 'The validated map is empty'.
Parameters: map—the map to check is not empty
Throws: `java.lang.IllegalArgumentException`—if the map is empty

```
public static void notEmpty(java.lang.String string, java.lang.String message)
```

Validate an argument, throwing `IllegalArgumentException` if the argument String is empty (`null` or zero length).

```
Validate.notEmpty(myString, "The string must not be empty");
```

Parameters: string—the string to check is not empty
message—the exception message you would like to see if the string is empty
Throws: `java.lang.IllegalArgumentException`—if the string is empty

```
public static void notEmpty(java.lang.String string)
```

Validate an argument, throwing `IllegalArgumentException` if the argument `String` is empty (`null` or zero length).

```
Validate.notEmpty(myString);
```

The message in the exception is 'The validated string is empty'.
   Parameters: `string`—the string to check is not empty
   Throws: `java.lang.IllegalArgumentException`—if the string is empty

```
public static void noNullElements(java.lang.Object[] array,
java.lang.String message)
```

Validate an argument, throwing `IllegalArgumentException` if the argument array has `null` elements or is `null`.

```
Validate.notEmpty(myArray, "The array must not contain null
elements");
```

   Parameters: `array`—the array to check
   `message`—the exception message if the array has `null` elements
   Throws: `java.lang.IllegalArgumentException`—if the array has `null` elements or is `null`

```
public static void noNullElements(java.lang.Object[] array)
```

Validate an argument, throwing `IllegalArgumentException` if the argument array has `null` elements or is `null`.

```
Validate.notEmpty(myArray);
```

The message in the exception is 'The validated array contains `null` element at index:'.
   Parameters: `array`—the array to check
   Throws: `java.lang.IllegalArgumentException`—if the array has `null` elements or is `null`

```
public static void noNullElements(java.util.Collection collection,
java.lang.String message)
```

Validate an argument, throwing `IllegalArgumentException` if the argument collection has `null` elements or is `null`.

```
Validate.notEmpty(myCollection, "The collection must not contain null
elements");
```

   Parameters: `collection`—the collection to check
   `message`—the exception message if the array has `null` elements

Throws: `java.lang.IllegalArgumentException`—if the collection has `null` elements or is `null`

```
public static void noNullElements(java.util.Collection collection)
```

Validate an argument, throwing `IllegalArgumentException` if the argument collection has `null` elements or is `null`.

```
Validate.notEmpty(myCollection);
```

The message in the exception is 'The validated collection contains `null` element at index:'.

Parameters: `collection`—the collection to check
Throws: `java.lang.IllegalArgumentException`—if the collection has `null` elements or is `null`

org.apache.commons.lang.WordUtils

Operations on `Strings` that contain words. This class tries to handle `null` input gracefully. An exception will not be thrown for a `null` input. Each method documents its behavior in more detail.

Constructor Detail

```
public WordUtils()
```

`WordWrapUtils` instances should NOT be constructed in standard programming. Instead, the class should be used as `WordWrapUtils.wrap("foo bar", 20);`. This constructor is public to permit tools that require a JavaBean instance to operate.

Method Detail

```
public static java.lang.String wrap(java.lang.String str, int wrapLength)
```

Wraps a single line of text, identifying words by ' '. New lines will be separated by the system property line separator. Very long words, such as URLs, will not be wrapped. Leading spaces on a new line are stripped. Trailing spaces are not stripped.

```
WordUtils.wrap(null, *) = null
WordUtils.wrap("", *) = ""
```

Parameters: `str`—the `String` to be word wrapped, may be `null`
`wrapLength`—the column to wrap the words at, less than 1 is treated as 1

Returns: a line with newlines inserted, `null` if `null` input

```
public static java.lang.String wrap(java.lang.String str, int
wrapLength, java.lang.String newLineStr, boolean wrapLongWords)
```

Wraps a single line of text, identifying words by ' '. Leading spaces on a new line are stripped. Trailing spaces are not stripped.

```
WordUtils.wrap(null, *, *, *) = null
WordUtils.wrap("", *, *, *) = ""
```

Parameters: `str`—the `String` to be word wrapped, may be `null`
`wrapLength`—the column to wrap the words at, less than 1 is treated as 1
`newLineStr`—the string to insert for a new line, `null` uses the system property line separator
`wrapLongWords`—`true` if long words (such as URLs) should be wrapped
Returns: a line with newlines inserted, `null` if `null` input

```
public static java.lang.String capitalize(java.lang.String str)
```

Capitalizes all the whitespace separated words in a `String`. Only the first letter of each word is changed. To change all letters to the capitalized case, use `capitalizeFully(String)`. Whitespace is defined by `Character.isWhitespace(char)`. A `null` input `String` returns `null`. Capitalization uses the unicode title case, normally equivalent to upper case.

```
WordUtils.capitalize(null) = null
WordUtils.capitalize("") = ""
WordUtils.capitalize("i am FINE") = "I Am FINE"
```

Parameters: `str`—the `String` to capitalize, may be `null`
Returns: capitalized `String`, `null` if `null` `String` input
See Also: `uncapitalize(String)`, `capitalizeFully(String)`

```
public static java.lang.String capitalizeFully(java.lang.String str)
```

Capitalizes all the whitespace separated words in a `String`. All letters are changed, so the resulting string will be fully changed. Whitespace is defined by `Character.isWhitespace(char)`. A `null` input `String` returns `null`. Capitalization uses the unicode title case, normally equivalent to upper case.

```
WordUtils.capitalize(null) = null
WordUtils.capitalize("") = ""
WordUtils.capitalize("i am FINE") = "I Am Fine"
```

Parameters: `str`—the `String` to capitalize, may be `null`

Returns: capitalized `String`, `null` if `null String` input

```
public static java.lang.String uncapitalize(java.lang.String str)
```

Uncapitalizes all the whitespace separated words in a `String`. Only the first letter of each word is changed.

Whitespace is defined by `Character.isWhitespace(char)`. A `null` input `String` returns `null`.

```
WordUtils.uncapitalize(null) = null
WordUtils.uncapitalize("") = ""
WordUtils.uncapitalize("I Am FINE") = "i am fINE"
```

Parameters: str—the `String` to uncapitalize, may be `null`
Returns: uncapitalized `String`, `null` if `null String` input
See Also: `capitalize(String)`

```
public static java.lang.String swapCase(java.lang.String str)
```

Swaps the case of a `String` using a word based algorithm.

- Upper case character converts to Lower case
- Title case character converts to Lower case
- Lower case character after Whitespace or at start converts to Title case
- Other Lower case character converts to Upper case

Whitespace is defined by `Character.isWhitespace(char)`. A `null` input `String` returns `null`.

```
StringUtils.swapCase(null) = null
StringUtils.swapCase("") = ""
StringUtils.swapCase("The dog has a BONE") = "tHE DOG HAS A bone"
```

Parameters: str—the `String` to swap case, may be `null`
Returns: the changed `String`, `null` if `null String` input

ORG.APACHE.COMMONS.LANG.TIME

Provides classes and methods to work with dates and durations. This includes:

- `DateUtils`—A set of public utility methods for working with dates
- `FastDateFormat`—A replacement for `SimpleDateFormat` that is fast and thread-safe
- `DateFormatUtils`—A formatting class for dates
- `StopWatch`—A duration timer

Class Summary

- **DateFormatUtils** Date and time formatting utilites and constants.
- **DateUtils** A suite of utilities surrounding the use of the `Calendar` and `Date` object.
- **FastDateFormat** FastDateFormat is a fast and thread-safe version of `SimpleDateFormat`.
- **StopWatch** `StopWatch` provides a convenient API for timings.

org.apache.commons.lang.time.DateFormatUtils

Date and time formatting utilites and constants. Formatting is performed using the `FastDateFormat` class.

```
public static final FastDateFormat ISO_DATETIME_FORMAT
```

ISO8601 formatter for date-time witout time zone. The format used is `yyyy-MM-dd'T'HH:mm:ss`.

```
public static final FastDateFormat ISO_DATETIME_TIME_ZONE_FORMAT
```

ISO8601 formatter for date-time with time zone. The format used is `yyyy-MM-dd'T'HH:mm:ssZZ`.

```
public static final FastDateFormat ISO_DATE_FORMAT
```

ISO8601 formatter for date without time zone. The format used is `yyyy-MM-dd`.

```
public static final FastDateFormat ISO_DATE_TIME_ZONE_FORMAT
```

ISO8601-like formatter for date with time zone. The format used is `yyyy-MM-ddZZ`. This pattern does not comply with the formal ISO8601 specification as the standard does not allow a time zone without a time.

```
public static final FastDateFormat ISO_TIME_FORMAT
```

ISO8601 formatter for time without time zone. The format used is `'T'HH:mm:ss`.

```
public static final FastDateFormat ISO_TIME_TIME_ZONE_FORMAT
```

ISO8601 formatter for time with time zone. The format used is `'T'HH:mm:ssZZ`.

```
public static final FastDateFormat ISO_TIME_NO_T_FORMAT
```

ISO8601-like formatter for time without time zone. The format used is `HH:mm:ss`. This pattern does not comply with the formal ISO8601 specification as the standard requires the 'T' prefix for times.

```
public static final FastDateFormat ISO_TIME_NO_T_TIME_ZONE_FORMAT
```

ISO8601-like formatter for time with time zone. The format used is `HH:mm:ssZZ`. This pattern does not comply with the formal ISO8601 specification as the standard requires the 'T' prefix for times.

```
public static final FastDateFormat SMTP_DATETIME_FORMAT
```

SMTP (and probably other) date headers. The format used is `EEE, dd MMM yyyy HH:mm:ss z` in U.S. locale.

Constructor Detail

```
public DateFormatUtils()
```

DateFormatUtils instances should NOT be constructed in standard programming. This constructor is public to permit tools that require a JavaBean instance to operate.

Method Detail

```
public static java.lang.String formatUTC(long millis, java.lang.String pattern)
```

Format a date/time into a specific pattern using the UTC time zone.

Parameters: `millis`—the date to format expressed in milliseconds
`pattern`—the pattern to use to format the date
Returns: the formatted date

```
public static java.lang.String formatUTC(java.util.Date date,
    java.lang.String pattern)
```

Format a date/time into a specific pattern using the UTC time zone.

Parameters: `date`—the date to format
`pattern`—the pattern to use to format the date
Returns: the formatted date

```
public static java.lang.String formatUTC(long millis, java.lang.String
    pattern, java.util.Locale locale)
```

Format a date/time into a specific pattern using the UTC time zone.

Parameters: `millis`—the date to format expressed in milliseconds
`pattern`—the pattern to use to format the date
`locale`—the locale to use, may be `null`
Returns: the formatted date

```
public static java.lang.String formatUTC(java.util.Date date,
    java.lang.String pattern, java.util.Locale locale)
```

Format a date/time into a specific pattern using the UTC time zone.

> **Parameters:** `date`—the date to format
> `pattern`—the pattern to use to format the date
> `locale`—the locale to use, may be `null`
> **Returns:** the formatted date
>
> ```
> public static java.lang.String format(long millis, java.lang.String pattern)
> ```

Format a date/time into a specific pattern.

> **Parameters:** `millis`—the date to format expressed in milliseconds
> `pattern`—the pattern to use to format the date
> **Returns:** the formatted date
>
> ```
> public static java.lang.String format(java.util.Date date, java.lang.String pattern)
> ```

Format a date/time into a specific pattern.

> **Parameters:** `date`—the date to format
> `pattern`—the pattern to use to format the date
> **Returns:** the formatted date
>
> ```
> public static java.lang.String format(long millis, java.lang.String pattern, java.util.TimeZone timeZone)
> ```

Format a date/time into a specific pattern in a time zone.

> **Parameters:** `millis`—the time expressed in milliseconds
> `pattern`—the pattern to use to format the date
> `timeZone`—the time zone to use, may be `null`
> **Returns:** the formatted date
>
> ```
> public static java.lang.String format(java.util.Date date, java.lang.String pattern, java.util.TimeZone timeZone)
> ```

Format a date/time into a specific pattern in a time zone.

> **Parameters:** `date`—the date to format
> `pattern`—the pattern to use to format the date
> `timeZone`—the time zone to use, may be `null`
> **Returns:** the formatted date
>
> ```
> public static java.lang.String format(long millis, java.lang.String pattern, java.util.Locale locale)
> ```

Format a date/time into a specific pattern in a locale.

> **Parameters:** `millis`—the date to format expressed in milliseconds
> `pattern`—the pattern to use to format the date

locale—the locale to use, may be `null`
Returns: the formatted date

```
public static java.lang.String format(java.util.Date date,
java.lang.String pattern, java.util.Locale locale)
```

Format a date/time into a specific pattern in a locale.

Parameters: `date`—the date to format
`pattern`—the pattern to use to format the date
`locale`—the locale to use, may be `null`
Returns: the formatted date

```
public static java.lang.String format(long millis, java.lang.String
pattern, java.util.TimeZone timeZone, java.util.Locale locale)
```

Format a date/time into a specific pattern in a time zone and locale.

Parameters: `millis`—the date to format expressed in milliseconds
`pattern`—the pattern to use to format the date
`timeZone`—the time zone to use, may be `null`
`locale`—the locale to use, may be `null`
Returns: the formatted date

```
public static java.lang.String format(java.util.Date date,
java.lang.String pattern, java.util.TimeZone timeZone,
java.util.Locale locale)
```

Format a date/time into a specific pattern in a time zone and locale.

Parameters: `date`—the date to format
`pattern`—the pattern to use to format the date
`timeZone`—the time zone to use, may be `null`
`locale`—the locale to use, may be `null`
Returns: the formatted date

org.apache.commons.lang.time.DateUtils

A suite of utilities surrounding the use of the Calendar and Date object.

Field Detail

```
public static final java.util.TimeZone UTC_TIME_ZONE
```

The UTC time zone (often referred to as GMT).

```
public static final int MILLIS_IN_SECOND
```

Number of milliseconds in a standard second.

```
public static final int MILLIS_IN_MINUTE
```

Number of milliseconds in a standard minute.

    public static final int MILLIS_IN_HOUR

Number of milliseconds in a standard hour.

    public static final int MILLIS_IN_DAY

Number of milliseconds in a standard day.

    public static final int SEMI_MONTH

This is half a month, so this represents whether a date is in the top or bottom half of the month.

    public static final int RANGE_WEEK_SUNDAY

A week range, starting on Sunday.

    public static final int RANGE_WEEK_MONDAY

A week range, starting on Monday.

    public static final int RANGE_WEEK_RELATIVE

A week range, starting on the day focused.

    public static final int RANGE_WEEK_CENTER

A week range, centered around the day focused.

    public static final int RANGE_MONTH_SUNDAY

A month range, the week starting on Sunday.

    public static final int RANGE_MONTH_MONDAY

A month range, the week starting on Monday.

Constructor Detail

    public DateUtils()

DateUtils instances should NOT be constructed in standard programming. Instead, the class should be used as `DateUtils.parse(str);`. This constructor is public to permit tools that require a JavaBean instance to operate.

Method Detail

    public static java.util.Date round(java.util.Date date, int field) org.apache.commons.lang.time

Round this date, leaving the field specified as the most significant field. For example, if you had the datetime of 28 Mar 2002 13:45:01.231, if this was passed with HOUR, it would return 28 Mar 2002 14:00:00.000. If this was passed with MONTH, it would return 1 April 2002 0:00:00.000.

Parameters: `date`—the date to work with
`field`—the field from `Calendar` or `SEMI_MONTH`
Returns: the rounded date
Throws: `java.lang.IllegalArgumentException`—if the date is `null`

```
public static java.util.Calendar round(java.util.Calendar date, int field)
```

Round this date, leaving the field specified as the most significant field. For example, if you had the datetime of 28 Mar 2002 13:45:01.231, if this was passed with HOUR, it would return 28 Mar 2002 14:00:00.000. If this was passed with MONTH, it would return 1 April 2002 0:00:00.000.

Parameters: `date`—the date to work with
`field`—the field from `Calendar` or `SEMI_MONTH`
Returns: the rounded date (a different object)
Throws: `java.lang.IllegalArgumentException`—if the date is `null`

```
public static java.util.Date round(java.lang.Object date, int field)
```

Round this date, leaving the field specified as the most significant field. For example, if you had the datetime of 28 Mar 2002 13:45:01.231, if this was passed with HOUR, it would return 28 Mar 2002 14:00:00.000. If this was passed with MONTH, it would return 1 April 2002 0:00:00.000.

Parameters: `date`—the date to work with, either `Date` or `Calendar`
`field`—the field from `Calendar` or `SEMI_MONTH`
Returns: the rounded date
Throws: `java.lang.IllegalArgumentException`—if the date is `null`
`java.lang.ClassCastException`—if the object type is not a `Date` or `Calendar`

```
public static java.util.Date truncate(java.util.Date date, int field)
```

Truncate this date, leaving the field specified as the most significant field.

For example, if you had the datetime of 28 Mar 2002 13:45:01.231, if you passed with HOUR, it would return 28 Mar 2002 13:00:00.000. If this was passed with MONTH, it would return 1 Mar 2002 0:00:00.000.

Parameters: `date`—the date to work with
`field`—the field from `Calendar` or `SEMI_MONTH`
Returns: the rounded date
Throws: `java.lang.IllegalArgumentException`—if the date is `null`

```
public static java.util.Calendar truncate(java.util.Calendar date, int field)
```

Truncate this date, leaving the field specified as the most significant field. For example, if you had the datetime of 28 Mar 2002 13:45:01.231, if you passed with HOUR, it would return 28 Mar 2002 13:00:00.000. If this was passed with MONTH, it would return 1 Mar 2002 0:00:00.000.

> **Parameters:** `date`—the date to work with
> `field`—the field from `Calendar` or `SEMI_MONTH`
> **Returns:** the rounded date (a different object)
> **Throws:** `java.lang.IllegalArgumentException`—if the date is `null`

```
public static java.util.Date truncate(java.lang.Object date, int
field)
```

Truncate this date, leaving the field specified as the most significant field. For example, if you had the datetime of 28 Mar 2002 13:45:01.231, if you passed with HOUR, it would return 28 Mar 2002 13:00:00.000. If this was passed with MONTH, it would return 1 Mar 2002 0:00:00.000.

> **Parameters:** `date`—the date to work with, either `Date` or `Calendar`
> `field`—the field from `Calendar` or `SEMI_MONTH`
> **Returns:** the rounded date
> **Throws:** `java.lang.IllegalArgumentException`—if the date is `null`
> `java.lang.ClassCastException`—if the object type is not a `Date` or `Calendar`

```
public static java.util.Iterator iterator(java.util.Date focus, int
rangeStyle)
```

This constructs an Iterator that will start and stop over a date range based on the focused date and the range style. For instance, passing Thursday, July 4, 2002 and a RANGE_MONTH_SUNDAY will return an Iterator that starts with Sunday, June 30, 2002 and ends with Saturday, August 3, 2002.

> **Parameters:** `focus`—the date to work with
> `rangeStyle`—the style constant to use. Must be one of the range styles listed for the `iterator(Calendar, int)` method.
> **Returns:** the date iterator
> **Throws:** `java.lang.IllegalArgumentException`—if the date is `null` or if the rangeStyle is not

```
public static java.util.Iterator iterator(java.util.Calendar focus,
int rangeStyle)
```

This constructs an Iterator that will start and stop over a date range based on the focused date and the range style. For instance, passing Thursday, July 4, 2002 and a RANGE_MONTH_SUNDAY will return an Iterator that starts with Sunday, June 30, 2002 and ends with Saturday, August 3, 2002.

> **Parameters:** `focus`—the date to work with
> `rangeStyle`—the style constant to use. Must be one of RANGE_MONTH_SUNDAY, RANGE_MONTH_MONDAY, RANGE_WEEK_SUNDAY, RANGE_WEEK_MONDAY, RANGE_WEEK_RELATIVE, RANGE_WEEK_CENTER

Returns: the date iterator

Throws: `java.lang.IllegalArgumentException`—if the date is `null`

```
public static java.util.Iterator iterator(java.lang.Object focus, int
rangeStyle)
```

This constructs an Iterator that will start and stop over a date range based on the focused date and the range style. For instance, passing Thursday, July 4, 2002 and a RANGE_MONTH_SUNDAY will return an Iterator that starts with Sunday, June 30, 2002 and ends with Saturday, August 3, 2002.

Parameters: `focus`—the date to work with, either `Date` or `Calendar`

`rangeStyle`—the style constant to use. Must be one of the range styles listed for the `iterator(Calendar, int)` method.

Returns: the date iterator

Throws: `java.lang.IllegalArgumentException`—if the date is `null`

`java.lang.ClassCastException`—if the object type is not a `Date` or `Calendar`

org.apache.commons.lang.time.FastDateFormat

```
public class FastDateFormat extends java.text.Format
```

FastDateFormat is a fast and thread-safe version of SimpleDateFormat.

This class can be used as a direct replacement to SimpleDateFormat in most formatting situations. This class is especially useful in multi-threaded server environments. SimpleDateFormat is not thread-safe in any JDK version, nor will it be as Sun has closed the bug/RFE.

Only formatting is supported, but all patterns are compatible with SimpleDateFormat (except time zones—see below).

Java 1.4 introduced a new pattern letter, 'Z', to represent time zones in RFC822 format (e.g., +0800 or -1100). This pattern letter can be used here (on all JDK versions). In addition, the pattern 'ZZ' has been made to represent ISO8601 full format time zones (e.g., +08:00 or -11:00). This introduces a minor incompatability with Java 1.4, but at a gain of useful functionality.

Nested Class Summary

Nested classes inherited from class `java.text.Format`

```
java.text.Format.Field
```

Methods inherited from class `java.text.Format`
`clone, format, formatToCharacterIterator, parseObject`

Field Detail

```
public static final int FULL
```

FULL locale dependent date or time style.

```
public static final int LONG
```

LONG locale dependent date or time style.

```
public static final int MEDIUM
```

MEDIUM locale dependent date or time style.

```
public static final int SHORT
```

SHORT locale dependent date or time style.

Method Detail

```
public static FastDateFormat getInstance()
```

Gets a formatter instance using the default pattern in the default locale.
Returns: a date/time formatter

```
public static FastDateFormat getInstance(java.lang.String pattern)
```

Gets a formatter instance using the specified pattern in the default locale.

Parameters: `pattern`—`SimpleDateFormat` compatible pattern
Returns: a pattern based date/time formatter
Throws: `java.lang.IllegalArgumentException`—if pattern is invalid

```
public static FastDateFormat getInstance(java.lang.String pattern,
java.util.TimeZone timeZone)
```

Gets a formatter instance using the specified pattern and time zone.

Parameters: `pattern`—`SimpleDateFormat` compatible pattern
`timeZone`—optional time zone, overrides time zone of formatted date
Returns: a pattern based date/time formatter
Throws: `java.lang.IllegalArgumentException`—if pattern is invalid

```
public static FastDateFormat getInstance(java.lang.String pattern,
java.util.Locale locale)
```

Gets a formatter instance using the specified pattern and locale.

Parameters: `pattern`—`SimpleDateFormat` compatible pattern
`locale`—optional locale, overrides system locale
Returns: a pattern based date/time formatter
Throws: `java.lang.IllegalArgumentException`—if pattern is invalid

```
public static FastDateFormat getInstance(java.lang.String pattern,
java.util.TimeZone timeZone, java.util.Locale locale)
```

Gets a formatter instance using the specified pattern, time zone and locale.

Parameters: `pattern`—`SimpleDateFormat` compatible pattern
`timeZone`—optional time zone, overrides time zone of formatted date
`locale`—optional locale, overrides system locale

Returns: a pattern based date/time formatter
Throws: `java.lang.IllegalArgumentException`—if pattern is invalid or `null`

```
public static FastDateFormat getDateInstance(int style,
java.util.TimeZone timeZone, java.util.Locale locale)
```

Gets a date formatter instance using the specified style, time zone and locale.

Parameters: `style`—date style: FULL, LONG, MEDIUM, or SHORT
`timeZone`—optional time zone, overrides time zone of formatted date
`locale`—optional locale, overrides system locale
Returns: a localized standard date formatter
Throws: `java.lang.IllegalArgumentException`—if the Locale has no date pattern defined

```
public static FastDateFormat getTimeInstance(int style,
java.util.TimeZone timeZone, java.util.Locale locale)
```

Gets a time formatter instance using the specified style, time zone and locale.

Parameters: `style`—time style: FULL, LONG, MEDIUM, or SHORT
`timeZone`—optional time zone, overrides time zone of formatted time
`locale`—optional locale, overrides system locale
Returns: a localized standard time formatter
Throws: `java.lang.IllegalArgumentException`—if the Locale has no time pattern defined

```
public static FastDateFormat getDateTimeInstance(int dateStyle, int
timeStyle, java.util.TimeZone timeZone, java.util.Locale locale)
```

Gets a date/time formatter instance using the specified style, time zone and locale.

Parameters: `dateStyle`—date style: FULL, LONG, MEDIUM, or SHORT
`timeStyle`—time style: FULL, LONG, MEDIUM, or SHORT
`timeZone`—optional time zone, overrides time zone of formatted date
`locale`—optional locale, overrides system locale
Returns: a localized standard date/time formatter
Throws: `java.lang.IllegalArgumentException`—if the Locale has no date/time pattern defined

```
public java.lang.StringBuffer format(java.lang.Object obj,
java.lang.StringBuffer toAppendTo, java.text.FieldPosition pos)
```

Format either a Date or a Calendar object.

Parameters: `obj`—the object to format
`toAppendTo`—the buffer to append to
`pos`—the position—ignored
Returns: the buffer passed in

```
public java.lang.String format(java.util.Date date)
```

Formats a Date object.

> **Parameters:** `date`—the date to format
> **Returns:** the formatted string

```
public java.lang.String format(java.util.Calendar calendar)
```

Formats a Calendar object.

> **Parameters:** `calendar`—the calendar to format
> **Returns:** the formatted string

```
public java.lang.StringBuffer format(java.util.Date date,
java.lang.StringBuffer buf)
```

Formats a Date object into the supplied StringBuffer.

> **Parameters:** `date`—the date to format
> `buf`—the buffer to format into
> **Returns:** the specified string buffer

```
public java.lang.StringBuffer format(java.util.Calendar calendar,
java.lang.StringBuffer buf)
```

Formats a Calendar object into the supplied StringBuffer.
> **Parameters:** `calendar`—the calendar to format
> `buf`—the buffer to format into
> **Returns:** the specified string buffer

```
public java.lang.Object parseObject(java.lang.String source,
java.text.ParsePosition pos)
```

Parsing not supported.
> **Parameters:** `source`—the string to parse
> `pos`—the parsing position
> **Returns:** `null` as not supported

```
public java.lang.String getPattern()
```

Gets the pattern used by this formatter.
> **Returns:** the pattern, `SimpleDateFormat` compatible

```
public java.util.TimeZone getTimeZone()
```

Gets the time zone used by this formatter. This zone is always used for Date formatting. If a Calendar is passed in to be formatted, the time zone on that may be used depending on `getTimeZoneOverridesCalendar()`.
> **Returns:** the time zone

```
public boolean getTimeZoneOverridesCalendar()
```

org.apache.commons.lang.time

Returns true if the time zone of the calendar overrides the time zone of the formatter.
Returns: true if time zone of formatter overridden for calendars

```
public java.util.Locale getLocale()
```

Gets the locale used by this formatter.
Returns: the locale

```
public int getMaxLengthEstimate()
```

Gets an estimate for the maximum string length that the formatter will produce.

The actual formatted length will almost always be less than or equal to this amount.
Returns: the maximum formatted length

```
public boolean equals(java.lang.Object obj)
```

Compare two objects for equality.
Parameters: obj—the object to compare to
Returns: true if equal

```
public int hashCode()
```

A suitable hashcode.
Returns: a hashcode compatable with equals

```
public java.lang.String toString()
```

Gets a debugging string version of this formatter.
Returns: a debugging string

org.apache.commons.lang.time.StopWatch

StopWatch provides a convenient API for timings. The methods do not protect against inappropriate calls. Thus you can call stop before start, resume before suspend, or unsplit before split. The results are indeterminate in these cases.
To start the watch, call start(). At this point you can:

- ☞ split() the watch to get the time whilst the watch continues in the background. unsplit() will remove the effect of the split. At this point, these three options are available again.
- ☞ suspend() the watch to pause it. resume() allows the watch to continue. Any time between the suspend and resume will not be counted in the total. At this point, these three options are available again.
- ☞ stop() the watch to complete the timing session.

It is intended that the output methods `toString()` and `getTime()` should only be called after stop, split or suspend, however a suitable result will be returned at other points.

Constructor Detail

```
public StopWatch()
```

Method Detail

```
public void start()
```

Start the stopwatch. This method starts a new timing session, clearing any previous values.

```
public void stop()
```

Stop the stopwatch. This method ends a new timing session, allowing the time to be retrieved.

```
public void reset()
```

Reset the stopwatch. This method clears the internal values to allow the object to be reused.

```
public void split()
```

Split the time. This method sets the stop time of the watch to allow a time to be extracted. The start time is unaffected, enabling `unsplit()` to contine the timing from the original start point.

```
public void unsplit()
```

Remove a split. This method clears the stop time. The start time is unaffected, enabling timing from the original start point to continue.

```
public void suspend()
```

Suspend the stopwatch for later resumption. This method suspends the watch until it is resumed. The watch will not include time between the suspend and resume calls in the total time.

```
public void resume()
```

Resume the stopwatch after a suspend. This method resumes the watch after it was suspended. The watch will not include time between the suspend and resume calls in the total time.

```
public long getTime()
```

Get the time on the stopwatch. This is either the time between start and latest split, between start and stop, or the time between the start and the moment this method is called.
Returns: the time in milliseconds

```
public java.lang.String toString()
```

Gets a summary of the time that the stopwatch recorded as a string. The format used is ISO8601-like, hours:minutes:seconds.milliseconds.
Returns: the time as a `String`

APPENDIX **B**

Apache License, Version 2.0

Apache License
Version 2.0, January 2004
http://www.apache.org/licenses/

TERMS AND CONDITIONS FOR USE, REPRODUCTION, AND DISTRIBUTION

1. Definitions. "License" shall mean the terms and conditions for use, reproduction, and distribution as defined by Sections 1 through 9 of this document.

"Licensor" shall mean the copyright owner or entity authorized by the copyright owner that is granting the License.

"Legal Entity" shall mean the union of the acting entity and all other entities that control, are controlled by, or are under common control with that entity. For the purposes of this definition, "control" means (i) the power, direct or indirect, to cause the direction or management of such entity, whether by contract or otherwise, or (ii) ownership of fifty percent (50%) or more of the outstanding shares, or (iii) beneficial ownership of such entity.

"You" (or "Your") shall mean an individual or Legal Entity exercising permissions granted by this License.

"Source" form shall mean the preferred form for making modifications, including but not limited to software source code, documentation source, and configuration files.

"Object" form shall mean any form resulting from mechanical transformation or translation of a Source form, including but not limited to compiled object code, generated documentation, and conversions to other media types.

"Work" shall mean the work of authorship, whether in Source or Object form, made available under the License, as indicated by a copyright notice that is included in or attached to the work (an example is provided in the Appendix below).

"Derivative Works" shall mean any work, whether in Source or Object form, that is based on (or derived from) the Work and for which the editorial revisions, annotations, elaborations, or other modifications represent, as a whole, an original work of authorship. For the purposes of this License, Derivative Works shall not include works that remain separable from, or merely link (or bind by name) to the interfaces of, the Work and Derivative Works thereof.

"Contribution" shall mean any work of authorship, including the original version of the Work and any modifications or additions to that Work or Derivative Works thereof, that is intentionally submitted to Licensor for inclusion in the Work by the copyright owner or by an individual or Legal Entity authorized to submit on behalf of the copyright owner. For the purposes of this definition, "submitted" means any form of electronic, verbal, or written communication sent to the Licensor or its representatives, including but not limited to communication on electronic mailing lists, source code control systems, and issue tracking systems that are managed by, or on behalf of, the Licensor for the purpose of discussing and improving the Work, but excluding communication that is conspicuously marked or otherwise designated in writing by the copyright owner as "Not a Contribution."

"Contributor" shall mean Licensor and any individual or Legal Entity on behalf of whom a Contribution has been received by Licensor and subsequently incorporated within the Work.

2. Grant of Copyright License. Subject to the terms and conditions of this License, each Contributor hereby grants to You a perpetual, worldwide, non-exclusive, no-charge, royalty-free, irrevocable copyright license to reproduce, prepare Derivative Works of, publicly display, publicly perform, sublicense, and distribute the Work and such Derivative Works in Source or Object form.

3. Grant of Patent License. Subject to the terms and conditions of this License, each Contributor hereby grants to You a perpetual, worldwide, non-exclusive, no-charge, royalty-free, irrevocable (except as stated in this section) patent license to make, have made, use, offer to sell, sell, import, and otherwise transfer the Work, where such license applies only to those patent claims licensable by such Contributor that are necessarily infringed by their Contribution(s) alone or by combination of their Contribution(s) with the Work to which such Contribution(s) was submitted. If You institute patent litigation against any entity (including a cross-claim or counterclaim in a lawsuit) alleging that the Work or a Contribution incorporated within the Work constitutes direct or contributory patent infringement, then any patent licenses granted to You under this License for that Work shall terminate as of the date such litigation is filed.

4. Redistribution. You may reproduce and distribute copies of the Work or Derivative Works thereof in any medium, with or without modifications, and in Source or Object form, provided that You meet the following conditions:

    a. You must give any other recipients of the Work or Derivative Works a copy of this License; and

    b. You must cause any modified files to carry prominent notices stating that You changed the files; and

c. You must retain, in the Source form of any Derivative Works that You distribute, all copyright, patent, trademark, and attribution notices from the Source form of the Work, excluding those notices that do not pertain to any part of the Derivative Works; and

d. If the Work includes a "NOTICE" text file as part of its distribution, then any Derivative Works that You distribute must include a readable copy of the attribution notices contained within such NOTICE file, excluding those notices that do not pertain to any part of the Derivative Works, in at least one of the following places: within a NOTICE text file distributed as part of the Derivative Works; within the Source form or documentation, if provided along with the Derivative Works; or, within a display generated by the Derivative Works, if and wherever such third-party notices normally appear. The contents of the NOTICE file are for informational purposes only and do not modify the License. You may add Your own attribution notices within Derivative Works that You distribute, alongside or as an addendum to the NOTICE text from the Work, provided that such additional attribution notices cannot be construed as modifying the License.

You may add Your own copyright statement to Your modifications and may provide additional or different license terms and conditions for use, reproduction, or distribution of Your modifications, or for any such Derivative Works as a whole, provided Your use, reproduction, and distribution of the Work otherwise complies with the conditions stated in this License.

5. Submission of Contributions. Unless You explicitly state otherwise, any Contribution intentionally submitted for inclusion in the Work by You to the Licensor shall be under the terms and conditions of this License, without any additional terms or conditions. Notwithstanding the above, nothing herein shall supersede or modify the terms of any separate license agreement you may have executed with Licensor regarding such Contributions.

6. Trademarks. This License does not grant permission to use the trade names, trademarks, service marks, or product names of the Licensor, except as required for reasonable and customary use in describing the origin of the Work and reproducing the content of the NOTICE file.

7. Disclaimer of Warranty. Unless required by applicable law or agreed to in writing, Licensor provides the Work (and each Contributor provides its Contributions) on an "AS IS" BASIS, WITHOUT WARRANTIES OR CONDITIONS OF ANY KIND, either express or implied, including, without limitation, any warranties or conditions of TITLE, NON-INFRINGEMENT, MERCHANTABILITY, or FITNESS FOR A PARTICULAR PURPOSE. You are solely responsible for determining the appropriateness of using or redistributing the Work and assume any risks associated with Your exercise of permissions under this License.

8. Limitation of Liability. In no event and under no legal theory, whether in tort (including negligence), contract, or otherwise, unless required by applicable law (such as deliberate and grossly negligent acts) or agreed to in writing, shall any Contributor be liable to You for damages, including any direct, indirect, special, incidental, or consequential damages of any character arising as a result of this License or out of the use or inability to use the Work (including but not limited to damages for loss of goodwill, work stoppage, computer failure or malfunction, or any and all other commercial damages or losses), even if such Contributor has been advised of the possibility of such damages.

9. Accepting Warranty or Additional Liability. While redistributing the Work or Derivative Works thereof, You may choose to offer, and charge a fee for, acceptance of support, warranty, indemnity, or other liability obligations and/or rights consistent with this License. However, in accepting such obligations, You may act only on Your own behalf and on Your sole responsibility, not on behalf of any other Contributor, and only if You agree to indemnify, defend, and hold each Contributor harmless for any liability incurred by, or claims asserted against, such Contributor by reason of your accepting any such warranty or additional liability.

APPENDIX: HOW TO APPLY THE APACHE LICENSE TO YOUR WORK

To apply the Apache License to your work, attach the following boilerplate notice, with the fields enclosed by brackets "[]" replaced with your own identifying information. (Don't include the brackets!) The text should be enclosed in the appropriate comment syntax for the file format. We also recommend that a file or class name and description of purpose be included on the same "printed page" as the copyright notice for easier identification within third-party archives.

```
Copyright [yyyy] [name of copyright owner]

Licensed under the Apache License, Version 2.0 (the "License");
you may not use this file except in compliance with the License.
You may obtain a copy of the License at

    http://www.apache.org/licenses/LICENSE-2.0

Unless required by applicable law or agreed to in writing, software
distributed under the License is distributed on an "AS IS" BASIS,
WITHOUT WARRANTIES OR CONDITIONS OF ANY KIND, either express or implied.
See the License for the specific language governing permissions and
limitations under the License.
```

Copyright © 1999–2004, The Apache Software Foundation
Licensed under the Apache License, Version 2.0.

INDEX

Symbols
== (equality) operation, 153

A
Apache Jakarta Commons project
  configuration under Eclipse, 5–9
  license for, 4
  obtaining and installing, 4
  overview, 1
Apache Software Foundation license, 4
applications
  BeanUtils example application, 94–103
  ClassPathTool utility (CLI package), 179–184
    complete source code, 186–191
    running command line, 184–185
  custom DataSources (DBCP package), 81–86
  FileUpload example, 16–26
  FTP example (Net package), 48–54
  JXPath object graph example
    hierarchy exploration, 110–113
    setup, 107–110
  legacy JDBC driver example (DBCP package), 86–88
  Logging package example, 120–122
    output, 122–125
  NNTP example (Net package), 54–66
  object factory example (Pool package), 74–75
  Swing client example (HttpClient package), 37–43
  thread pool example (Pool package), 69–74
  worker thread example (Pool package), 75–77
ArrayUtils class (Lang package), 128, 201–225
ASCII, 166
Attributes package, 196

B
Bag class (Collections package), 140–142
Base64 encoding (Codec package), 170–171
BasePoolableObjectFactory class (Pool package), 69
BeanMap class (Collections package), 142–144
BeanUtils package, 92–93
  classes, 93
  FormBean application example, 94–103
  project ideas, 103
Betwixt package, 193
BidiMap class (Collections package), 144–145, 148
BitField class (Lang package), 128, 201, 225–228
BlockingBuffer class (Collections package), 145
BooleanUtils class (Lang package), 128–129, 201, 228–234
Bounded class (Collections package), 145–147
BSD R commands, 46
Buffer class (Collections package), 147
Builder package (Lang package), 135

C
Cache package, 196
Chain package, 193
character encoding (Codec package), 166–170
CharRange class (Lang package), 129, 201, 234–236
CharSet class (Lang package), 129, 201, 236–238
CharSetUtils class (Lang package), 129, 201, 238–241
CircularFifoBuffer class (Collections package), 147
classes. *See also* interfaces
  ArrayUtils (Lang package), 128, 201–225
  Bag (Collections package), 140–142

Index

BeanMap (Collections package), 142–144
BeanUtils package, 93
BidiMap (Collections package), 144–145, 148
BitField (Lang package), 128, 201, 225–228
BlockingBuffer (Collections package), 145
BooleanUtils (Lang package), 128–129, 201, 228–234
Bounded (Collections package), 145–147
Buffer (Collections package), 147
Builder package, 135
CharRange (Lang package), 129, 201, 234–236
CharSet (Lang package), 129, 201, 236–238
CharSetUtils (Lang package), 129, 201, 238–241
CircularFifoBuffer (Collections package), 147
ClassUtils (Lang package), 130, 202, 241–244
Closure (Collections package), 147–149
Codec package, 166
CollatingIterator (Collections package), 150
Collections package, 140
Comparator (Collections package), 150–151
Composite (Collections package), 151
CopyUtils (IO package), 194
CursorableLinkedList (Collections package), 151–152
DataSource (DBCP package), 81–86
DateFormatUtils (Time package), 312–315
DateUtils (Time package), 315–319
DiskFileUpload (FileUpload package), 13–15
EnumUtils (Enum package), 136
Factory (Collections package), 152
Fast (Collections package), 152
FastDateFormat (Time package), 319–323
Fifo (Collections package), 152
FileUploadHelper (FileUpload application example), 20–23
FileUtils (IO package), 194
FixedSize (Collections package), 152
Flat3Map (Collections package), 153
FormBean (BeanUtils package), 94–103
ftp package classes (Net package), 46
FTPConnection (Net package), 49–50
Functor (Collections package), 153

Hash (Collections package), 153
HttpClient package, 29, 32–37
Identity (Collections package), 153
IOUtils (IO package), 194
Lazy (Collections package), 154
Linked (Collections package), 154
List (Collections package), 154–156
LRUMap (Collections package), 156
Map (Collections package), 156
Math package, 136–137
Multi (Collections package), 158
Net package, 46
NewsgroupInfo (Net package), 57
NNTPConnection (Net package), 59
NodeCachingLinkedList (Collections package), 158
ObjectGraph (Collections package), 158–159
ObjectUtils (Lang package), 130, 202, 245–247
ObjectUtils.Null (Lang package), 130, 202, 247
Ordered (Collections package), 159
Person (JXPath package), 105–108
Pool package, 68–69
PoolingDriver (DBCP package), 79, 86
Predicate (Collections package), 160
RandomStringUtils (Lang package), 130–131, 202, 247–250
ReferenceMap (Collections package), 160
SerializationUtils (Lang package), 131, 202, 250–252
Set (Collections package), 160
Singleton (Collections package), 160
StaticBucketMap (Collections package), 162
StopWatch (Time package), 323–325
StringEscapeUtils (Lang package), 131, 202, 252–256
StringUtils (Lang package), 132–133, 202, 256–295
Synchronized (Collections package), 162
SystemUtils (Lang package), 134, 202, 295–303
Time package, 137, 311–312
Transformer (Collections package), 162
Typed (Collections package), 163
Unmodifiable (Collections package), 163
Validate (Lang package), 134, 202, 303–309
WordUtils (Lang package), 134–135, 202, 309–311
WorkerThreadFactory (Pool package), 69

Index   333

ClassPathTool utility, 179
    building command-line interface with CLI
        package, 181–184
    complete source code, 186–191
    running command line, 184–185
ClassUtils class (Lang package), 130, 202,
    241–244
Clazz package, 196
CLI package, 179
    ClassPathTool utility example, 179–184
        complete source code, 186–191
        running command line, 184–185
    project ideas, 191
clients. *See* HttpClient package
Closure class (Collections package), 147–149
Codec package, 165
    Base64 encoding, 170–171
    character encoding, 166–170
    classes, 166
    hash generation, 173–175
    phonetic analysis, 175–176
    project ideas, 177
    URL parameter encoding, 171–172
CollatingIterator class (Collections
    package), 150
Collections package, 139–140
    Bag class, 140–142
    BeanMap class, 142–144
    BidiMap class, 144–145, 148
    BlockingBuffer class, 145
    Bounded class, 145–147
    Buffer class, 147
    CircularFifoBuffer class, 147
    Closure class, 147–149
    CollatingIterator class, 150
    Comparator class, 150–151
    Composite class, 151
    CursorableLinkedList class, 151–152
    Factory class, 152
    Fast class, 152
    Fifo class, 152
    FixedSize class, 152
    Flat3Map class, 153
    Functor class, 153
    Hash class, 153
    Identity class, 153
    Lazy class, 154
    Linked class, 154
    List class, 154–156
    LRUMap class, 156
    Map class, 156
    Multi class, 158
    NodeCachingLinkedList class, 158
    ObjectGraph class, 158–159
    Ordered class, 159
    Predicate class, 160
    project ideas, 164
    ReferenceMap class, 160
    Set class, 160
    Singleton class, 160
    StaticBucketMap class, 162
    Synchronized class, 162
    Transformer class, 162
    Typed class, 163
    Unmodifiable class, 163
command-line interface. *See* CLI package
Commons project. *See* Apache Jakarta
    Commons project
Comparator class (Collections package),
    150–151
CompareToBuilder class (Builder
    package), 135
components of Commons project. *See names
    of specific components*
Composite class (Collections package), 151
Compress package, 196
compression. *See* Codec package
configuration of Apache Jakarta Commons
    packages under Eclipse, 5–9
Configuration package, 193
connection pooling. *See* DBCP package;
    Pool package
constructors
    ArrayUtils class (Lang package), 204
    BitField class (Lang package), 225
    BooleanUtils class (Lang package), 228
    CharRange class (Lang package), 234–235
    CharSetUtils class (Lang package), 238
    ClassUtils class (Lang package), 241
    DateFormatUtils class (Time
        package), 313
    DateUtils class (Time package), 316
    ObjectUtils class (Lang package), 245
    RandomStringUtils class (Lang
        package), 247
    SerializationUtils class (Lang
        package), 251
    StopWatch class (Time package), 324
    StringEscapeUtils class (Lang
        package), 252
    StringUtils class (Lang package), 257
    SystemUtils class (Lang package), 303
    Validate class (Lang package), 303
    WordUtils class (Lang package), 309
content types, 34
Convert package, 196
Converter package (BeanUtils package),
    93, 101

cookie-based web site example, 31–32
CopyUtils class (IO package), 194
CursorableLinkedList class (Collections package), 151–152

D

Daemon package, 193
data types, JXPath package support, 116
Database Connection Pool. *See* DBCP package
DataSource class (DBCP package), 81–86
DateFormatUtils class (Time package), 137, 312–315
DateUtils class (Time package), 137, 315–319
DBCP package, 79–81. *See also* Pool package
　custom DataSources, 81–86
　legacy JDBC driver application example, 86–88
　project ideas, 89
DbUtils package, 194
debugging information, printing. *See* Logging package
Digester package, 194
directory naming conventions, 5, 24
Discovery package, 194
DiskFileUpload class (FileUpload package), 13–15
DoubleRange class (Math package), 136
downloading files. *See* HttpClient package
DynaBean class (BeanUtils package), 93
DynaClass class (BeanUtils package), 93

E

echo() method, 140
Eclipse, configuration of Apache Jakarta Commons packages, 5–9
EL package, 194
Email package, 197
email protocols, JavaMail support for, 45
encoding. *See* Codec package
Enum package (Lang package), 136
EnumUtils class (Enum package), 136
equality (==) operation, 153
EqualsBuilder class (Builder package), 135
escaping strings, StringEscapeUtils class (Lang package), 131, 202, 252–256
Events package, 197
Exception package (Lang package), 136
Expression Language, 194–195
extensions, JXPath package, 115–116

F

Factory class (Collections package), 152
family tree example. *See* object graphs
Fast class (Collections package), 152
FastDateFormat class (Time package), 137, 319–323
Feedparser package, 197
Fifo class (Collections package), 152
FileItem interface (FileUpload package), 15
FileUpload package, 11
　application example, 16–26
　DiskFileUpload class, 13–15
　FileItem interface, 15
　limitations and security issues, 26–27
　project ideas, 27
　user interface, 13
FileUploadHelper class (FileUpload application example), 20–23
FileUtils class (IO package), 194
Finger, 45
FixedSize class (Collections package), 152
Flat3Map class (Collections package), 153
FloatRange class (Math package), 136
FormBean class (BeanUtils package), 94–103
Fraction class (Math package), 136–137
FTP, 45, 48–54
ftp package (Net package)
　application example, 48–54
　classes, 46
FTPClient class (Net package), 46
FTPConnection class (Net package), 49–50
functions, Functor package, 197
Functor class (Collections package), 153
Functor package, 197

G–H

GenericObjectPool class (Pool package), 69
GET method, 34
　HttpClient package, 31
　Swing client example (HttpClient package), 39–40
graphs of objects. *See* object graphs

Hash class (Collections package), 153
hash generation, Codec package, 173–175
HashCodeBuilder class (Builder package), 135
Hibernate, 92
hierarchy exploration, JXPath object graph example, 110–113
HttpClient package
　classes, 29, 32–37
　methods, 34
　MIME types, 34

Index   335

project ideas, 44
server redirects, 31
Swing client example, 37–43
HttpMethod interface (HttpClient
  package), 34
HttpState class (HttpClient package), 34
HttpUrlMethod interface (HttpClient
  package), 34

I

Id package, 197
Identity class (Collections package), 153
index.jsp page (FileUpload application
  example), 18
interfaces. *See also* classes
  FileItem (FileUpload package), 15
  HttpMethod (HttpClient package), 34
  HttpUrlMethod (HttpClient package), 34
  Pool package, 69
  PoolableObjectFactory (Pool package), 74
Internet protocols
  JavaMail support for, 45
  Net package support for, 45–46
IntRange class (Math package), 136
IO package, 194
IOUtils class (IO package), 194

J

Jakarta JAR Archive Repository, 197
Jakarta projects, examples of, 4
James (Java-based mail and NNTP
  server), 66
Java, mapping XML to, 194
JavaBeans specification, 91–92
  BeanUtils package, 92–103
  mapping JavaBeans to XML
    documents, 193
JavaMail, Internet protocols supported, 45
JDBC connections, DBCP package, 79–81
JDBC driver application example (DBCP
  package), 86–88
Jelly package, 195
Jexl package, 195
JJar package, 197
JSP, retrieving data, 11–13
JVMRandom class (Math package), 137
JXPath package, 105–106
  data types supported, 116
  hierarchy exploration, 110–113
  object graph setup, 107–110
  performance, 116
  project ideas, 117
  XPath syntax, 113–116

K–L

KeyedObjectPool class (Pool package), 69

Lang package, 127
  ArrayUtils class, 128, 201–225
  BitField class, 128, 201, 225–228
  BooleanUtils class, 128–129, 201,
    228–234
  Builder package, 135
  CharRange class, 129, 201, 234–236
  CharSet class, 129, 201, 236–238
  CharSetUtils class, 129, 201, 238–241
  ClassUtils class, 130, 202, 241–244
  Enum package, 136
  Exception package, 136
  Math package, 136–137
  ObjectUtils class, 130, 202, 245–247
  ObjectUtils.Null class, 130, 202, 247
  packages in, 127
  project ideas, 138
  RandomStringUtils class, 130–131, 202,
    247–250
  SerializationUtils class, 131, 202,
    250–252
  StringEscapeUtils class, 131, 202,
    252–256
  StringUtils class, 132–133, 202, 256–295
  SystemUtils class, 134, 202, 295–303
  Time package, 137, 311–312
    DateFormatUtils class, 312–315
    DateUtils class, 315–319
    FastDateFormat class, 319–323
    StopWatch class, 323–325
  Validate class, 134, 202, 303–309
  WordUtils class, 134–135, 202, 309–311
Latka package, 195
Launcher package, 195
Lazy class (Collections package), 154
legacy JDBC driver application example
  (DBCP package), 86–88
libraries. *See names of specific libraries*
licenses, Apache Software Foundation
  license, 4
limitations, FileUpload package, 26–27
Linked class (Collections package), 154
List class (Collections package), 154–156
Log4j toolkit, 119
Logging package, 119
  application example, 120–122
  levels of messages, 119–120
  output examples, 122–125
  project ideas, 125
LongRange class (Math package), 136
LRUMap class (Collections package), 156

M

Map class (Collections package), 156
Mapper package, 197
Math package (Lang package), 136–137, 195
MD5 hash generation, Codec package, 173–175
Messenger package, 198
Metaphone phonetic analysis, 175
methods
   ArrayUtils class (Lang package), 204–225
   BitField class (Lang package), 225–228
   BooleanUtils class (Lang package), 228–234
   CharRange class (Lang package), 235–236
   CharSet class (Lang package), 237–238
   CharSetUtils class (Lang package), 238–241
   ClassUtils class (Lang package), 241–244
   DateFormatUtils class (Time package), 313–315
   DateUtils class (Time package), 317–319
   FastDateFormat class (Time package), 320–323
   HttpClient package, 34
   ObjectUtils class (Lang package), 245–247
   RandomStringUtils class (Lang package), 248–250
   SerializationUtils class (Lang package), 251–252
   StopWatch class (Time package), 324–325
   StringEscapeUtils class (Lang package), 252–256
   StringUtils class (Lang package), 257–295
   SystemUtils class (Lang package), 303
   Validate class (Lang package), 304–309
   WordUtils class (Lang package), 309–311
MIME types, 34
Modeler package, 195
Multi class (Collections package), 158

N

naming conventions
   directories, 5
   uploaded files, 24
Net package
   ftp package
      application example, 48–54
      classes, 46
   Internet protocols supported, 45–46
   nntp package, application example, 54–66
   origins of, 47
   packages included, list of, 46
   project ideas, 66
NetComponents, 47
NewsgroupInfo class (Net package), 57
newsgroups, hierarchy of, 55
NNTP, 45
   Net package application example, 54–66
   newsgroup hierarchy, 55
nntp package (Net package), application example, 54–66
NNTPConnection class (Net package), 59
NodeCachingLinkedList class (Collections package), 158
null values
   ArrayUtils class (Lang package), 203
   ObjectUtils.Null class (Lang package), 130, 202, 247
   StringUtils class (Lang package), 132–133, 202, 256–295
NumberRange class (Math package), 136
NumberUtils class (Math package), 137

O

object factory application, Pool package example, 74–75
object graphs, JXPath package, 105–106
   data types supported, 116
   hierarchy exploration, 110–113
   object graph setup, 107–110
   performance, 116
   XPath syntax, 113–116
ObjectGraph class (Collections package), 158–159
ObjectPool class (Pool package), 69
ObjectPoolFactory class (Pool package), 69
ObjectUtils class (Lang package), 130, 202, 245–247
ObjectUtils.Null class (Lang package), 130, 202, 247
optimizing object creation, avoiding preoptimization, 67
Ordered class (Collections package), 159
output
   echo() method, 140
   Logging package application example, 122–125

P

packages. *See* Apache Jakarta Commons project; *names of specific packages*
performance
   JXPath package, 116
   threads, impact of, 13
Person class (JXPath package), 105–108

Index

phonetic analysis, Codec package, 175–176
Pool package, 67. *See also* DBCP package
   classes, 68–69
   object factory example, 74–75
   project ideas, 77
   thread pool example, 69, 71–74
   worker thread example, 75–77
PoolableObjectFactory interface (Pool package), 69, 74
PoolingDriver class (DBCP package), 79, 86
POST method, 34
   Swing client example (HttpClient package), 40–41
Predicate class (Collections package), 160
preoptimization, avoiding, 67
Primitives package, 195
printing debugging information. *See* Logging package
project ideas
   BeanUtils package, 103
   CLI package, 191
   Codec package, 177
   Collections package, 164
   DBCP package, 89
   FileUpload package, 27
   HttpClient package, 44
   JXPath package, 117
   Lang package, 138
   Logging package, 125
   Net package, 66
   Pool package, 77
proper components
   list of, 2–3
   versus sandbox components, 2
proper projects, web site for information, 193
protocols. *See* Internet protocols

Q–R

RandomStringUtils class (Lang package), 130–131, 202, 247–250
RandomUtils class (Math package), 137
Range class (Math package), 136
redirects, HttpClient package, 31
ReferenceMap class (Collections package), 160
ReflectionToStringBuilder class (Builder package), 135
Resources package, 198
retrieving
   data with JSP or servlets, 11–13
   object graph data. *See* JXPath package

S

sandbox components versus proper components, 2
sandbox projects, 196
Scaffold package, 198
Secure Hash Algorithm. *See* SHA
security issues, FileUpload package, 26–27
SerializationUtils class (Lang package), 131, 202, 250–252
server redirects, HttpClient package, 31
servlets
   performance impact of threads, 13
   retrieving data, 11–13
Set class (Collections package), 160
SHA (Secure Hash Algorithm), 173
   hash generation, Codec package, 173–175
Singleton class (Collections package), 160
SoftReferenceObjectPool class (Pool package), 69
SoundEx phonetic analysis, 175
spell-checking (phonetic analysis), 175
SQL package, 198
StackObjectPool class (Pool package), 69
StandardToStringStyle class (Builder package), 135
StaticBucketMap class (Collections package), 162
StopWatch class (Time package), 137, 323–325
StringEscapeUtils class (Lang package), 131, 202, 252–256
StringUtils class (Lang package), 132–133, 202, 256–295
Swing client
   HttpClient package example, 37–43
   JXPath object graph example, 110–113
Synchronized class (Collections package), 162
SystemUtils class (Lang package), 134, 202, 295–303

T

Telnet, 45
TFTP, 45
ThreadPool package, 198
threads
   performance impact, 13
   Pool package application example, 69–77
   Swing client example (HttpClient package), 41
   ThreadPool package, 198
Time package (Lang package), 137, 311–312
   DateFormatUtils class, 312–315
   DateUtils class, 315–319

FastDateFormat class, 319–323
StopWatch class, 323–325
timeouts, Swing client example (HttpClient package), 41
toolkits for logging, 119
ToStringBuilder class (Builder package), 135
ToStringStyle class (Builder package), 135
Transaction package, 198
Transformer class (Collections package), 162
translations. *See* Codec package
Typed class (Collections package), 163

U

Unicode, 168
Unmodifiable class (Collections package), 163
uploading files. *See* FileUpload package
URL parameter encoding, Codec package, 171–172
USENET newsgroup hierarchy, 55
user interface. *See also* CLI package
  FileUpload application example, 16–17
  FileUpload package, 13
  FTP example (Net package), 49
  Swing client example (HttpClient package), 37–39
utilities, Lang package. *See* Lang package

V–W

Validate class (Lang package), 134, 202, 303–309
Validator package, 196
VFS package, 198
Virtual File System, 198

web pages, cookie-based web site example, 31–32
Whois, 45
WordUtils class (Lang package), 134–135, 202, 309–311
worker thread application, Pool package example, 75–77
WorkerThreadFactory class (Pool package), 69
Workflow package, 199

X–Z

XML documents
  logging output, 123–125
  mapping JavaBeans to, 193
  mapping to Java, 194
XML-based scripting, 195
XPath syntax, JXPath package, 105–116
  data types supported, 116
  hierarchy exploration, 110–113
  object graph setup, 107–110
  performance, 116

informIT

www.informit.com

YOUR GUIDE TO IT REFERENCE

Articles

Keep your edge with thousands of free articles, in-depth features, interviews, and IT reference recommendations — all written by experts you know and trust.

Online Books

Answers in an instant from **InformIT Online Book's** 600+ fully searchable on line books. For a limited time, you can get your first 14 days **free**.

POWERED BY
Safari
TECH BOOKS ONLINE

Catalog

Review online sample chapters, author biographies and customer rankings and choose exactly the right book from a selection of over 5,000 titles.

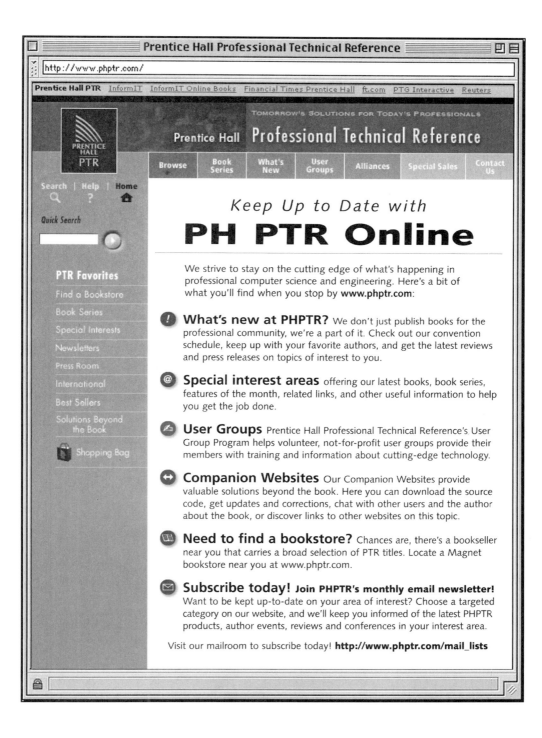

Wouldn't it be great

if the world's leading technical publishers joined forces to deliver their best tech books in a common digital reference platform?

They have. Introducing
**InformIT Online Books
powered by Safari.**

- **Specific answers to specific questions.**
InformIT Online Books' powerful search engine gives you relevance-ranked results in a matter of seconds.

- **Immediate results.**
With InformIT Online Books, you can select the book you want and view the chapter or section you need immediately.

- **Cut, paste and annotate.**
Paste code to save time and eliminate typographical errors. Make notes on the material you find useful and choose whether or not to share them with your work group.

- **Customized for your enterprise.**
Customize a library for you, your department or your entire organization. You only pay for what you need.

Get your first 14 days FREE!

For a limited time, InformIT Online Books is offering its members a 10 book subscription risk-free for 14 days. Visit **http://www.informit.com/onlinebooks** for details.